A comprehensive manual of
HUMAN RESOURCE MANAGEMENT
for Competitive Examinations

- An introducton to every topic
- Definitions of Key Concepts
- Well planned MCQs
- Explanations, where necessary for answers of MCQs have been endorsed
- Features of Japanese Management
- Learner friendly overviews of subjects
- OB, Organisational Culture and IHRM
- Topics like Creativity, Personality and Attitudes

Dr. P.K.S. MENON
M.A., LL B, MIRPM, Ph.D.
Former Senior Faculty,
Dr. Punjabrao Deshmukh Institute of
Management Technology and Research,
Congressnagar, NAGPUR

Himalaya Publishing House
MUMBAI • DELHI • NAGPUR • BANGALORE • HYDERABAD • CHENNAI • PUNE • LUCKNOW

First Edition : 2008
Edition : 2012
Edition : 2014

Published by : Mrs. Meena Pandey
for **HIMALAYA PUBLISHING HOUSE PVT. LTD.,**
"Ramdoot", Dr. Bhalerao Marg, Girgaon, Mumbai - 400 004.
Phones: 23860170, 23863863, Fax: 022-23877178.
Email: himpub@vsnl.com + Website: www.himpub.com

Branch Offices:

New Delhi : "Pooja Apartments", 4-B, Murari Lal Street, Ansari Road, Darya Ganj, New Delhi-110 002. Phones: 23270392, 23278631, Fax: 011-23256286

Nagpur : Kundanlal Chandak Industrial Estate, Ghat Road, Nagpur - 440 018. Phones: 2738731, 3296733 Telefax: 0712-2721216.

Bengaluru : No. 16/1 (Old 12/1), 1st Floor, Next to Hotel Highlands, Madhava Nagar, Race Course Road, Bengaluru - 560 001. Phones: 22281541, 22385461, Telefax: 080-22286611.

Hyderabad : No. 3-4-184, Lingampally, Besides Raghavendra Swamy Matham,Kachiguda, Hyderabad - 500 027. Phones: 040-27560041, 27550139.

Chennai : No. 85/50, Bazullah Road, T. Nagar, Chennai - 600 017. Phones: 044-32463737, 42124860.

Pune : First Floor, "Laksha" Apartment, No. 527, Mehunpura, Shaniwarpeth, (Near Prabhat Theatre), Pune - 411 030. Phones: 020-24496323, 24496333.

Lucknow : House No. 731, Shekhupura Colony, Near B.D. Convent School, Vikas Nagar, Aliganj, Lucknow - 226022. Mob: 09307501549.

Ahmedabad : 114, "SHAIL",1st Floor, Opp. Madhu Sudan House, C.G.Road, Navrang Pura, Ahmedabad - 380 009. Phone: 079-26560126.

Ernakulam : 39/176 (New No: 60/251) 1ST Floor,Karikkamuri Road,Ernakulam, Kochi - 682011, Kerala. Tel : (91) (0484) 2378012, 2378016.

Bhubaneswar : 5 Station Square, Bhubaneswar (Orissa) - 751 001. Phone: 0674-2532129,9338746007.

Indore : Kesardeep Avenue Extension, 73 Narayan Bagh, Flat No. 302, IIIrd Floor, Near Humpty Dumpty School, Narayan Bagh, Indore (M.P.).

Kolkata : 108/4, Beliaghata Main Road, Near ID Hospital, Opp. SBI Bank, Kolkata - 700 010. Phone: 033-32449649.

Guwahati : House No. 15, Behind Pragjyotish College Near Sharma Printing Press, P.O. Bharalumukh, Guwahati-781 009 (Assam). Mobile: 09883055590/36.

Printed at : Geetanjali Press Pvt.Ltd., Nagpur on behalf of H.P.H.

Dedicated with love and regards

in memory of my

Wife

PRABHA

PREFACE TO FIRST EDITION

Patterns of examinations and interviews for selection of various jobs are frequently changed according to requirements like evaluation of skills, experience and other personality attributes of the candidates.

It has become a common practice to conduct objective tests for selection when a large number of candidates are appearing for selection tests. For answering the multiple choice objective questions correctly, an individual must possess thorough knowledge of the subject. Therefore, It is, necessary that the book the individual selects for reference must provide him a clear concept of the subject in totality. The same has been ensured through the appropriate questions and options of answers provided in this book with regard to 'Human Resource Management. Over and above, it is intended for the future managers to have the basic concepts of HRM within the context of Business environment which will enable them to face the challenges at work places, inclusive of international arena, effectively.

The book creates a perfect balance between research oriented and application oriented studies of HRM and organisational behaviour to facilitate the required understanding, especially to management aspirants. The book will be a useful guide for students of MBA and also for BBM, BBA, BCA, B Com, M Com, and professional examinations.

This publication has 1200 multiple choice-objective questions with answers, covering all important topics of HRM and its connected subjects.

I would like to thank Shri. G.N. Pandey and Shri. Niraj Pandey of Himalaya Publishing House for their interest and painstaking efforts in bringing out this book expeditiously.

NAGPUR

Dr PKS Menon

CONTENTS

CHAPTER-1 1-30

Management Perspective

CHAPTER-2 31-68

Recruitment and Selection, Promotion and Transfers,
Job Analysis, Job Evaluation and Job Design,
Merit rating and Performance Appraisals,
Wage and Salary Administration

CHAPTER-3 69-105

Training and Development, Welfare and Social Security,
Personal Records (Each employee), Research and Audit,
Grievance and Discipline, Collective Bargaining,
Settlement of Industrial Disputes, Industrial Democracy

CHAPTER-4 106-134

Human Resource Planning and Labour Market,
Concept of Motivation, Organisation Dynamics,
Organisation Development (OD)

CHAPTER-5 135-165

Concept of Leadership, Developing Creativity,
Developing Creativity, Managerial Skills,
Fundamentals of Decision Making

CHAPTER-6 166-196

Communication, Transactional Analysis in Communication,
Group Dynamics, Informal Organisation, Counselling,
Job Satisfaction, Human Relation

CHAPTER-7 197-225

Influence and Power in Organisation, Organisational Culture,
Industrial Planning, Concepts of Organisational Behaviour (OB),
Stress Management, Concepts of Human Accounting System

CHAPTER-8 226-265

International Human Resource Management (IRHM),
Career Planning (An Overview), Personality, Attitude

BIBLIOGRAPHY 266

CHAPTER - 1

- ***MANAGEMENT PERSPECTIVE***
- ***MANAGEMENT PROCESS***
- ***HUMAN FACTOR IN ORGANISATION***
- ***HUMAN RESOURCE MANAGEMENT***
- ***IMAGE AND QUALITIES OF HRM MANAGER***
- ***INDIAN APPROACH TO HRM***
- ***JAPANESE MANAGEMENT (AN OVERVIEW)***

FEATURES :

- *Management process*
- *Meaning*
- *Planning*
- *Organising*
- *Staffing*
- *Directing*
- *Controlling*
- *Decision making*
- *Human factor in organisation*
- *Nature*
- *Understanding the human factor*
- *Study of human behaviour*
- *HRM, nature concept*
- *Importance*
- *Speciality of HRM*
- *Objective*
- *HRM strategy*
- *Protective approach*
- *Qualities of HRM Manager*
- *Performance management*
- *Indian approach to HRM*
- *Challenges of HRM in Indian context*
- *Value system of Indian Management*
- *Changing role of HRM*
- *Technological changes*
- *Quality of work life*
- *Japanese management*
- *Organic character*
- *Japanese management and Western countries*
- *'Ringi method*
- *Target and productivity*
- *'Z' theory*
- *'7S' model*

MANAGEMENT PRESPECTIVE

ORIGIN OF HRM

The origin of HRM is indistinct, whereas this concept was created by a group of US analysts in early 1980s. Some of the essential propositions like proactiveness, commitment, strategic integration and flexibility are closely associated with modern business strategy. Recent developments in HRM are globalisation, transfer of sectorial employment to global level, technology change in organisation structure (especially in the information technology). According to Terry, HRM is a continuous function that requires constant awareness of the people at work. The resource (i.e., human resource) available to management is only one part of the resources. This has to be properly coordinated with other material resources to achieve the objectives. The most effective way to get results in any organisation is to work with the people than through them. The quality of relationship within the work place must be 'coaction' and not 'coercion'. Mutual goal setting of employers and employees plays a vital role in understanding each other; and leads to commitment, which in turn, produce better performance. Therefore, objective of HRM is to satisfy people at work place for better results. The challenge before HRM today is to evaluate the international scene under the business perspective and acquire the competitive skills among workers to match with changing situations.

KEY NOTE

Management process : It is a series of management activities. In other words, it is a unified concept of management functions and activities. It is primarily concerned with important task of goal achievement. Every organisation has certain pre-planned objectives.

Human factor in organisation : Macro and micro issues of socio-economic factors which are interrelated with physiological, psychological and socio-ethical aspects of human being. This represents the entire concept of human behaviour. Human factor can be understood through determinants of human behaviour at work.

Human resource management : Human resource management is a method of developing employees, in order to get the highest satisfaction from their work and also contribute their best efforts to the work to improve productivity. It is a concept of development of human resource for better results. HRM aims at good industrial relations and high morale of workers.

Image and qualities of HRM manager : Their sense of vocation capacity for persuasion and leadership must be able to rate them to that group of rare men, who are aware of what is to be achieved. They also must have special skills like-human skill, conceptual skill, technical skill, perceptual skill, self-management skill and attitude and interest skill according to the need of management, to the level of management position they occupy in an organisation.

Indian approach to HRM : According to Mr. Amartya Sen, "The growth of any country lies not in the physical development alone, but on the development of its human resource." Due to globalisation change in organisational structure, change in social actions of collectivism to individualism bring a new approach in human resource management. Even though Indian management is autocratic in nature, when people are employed in an organisation, they evolve a culture consequently at work place. In the recent past, management has become an integrated subject of various view points and come as a challenge in the field of business administration, while dealing with various aspects of human relations to enhance the development of individual as well as the productivity.

Japanese management (an overview) : When we talk about Japanese management, it has distinct value and nature. Japan has adopted their traditional values in business approach along with the western management principles and made a new principle of Seven S's' like strategy, structure systems, staff, skills, styles and superordinate goals. Japanese emphasise the first three S's' as 'Hard' and dry, uninteresting nature, whereas the last four S's' which are called 'Soft-S's' make the life line of the organisation. Japanese organisations could produce tremendous success by using the Soft 'S's' creatively. These Soft 'S's' provide a smooth way of functioning, at the same time 'Hard 'S's' like strategy, structure and system of western management are not able to provide a cordial atmosphere in the organisation, as they lack 'Human relation' principles. Japanese, therefore, advocate the combination of '7S's' as an ideal one.

It is, rightly quoted by 'Washington Post Review'- that "If there is one major lesson to be learned from the Japanese business structures, it is how to manage. If we don't want to lose out even more in the competitive race, we better try to learn (it)."

QUESTIONS

1. **What is management?**
(a) Managing people,
(b) The art of getting things done,
(c) The action of managing,
(d) Getting the job completed by people.

2. **Do you agree that the management and administration are the same?**
(a) Yes,
(b) No,
(c) Parallel,
(d) Having certain differences.

3. **What do you mean by management skill?**
(a) Conceptual skill,
(b) Human skill,
(c) Technical skill,
(d) All the three above.

4. **Is management a science or an art?**
(a) It is a scientific discipline,
(b) Management is a profession,
(c) An act of getting things done,
(d) It is an art as well as a science.

5. **Management by objectives refers to –**
(a) Concept of getting results through people,
(b) Popular management technique.
(c) Effective way of practising basic functions of management,
(d) A modern concept originated in USA.

6. **What is Peter Drucker's opinion about MBO?**
(a) Development of an action plan,
(b) A scientific approach to management,
(c) Philosophy based on human behaviour and motivation,
(d) An appraisal of individual performance.

7. **Who is called the father of scientific management?**
(a) Charles Babbage
(b) Henry L. Gnatt
(c) Henry Robinson Towne
(d) F.W. Taylor

8. **What does unity of command indicate?**
(a) Person giving command must have authority.
(b) An employee should receive orders from one superior.
(c) Unified command and control.
(d) None of the above.

9. **What does scalar chain mean?**

(a) Chain of services provided by management.
(b) Chain of relations between superior and subordinate.
(c) A line of authority from superior to subordinate used for proper communication.
(d) A process of communication in management.

10. What is authority?
(a) Capacity to make others act according to your wish.
(b) Ability to dominate the values of others
(c) It is used through persuasion and coercion.
(d) A relationship between superior and subordinate.

11. How does the executive use his power?
(a) Through persuasion,
(b) Through formal sanction,
(c) Referential or identification method.
(d) All the above.

12. What is the meaning of 'impersonal nature'?
(a) Proper dispensation of justice,
(b) Making an impression of fair deed,
(c) As far as possible, dispensation of impartiality,
(d) Conducting without fear or favour.

13. What do you mean'by staff duties ?'
(a) Duties performed by the staff of an organisation
(b) Professional duties by experts.
(c) Providing the advisory services to managers by the experts in the organisation.
(d) None of the above.

14. What does Esprit-de-corps mean?
(a) Word of French origin. Spirit of the body
(b) A feeling of pride and loyalty, uniting members of a group.
(c) A feeling of part and parcel of an organisation.
(d) Cooperation among the people.

15. How is Henry Fayol related to management?
(a) Proponent of theory,
(b) Related to Administrative theory,
(c) Great observer of scientific management,
(d) Principles of division of work.

16. What is the contribution of Robert Owen to the history of Management?
(a) He was the manager of different Cotton Mills between 1800 and 1828 AD.
(b) Man should not be treated as secondary and inferior to machine.
(c) Made changes in the attitude of industrialists.
(d) Advocated that men are the product of physical and moral environment.

17. Who did suggest time study technique in management?
(a) F.W. Taylor, (b) Charles Babbage,
(c) Henry Fayol, (d) Joseph L. Massie

18. Who is the author of the book "General & Industrial Administration?"
(a) Edwin B. Flippo, (b) Henry Fayol,
(c) Leonard Nadler, (d) Keith Davis

19. State the importance of 'Power' from the following :
(a) The force that is being used to influence a person.
(b) One's ability to influence others,
(c) Political ability of an individual,
(d) None of the above.

20. What is status?
(a) An individual's position in the society.
(b) Position of an individual in an organisation.

(c) Social rating of an individual in comparison with others.
(d) The relative rank in a system.

21. What do you understand by 'role'?
(a) Role is the performance of a person.
(b) Occupational duty of an employee.
(c) The pattern of action expected of a person.
(d) All the above.

22. What is an organisation?
(a) Essential for any one, who likes to work or manage.
(b) Rational coordination of activities.
(c) It is a social entity.
(d) It is an accomplishment of mentally agreed purpose.

23. "The principles of 'Division of work' should be applied to all kinds of work-Technical, as well as managerial." Whose view is this?
(a) Henry Fayol, (b) E.B. Flippo,
(c) Roger Bennett, (d) Peter F. Drucker

24. Centralisation and Decentralisation are required to achieve-
(a) The excellence of management.
(b) A process by which optimum degree of authority distribution
(c) Ensure the best overall performance.
(d) All the above.

25. What does creation of organisational environment mean?
(a) Cordial relations between employer and employees.
(b) Proper behavioural pattern in an orgasnisation.
(c) Application of social norms, values and goals in work culture.
(d) Following the principles of organisational behaviour.

26. How can an organisation be distinguished?
(a) Body of units, which are interdependent.
(b) Departments, which have definite functions.
(c) In an organisation, units have their own functions,
(d) All the above.

27. What does relationship mean in management?
(a) Interpersonal influence exercised in a situation and directed to achieve the results.
(b) Quality of an individual for achieving specified goals.
(c) Quality of an individual to accomplish the job.
(d) None of the above.

28. Who did originate bureaucracy?
(a) Henry Fayol. (b) Tannenbaum.
(c) Max Webber. (d) Skinner, B.K.

29. What do you understand by management policies?
(a) Directions to management activities,
(b) Guiding principles of management,
(c) Management action plans,
(d) Guidelines for decision making.

30. What does strategy indicate?
(a) A method for a particular plan.
(b) An indication of correct action.
(c) Programme of actions to achieve objectives.
(d) Specific indication to an action.

31. Organisational efficiency is the contribution of —
(a) Leader,
(b) Members of the organisation,
(c) Employees' contribution,
(d) Individual's contribution.

32. What does organisational structure denote?
(a) Structure as per the objectives,
(b) Creation of proper coordination,
(c) Efficient leadership
(d) A framework of formal relationship that has been established.

33. How does management pursue its objectives?

(a) Proper and meticulous planning and control methods.

(b) Utilization of adequate skilled persons of all categories,

(c) Through men, money, materials, machines and methods.

(d) None of the above.

34. What do you understand by Information Technology (IT)?

(a) Application of scientific knowledge in information process.

(b) The manner in which organisational input is transformed into output of information.

(c) Use of systems like telecommunication and computer for storing, retrieving and sending information.

(d) Use of computer software and hardware technology in the process of information receipt and despatch.

35. "Management means what a manager does," who said this?

(a) William Spriegel,

(b) Lawrence A. Appley,

(c) Sir Charles Reynold,

(d) Louis Allen

36. Who did contributed the principles of group dynamics and human relation theory of Management?

(a) Eltan Mayo,

(b) R.J. Rothlisberger,

(c) Mary Parker Follet,

(d) Robbins, S.P.

37. What is the importance of management in modern social system?

(a) Through interaction it creates awareness in public.

(b) Interaction between management and society brings better results.

(c) Creates a strong social awareness about moral and social obligations of business in society.

(d) All the above.

MANAGEMENT PROCESS

38. What does the process of management mean?

(a) Help in the end result of management.

(b) Goal is achieved through certain fundamental management functions.

(c) Clear and complete functions of management.

(d) To achieve certain objectives of management.

39. What does planning refer to?

(a) Achieve desired results

(b) What is to be done and where,

(c) Completing a job as per the time.

(d) Planning to bridge the gap from where we are and where we want to go.

40. What does organising stand for?

(a) A process of systematic bringing together.

(b) Integration of available factors to an optimum relationship

(c) Establishing of various departments and allotting functional duties.

(d) Integrating between people and work in a systematic manner.

41. What does staffing indicate?

(a) Selection of right type of people for right jobs.

(b) Adoption of anticipating needs in man-power distribution.

(c) An attempt to select and develop right type of personnel as per requirement

(d) The distribution of personnel in an organisation.

42. What is directing?

(a) An instruction has to reach the destination.

(b) It is an important activity of the manager.

(c) Inspiring the people of their activities for implementation.

(d) Instructions on how to do something, or how to reach the destination or a goal.

43. What is the importance of controlling?

(a) Ensure that activities are in accordance with the terms of the plan.

(b) An important mental process on the part of a manager

(c) power to influence people's behaviour

(d) Process of regulating the activities.

44. What are the elements of organisation process?

(a) Assignment of responsibilities to employees

(b) Determination of activities to be performed.

(c) Departmentation, delegation and decentralisation.

(d) Delegation of proper authority to subordinates.

45. Management expert Terry, said, "Today's efforts are tomorrow's work that manager thought about yesterday." What is it?

(a) Planning involves thinking analysis of information before action.

(b) The planner must be able to look into the future and visualise proposed activities for completion in time.

(c) The planner must deal with the proposed action in time.

(d) None of the above.

46. When a planning problem does arise, what is the next action?

(a) Making adequate change in the programme of action.

(b) Developing alternative course of action to rectify the problem.

(c) Ensuring proper evaluation of effectiveness in the existing plan.

(d) Selecting the optimum plan.

47. Planning is essentially a decision making, since it involves...What?

(a) Determination of organisational objectives.

(b) Important step in planning process.

(c) Selection from alternatives

(d) All the above.

48. What is a decision in management?

(a) Reaching at a proper conclusion after consideration.

(b) A decision involves choosing of alternatives.

(c) A decision is the outcome of a group of people or an individual.

(d) None of the above.

49. Quantitative Technique refers to-

(a) Models, simulation, resource allocation technique.

(b) Waiting line problems and the queuing theory

(c) Gaming and Game theory and Probability theory

(d) All the above.

50. What does operation research (OR) mean?

(a) A theory practised by Charles Babbage and F.W. Taylor

(b) All quantitative decision making technique

(c) Use of mathematics in management decision making

(d) An aid to proper decision making.

HUMAN FACTOR IN ORGANIZATION

51. What is the most critical factor in an organisation for achieving results?

(a) Infrastructure and resource mobilisation
(b) Financial stability
(c) Human behaviour motivation and performance
(d) Production and marketing.

52. The major economic and management issues facing the Indian economy are the removal of -

(a) Strikes and lock-outs.
(b) Absenteeism and turn over.
(c) Unemployment and poverty.
(d) All the above.

53. What is human factor?

(a) Micro and macro issues of socio-economic factor.
(b) Interrelated Physiological, Psychological and Socio-ethical aspects of human being.
(c) The entire concept of human behaviour
(d) None of the above.

54. How can we understand the nature of human factor?

(a) Through determinants of human behaviour
(b) According to the behaviour of people at work
(c) The way the management influences an individual and a group.
(d) Through the study of human behaviour in organisation.

55. "Organisational behaviour is an academic discipline concerned with understanding and describing human behaviour in organisational environment. It seeks to shed light on the whole complex of 'human factor' in organisation by identifying causes and effect of that behaviour." Who said this?

(a) Mc Gregor, (b) Frank Gilberth,
(c) J.H. Miller, (d) Kaith Davis.

56. There is no single correct managerial strategy that will work for all men at all time — What is the solution?

(a) The complex nature of man.
(b) Manager must possess good diagnostic ability to find out the causes.
(c) Manager must have the ability to change his own behaviour according to the requirement of a certain situation.
(d) All the above.

57. Since human beings are complex in nature; to understand the 'human factor' at work, what must be the role of manager?

(a) Man is responsive to management, therefore, a superior must meet the subordinates' needs.
(b) Manager must perform the role of a controller and motivator.
(c) A catalyst and facilitator.
(d) Management must understand the need of autonomy and independence of men at work.

58. Study of human behaviour in organisation has to rely on certain important aspects — What are they?

(a) Attitude, motivation and skills.
(b) Role, concepts and role dynamics.
(c) Individual factors, informal group factors and formal organisational factors.
(d) Organisational structure, climate and culture.

HUMAN RESOURCE MANAGEMENT

HRM-NATURE, CONCEPT & IMPORTANCE

59. "HRM as a method of developing potentialities of employees, so that they get maximum satisfaction out of their work and contribute the best efforts to business organisations." Who said this?

(a) Dale Yoder, (b) G. Terry
(c) Pigors and Myers (d) G. Stainer.

60. What is the concept of human resource?

(a) It is the concept of development of human for better results.
(b) Men are valuable assets of the organisation. There must be efforts to realise the organisational goals by satisfying the needs of employees and also developing their potentials.
(c) Human resource development must aim to acquire competence to perform the task efficiently.
(d) All the above.

61. What does importance of HRM refer to?

(a) Promotion of excellent growth opportunities for people, who will have to develop potentials.
(b) Promote teamwork and cooperation among people.
(c) Induce the people to work with whole hearted commitment.'
(d) HRM combined with all other resources, produce better results for any organisation.

62. How HRM has become a highly specialised job?

(a) It is concerned with obtaining and maintaining a satisfied work force.
(b) It maximises the output and satisfaction of the employees.
(c) Promote group satisfaction and individual development.
(d) Optimum utilisation of man-power by motivation and improving the efficiency.

63. What is the scope of HRM?

(a) Training and development of employees for their growth.
(b) Maintenance of good industrial relations and workers' high morale for higher productivity
(c) Further researches in behavioural science, new ideas in man, management and advances in the field of training and development.
(d) None of the above.

64. Which are the objectives of HRM?

(a) Optimum productivity, group satisfaction and individual development.
(b) To achieve maximum individual progress.
(c) Aims to achieve best result from workers.
(d) All the above.

65. What is effective moulding of human resource in contrast with physical resource?

(a) Selection of right and adequate number of persons required.
(b) Man is the only active factor of production, who engages all other factors of production to work.
(c) Proper orientation and introduction of needs of employees at work for better results.
(d) Availability of suitable training opportunities to facilitate better performance and to accept challenges of business.

66. What should be the strategy of HRM?
(a) Making the long-term and short-term planning.
(b) Planning the optimum level of man-power.
(c) Introducing training programmes to personnel.
(d) All the above.

67. "Human relation, as an area of management practice is the integration of people into a work situation, in a way that motivates them to work together productively, cooperatively and with economic, psychological and social satisfaction." Who said this?
(a) Kaith Davis
(b) Mc Farland
(c) Koontz and O'Donnel
(d) Herzberg.

68. Who laid the foundation of HRM practice?
(a) Elton Mayo
(b) Roethlisberger and Dickinson
(c) Peter Drucker and Douglas McGregor
(d) David C. McClelland.

69. How can we evaluate the efficiency of HRM?
(a) Through HRM policies and process.
(b) Efficiency depends on the HRM Manager.
(c) Through commitments, competence, Congruence and cost effectiveness.
(d) None of the above.

70. What does the philosophy of HRM indicate?
(a) Different approaches adopted by the management in dealing with employees .
(b) Attitude and behaviour of management towards its work force.
(c) Provision of welfare, recreational and medical facilities for employees.
(d) Development programmes of HRM.

71. What does the commodity approach to labour mean?
(a) Law of supply and demand like a commodity.
(b) Mechanical concept of a labour as a factor of production.
(c) The observation that wages where high when labour was scarce and low when labour was excess.
(d) All the above.

72. What is a protective approach?
(a) Employers realise that welfare of their employees has a direct effect on the productivity.
(b) Introduction of safety means, mechanical aid, lunch rooms, etc., at the work place.
(c) Employers establishing a goodwill.
(d) All the above.

73. What does importance of social approach indicate?
(a) Human relation and the value of human assets.
(b) Workers have certain rights as human being.
(c) The experiment by Prof. Elton Mayo and his associates asserted that 'Factory' is a social system.
(d) All the above.

74. What are the factors responsible for the growth of HRM?
(a) Development of scientific management and awakened sense of social responsibility.
(b) The problem of how the available human resource could effectively minimise the cost and maximise the production.
(c) Technical factors, awakening amongst workers, attitude of the government, cultural and social system.
(d) All the above.

75. What is the 'Laissez fair' view point?

(a) A view popularised by Ronssean, Bentham and Hobbes.
(b) A minimum of public intervention in economic activities.
(c) Business enterprise must get opportunity to earn more profits.
(d) The change in the concept of labour from commodity approach to human concept.

76. How can business organisations avoid problems of coordination and control?

(a) Large-scale production create the problem of control over the large number of persons working in a unit.
(b) They can be sorted out by coordination and control between HRM objectives and new structural relationship.
(c) They require intensified study in the nature of human resource at work.
(d) Study on technical, social and scientific changes in the work environment.

77. Whom does Human relation approach refer to?

(a) Worker, who should be given humanly treatment at work.
(b) Mutual cooperation between employer and employee in solving the common problems.
(c) Integration of people into a work situation that motivates them to work together to achieve productivity and also economic, psychological and social satisfaction.
(d) None of the above.

78. "In CIOs' conference in Tokyo a famous management expert mentioned about a few years ago, "Major problem in the developing countries was the problem of ineffective management of a large quantity of human resource (especially in India), converting huge masses into human assets is not only a management problem but also a socio-economic issue." Who said this?

(a) J.H. Miller (b) Keith Davis
(c) Peter Drucker (d) Mc Gregor.

79 What is the outcome of Hawthrone experiment?

(a) An experiment carried out to understand the human behaviour at work place.
(b) Determination and analysis of social organistion at work.
(c) Informal organisation is created in the very organisation, when workers interact.
(d) It could change the attitude of management that an informal leader plays an important role in influencing workers' behaviour.

80. What does human resource approach mean?

(a) A developmental approach.
(b) It is concerned with growth and high level of competency.
(c) A supportive approach.
(d) Provides work satisfaction by making further use of capabilities of individuals.

81. What does organisational style indicate?

(a) Deals with emotional, intellectual and motivational characteristics of employees.
(b) Bureaucratic and participatory models.
(c) Organisation strictly follows rules of conduct and line of authority.
(d) None of the above.

82. How can a modern manager carry out his job with optimum resources? What process should he follow to achieve the target?

(a) Direct various activities as per the programme.

(b) While taking decision he must be careful to make a right decision.

(c) Planning, organising, staffing, coordinating and directing.

(d) All the above.

83 What is the aim of HRM department in a business organisation?

(a) To help the management in securing, using and developing appropriate man-power to achieve objectives.

(b) To attract and secure the human resource.

(c) To use the work force effectively.

(d) Generate maximum individual development in the organisation.

IMAGE AND QUALITIES OF HRM MANAGER

84. What are the important qualities of a human resource manager?

(a) Sense of vocation, capacity for persuasion and leadership.

(b) Dynamic personality attributes.

(c) Ability to motivate workers.

(d) Must be a result oriented individual.

85. What does make a manager supreme in an organisation?

(a) Management surpasses all other activities.

(b) Managers belong to that group of rare men, who are aware of what is to be achieved.

(c) Power of creating ideas and actions.

(d) None of the above.

86. "An effective management must direct the view of all managers towards common goal. His concept of visionary, directed leadership is fundamental to HRM." Who said this?

(a) Douglas Mc Gregor,

(b) Peter Drucker

(c) Armstrong Michael

(d) Flippo, E.B.

87. In human resource, normally you find four categories of people like- elated, depressed, irritable and unstable- why so?

(a) Due to cultural background,

(b) DNA factor,

(c) Emotionality,

(d) Natural phenomenon.

88. How can you identify an 'intelligent person'?

(a) Capacity to learn and understand.

(b) Mental awareness.

(c) In relation to others, during interaction.

(d) None of the above.

89. "The part of personality no matter what they are plus the way they are related to one and another constitute whole; that are personality theorists would call personality." Who said this?

(a) Marx Frisle

(b) Chris Agryris

(c) McLewis Terman

(d) Herzberg.

90. What is the nature of personality?

(a) One has to introspect so as to help improve upon his personality.

(b) Nature of every individual is attributed to his personality.

(c) A matured person takes an objective attitude towards himself and others.

(d) Generally, an individual asserts through his behavioural characteristics.

91. "Personality is not very easy to define." What is your idea?

(a) An impression of others formed by an individual.

(b) Psychologically the sum total of an individual.

(c) An individual's attributes to characteristics.

(d) An impression is the phenomenon, which may be seen at a glance.

92. Is HRM an international function?

(a) HRM makes claim to a fundamentally different relation between organisational employment function and its role.

(b) It has the capability in shaping and delivering international corporate strategies with desired results.

(c) Capable of making managerial approach to the employment relationship, which is culturally neutral within the perception of organisation and is capable of being translated across the organisational and natural boundaries.

(d) None of the above.

93. How Trade Unions are viewed by HRM?

(a) There is a diminishing trend in unionisation due to HRM activities.

(b) Employers the world over are making efforts to prevent unionisation at new work sites.

(c) Unions in most countries are considered as obstacles in the way to efficiency, competitiveness, introduction of new technology and labour flexibility.

(c) None of the above.

94. "Personnel function concerned with procurement, development, compensation, integration and maintenance of the personnel of a company towards the accomplishment of that organisation's goals or practice." Who said this?

(a) Edwin B. Flippo

(b) Leonard Nadler

(c) Douglas McGregor

(d) Dale, E

95. What is the speciality of Matrix organisations?

(a) Can define the objectives of a project clearly.

(b) Meet the increasing demand of companies and customers, final results or completed projects in record time.

(c) Undertake organisation and group development.

(d) Normal organisations may not be feasible forming a number of industries at a time.

96. What does performance management mean?

(a) Reviewing progress and estimating the potential for advancement.

(b) A technique of appraising performance systematically against defined criteria.

(c) Appraising the performance of individuals as per the programme of appraisal system.

(d) All the above.

INDIAN APPROACH TO HRM

97. "The growth of any country lies not in the physical development alone, but on the development of its human resource." Who said this?

(a) P.B. Smith (b) Amartya Sen
(c) Peter Drucker (d) Kaith Davis

98 What are the challenges of HRM in Indian context?

(a) How do we induce group effort to produce synergy and effectiveness for better results.

(b) Method of motivation to achieve the targets.

(c) How do we make our organisation dynamic and vibrant in all respects.

(d) All the above.

99 What is meant by the value system of Indian management?

(a) Indian management, by and large, is autocratic in nature.

(b) It is basically proprietary in nature.

(c) Some of the big business houses in India are still following the proprietary management.

(d) Every manager including the top professional manager is working at any level in the organisation ought to respect the proprietors.

100. What does organisational culture refer to?

(a) A set of fundamental assumptions and beliefs about reality that are shared by group of individuals for working for a common purpose.

(b) The art and customs of people or a group.

(c) A system of thinking or behaving shared by the values, attitudes and sanctions in an organisation.

(d) When people are employed in an organisation, they evolve a culture consequently at the work place.

101. What is the recent advancement in HRM?

(a) Globalisation, shifting of sectorial employment at international level and wide use of information technology.

(b) Change in organisational structure, change in social actions of collectivism to individualism.

(c) Society is moving from status to contract indicating the tendencies of individualism that can be seen in social process.

(d) All the above.

102 What is the changing role of HRM manager in the present scenario?

(a) Recognise the talent and improve the same to achieve more productivity.

(b) Technological advancement, globalised competition, change in population and the trend towards a service oriented society have undergone drastic transformation that require utmost consideration.

(c) HR Manager is shifting from protector and scanner to a catalytic agent in the present scenario.

(d) All the above.

103 "Management is the generic name for the total process of executive control in industry or commerce." Who said this?

(a) Oliver Sheldon

(b) Lawrence A. Appley

(c) E.F.L. Brech

(d) Peter Drucker.

104 What is the cause of recent bust interest for management in India?

(a) Over the last 30 years, professional management has become a major worldwide movement.

(b) The idea that management can be studied as an important social process is twentieth century concept.

(c) Many scholars of various disciplines have contributed their valuable view-points to management for all these days.

(d) In the recent past, only management has become an integrated 'grasp' of various viewpoints of specialists and came up as a challenging subject.

105. What is the new perspective of HRM?

(a) HRM develops an employment relationship with organisations.

(b) HRM's perspective means set of issues as well as set of practices having clarity and affirmation together with contradictions.

(c) It is a strategic fusion and developmental subject.

(d) Perspectives are the assumptions of HRM.

106. Following are the some of new sets of assumptions shaping their meaning of HRM. "Proactive system with wide intervention, strategic planning and cultural change. People are social capital capable of development. Coincidence of interest between stake holders can be developed, seeks power equalities for trust and collaboration. Open channels of communication to built trust and commitment and goal oriented participation." Who originated this?

(a) Beer and Spector (b) Barnett, C.

(c) Ralph C. Davis (d) Flippo, E.B.

107. What is the nature of contemporary employment relationship HRM has provided?

(a) Global decline in the population of employees in Trade Unions.

(b) More importance is given to individual's complaints than collective bargaining.

(c) Reduction in employment issues that is handled collectively and rise in short-term, part-time contract employments.

(d) All the above.

108. What are the major hurdles that require immediate action by HRM for the progress of Indian economy?

(a) Dishonesty and corruption

(b) Lack of interest in work and production loss,

(c) Unemployment and poverty

(d) Combating inflation and holding the price-line of essential commodities.

109. What does technological change refer to?

(a) The tendency has to make people learn new têchniques.

(b) Whenever technological change takes place, people have to acquire new skills to cope-up with the change.

(c) An organisation transforms its inputs into outputs according to the specific advancement of the time in its product and services.

(d) All the above.

110. What does the reengineering process indicate?

(a) It looks for quantum change in performance.

(b) When 70% of the work process in an organisation is evaluated and altered.

(c) It is initiated by the top mnagement in the organisation.

(d) Management has to follow an autocratic method for effective reengineering.

111. What is system approach in management?

(a) It is a modern theory of management.

(b) It integrates all demands for a proper functioning of an organisation.

(c) An approach leads to acquisition and maintenance of all resources.

(d) It has a capacity to adopt internal and external changes for growth.

112. What is the globalisation syndrome of HRM?

(a) Liberalisation programme and the concept of borderless economic world has been accepted by almost all countries.

(b) HRM has been viewed as a tool for development of the people to achieve the global market.

(c) HRM is considered as a proactive management, whereas the traditional personnel management is reactive in nature.

(d) Distinctive changes have taken place in many countries to promote liberalisation, privatisation and marketisation in line with globalisation programme.

113. What does commitment of top management mean?

(a) Top management must be accessible to personnel at lower level.

(b) Investment to develop people is an asset, it may not give immediate results; top management must visualise this factor carefully and act accordingly.

(c) Managerial, conceptual and human skill, etc., may be achieved through training, whereas ability, capacity and adaptability to situations be acquired through long-term practices.

(d) All the above.

114. What does it mean by quality of work life?

(a) Fair compensation, balance of work and codetermination in management decision making.

(b) Safe and healthy work environment and employees development.

(c) Congenial social integration and continued growth and security.

(d) All the above.

JAPANESE MANAGEMENT (AN OVERVIEW)

115. What are the factors behind Japanese economy to become an industrial power after the devastation in the Second World War?

(a) United States created infrastructure for free trade and also the political scenario of the world was conducive especially to oil market.

(b) Institutions in Japan post- II World War made reforms for new dimensions for change.

(c) Japanese culture has high values, commitments, diligence, self-discipline and great respect for authority.

(d) All the above.

116. Is there any speciality in Japanese management practices?

(a) Many of the Japanese management practices are not available in management books, whereas these features are found in personnel management as an integral part of Japanese style.

(b) Production and product development are people and work oriented.

(c) There is life time employment, seniority system, groupism, inclusive of special cultural characteristics of the management practices.

(d) The features of management practices have evolved as a result of the influence of cultural characteristics of Japanese society.

117. What is the main purpose of Japanese corporate organisation system?

(a) It interacts with departments, top mnagement and employees.

(b) Team work facilitates mental understanding and proper coordination.

(c) Managers are trained to be generalists rather than specialists and workers are trained to be multi-skilled rather than high-skilled in a particular field.

(d) Japanese companies not only emphasise the price but also quality of the product.

118. What are important achievements of the Japanese management?

(a) Transcends achievements of economic, technological growth and productivity during the post-II World War.

(b) Innovative progress of management.

(c) Harmonises industrial relations.

(d) Commitment and loyalty to work.

119. What is the main characteristics of Japanese management?

(a) Concerted activity by group and there is cordial interpersonal relationship between managers and employees.

(b) There is a strong feeling that all are part of the organisation.

(c) Japanese management being an organic organisation, encompasses the family and cultural norms, which are deeply rooted in Japanese society.

(d) All the above.

120 What is the reason for adopting Japanese management by western countries?

(a) Japanese management is developed from an organic system of culture.

(b) Egalitarian relations and democratic participation.

(c) Collective decision making.

(d) The problem of strikes by workers in UK enterprises and lack of commitment, quality ofmanagement and team work do not match with increase in quality of production in USA (especially automobile industries).

121. "Japan's greatest lesson to the world is putting to work. Her tradition of community and human values for the new ends of a modern industrialised state has succeed. Japanese know that management is both a science and humanity." Who said this?

(a) Taizo Ueda (b) Y. Yamashita

(c) Peter Drucker (d) Anthony G. Athos

122. How can one distinguish between the Japanese management system and other management systems?

(a) It encourages to perform constantly and consistently.

(b) Primarily concerned with high performance and quality standards.

(c) It is a system in contrast to American management system.

(d) None of the above.

123. What are the key factors of modern Japanese management system?

(a) Life time employment, wage and promotion system based on seniority.

(b) Work system based on quality and flexibility.

(c) Harmony, respect and loyalty to authority are consistently seniority based rewards.

(d) All the above.

124. What is 'Ringi' method of Japanese management?

(a) A method used for meeting the top mnagement by the personnel at lower strata.

(b) It encourages group decision making.

(c) Under this a subordinate can make a suggestion to the top management for improvement in work procedure through appropriate channel for approval.

(d) When suggestions are forwarded the individual may give his recommendations also.

125. Who is the author of the famous book, 'The Art of Japanese Management?'

(a) Richard Tanner, Pascale and Anthony G. Athos,

(b) Dr. Dakamia and Hajime Kinoshita,

(c) Dr. R.A. Mahelkar,

(d) Kunio Odaka.

126. What is the secret of Japanese management for its rapid progress?

(a) Japanese companies have survived after devastation of II World War with great struggle.

(b) Japanese biggest hardship has inspired their most impressive innovation.

(c) The integrated style of Japanese management.

(d) The 'genius' of turning adversity into advantage.

127. How does Japanese management make target productivity?

(a) Japanese are regarded, as industrious in natuare.

(b) In Japan cooperation is the word for productivity.

(c) Result oriented and concerted efforts by employer and employees for a common goal.

(d All the above.

128. Who founded the 'MITSUSHITA' Electric Company in Japan in 1918?

(a) Konosuke (b) Taizo Udea,

(c) Geneen (d) None of the above.

129. Is the Japanese management system of Corporate management developed at any one point of time?

(a) Japan involved her traditions of community and human values to achieve a new industralised state after II World War.

(b) If one looks back, one can understand that Pre-Meiji or Tokugawa period actually paved the way to Japanese social progress.

(c) Japan had effectively borrowed the best of American management and translated it into their own organic management system to strengthen it.

(d) All the above.

130. What is the Japanese management concept?

(a) The company is referred to 'family' of the traditional family system.

(b) Company is not a mechanism of capital, it is considered as an organic human group.

(c) It is not the maximisation of profit alone, and pursuit of profit means not an end.

(d) None of the above.

131. How do Japanese companies improve their productivity?

(a) Employees have the responsibility for improvement of production, as they are part and parcel of the company.

(b) The share and investment in plant and equipment in GNP in Japan is very high and the saving rate is about 20% of the disposable income.

(c) Permanent employment system is supported by managerial concept.

(d) Whenever Japanese companies suffer losses, they are made good by reducing dividends and not penalising workers.

132. What is the industrial relation scenario in Japanese companies?

(a) There is a 'saying' among Japanese that employers work for their employees.

(b) Organic characteristics of Japanese management are always striving to stabilise industrial harmony.

(c) It is in contrast to western UK and USA system of industrial relation.

(d) There is no class barrier in Japanese firms and the interaction between different classes induce strong faith and trust and also avoid difference of opinion among them.

133. What do you mean by new approach to integration?

(a) It is the integration of activities of human resource in an organisation.

(b) Schematic approach to group decision making.

(c) Group decision involves interaction of members closely related to a particular issue.

(d) An approach having integration with Japanese management and Western management.

134. Who did suggest the integration of Japanese management and Western management system?

(a) Takahashi (b) Sukkou,

(c) William Ouchi (d) Dr. Takamia.

135. What is the life time employment in Japanese companies for employees?

(a) The employment lasts throughout the working life in certain categories of staff.

(b) The employment is sponsored by 'Zaibatsu' a conglomerate trading company.

(c) These workers of Zaibatsu are specially identified category of work force.

(d) None of the above.

136. How the seniority wage system is implemented in Japan?

(a) The seniority system is regulated by Zaibatsu of Japan.

(b) Reward (wage) depends on the merit of service alone.

(c) Seniority rules of the company create opportunity for all to go upward, step by step, every year with certain proportion.

(d) Individuals, who go faster to their upward designation are recognised for seniority and merit.

137. What is known by JIT (just in time)?

(a) This has created an awareness in Japanese labour deployment for manufacturing and applying the same method in Western countries.

(b) The most significant work operation the western countries (USA and UK) have adopted is JIT.

(c) This process refers to delivery and use of components and supplies for manufacturing process, which are hold to a critical minimum to avoid excess holding of large quantity to avoid space problems of storage.

(d) All the above.

138. What is the brand name of the famous company 'Matsushita' of Japan?

(a) Zen (b) Panasonic,

(c) Gaman (d) National

139. How does Japanese management become successful in global scenario?

(a) Strong and vibrant company philosophy.

(b) Japanese culture encourages people to collaborate in groups to achieve the goal.

(c) The task of generation and proper direction of human energy.

(d) Japan made is in terms of long-term results.

140. What can be termed as essentials of Japanese management?

(a) A transparent corporate culture.

(b) Involvement of employees' group in problem solving.

(c) Long-term human resource development and attractive compensation.

(d) All the above.

141. How has 'Matsushita' succeeded in carrying out the business responsibility?

(a) Japanese have great expectations on the business achievements.

(b) Matasushita had a tacit agreement with the public to promote social progress and general welfare of the society.

(c) The aim of business must be the service to society first and then only the reward and profit.

(d) Matsushita recognises concepts of moral and social responsibility in business.

142. Who developed the latest productivity theory in the Japanese management technique?

(a) Mc Gregor (b) Hezberg

(c) William Ouchi (d) L.W. Porter

143. What are the principal suggestions of theory 'Z'?

(a) This is combination of elements of Japanese management and theory-Z.

(b) Ouchi has made many progressive approaches to the central characteristics of organisation and management.

(c) Ouchi has selected theory 'Y' of Mc Gregor and explained the view of workers, whose work is as natural like rest or a play. Also, about self-direction, self-control and commitment to objectives.

(d) It brings out a complete change of motivational principles responsible for high performance in pursuit of management practices.

144. What do special features of theory-'Z' indicate?

(a) In Japanese system one can find a successful industrial society in which the intimacy is seen at work place like any other place in society.

(b) In an organisation workers can bring cooperation and efficiency through sustained relations.

(c) Integrity, trust and fair interpersonal relations are vital aspects of organisational efficiency.

(d) Trust intimacy and cordial relations amongst people in the organisation.

145. What is the '7S' model of Japanese management?

(a) The model represents a simple but powerful insight, as to what makes an enterprise to succeed.

(b) Western companies have taken more interest in following 3S's, viz., Strategy, Structure and System.

(c) Organisations commonly follow the soft S's like staff, Skills, Styles and Super ordinate goals.

(d) None of the above.

146. What suggestions have been given to the American executives by the authors of the book 'The Art of Japanese Management'?

(a) Constant research into the practice of management is essential.

(b) The '7S' method has contributed to make strategies, structure (organisational) and system (useful) for managing business.

(c) The book has given a lot of scope for future research.

(d) Use of the best Japanese technique adds to your own strength, benefiting both the cultures.

147. What does the distinct corporate culture of Japan indicate?

(a) Traditions and social mores laid the impression for the evaluation of corporate culture.

(b) Traditional culture promotes a unique form of cooperation between management and labour.

(c) Company has certain commitments to

the employees and similarly, they are loyal to the company.

(d) Loyalty and commitment have great impact on the morale and motivation of both, workers and managers.

148. Does Japanese management encourage total involvement of employees in companies?

(a) There is total involvement of employees in problem solving and to arrive at a right decision.

(b) Japan has emerged as the largest and efficient producer of steel in the world market.

(c) The company culture encourages workers to offer suggestions on the productivity and other quality standards of the products to improve the quality to match international standards.

(d) Many such suggestions denote cutback the cost and improve production standards.

149. In Japanese management, employees' career path is non-specialised. Why?

(a) In Japanese industries job rotation is carried out for employees to have different skills and also for interdepartmental cooperation.

(b) In an organisation from the time of induction, employees are exposed to various types of jobs and training to enable them to have adaptability to any job.

(c) Japanese management system prefers to create capable workers to adapt organisational changes, as and when required.

(d) Rotation of job provides benefit of skills required for top quality executives.

150. What are self-discipline and cordial relations in Japanese organisations?

(a) There is no rivalry, as well as selfish motive amongst the groups of Japanese industries at their work places.

(b) All efforts are made to establish equality in terms of rank, salary, etc., among employees.

(c) Since there are no unhealthy practices of competitiveness, employees work in harmony, with trust and confidence.

(d) Harmony, cooperation, consensus are the special features of Japanese management.

INTROSPECTION

Any action is not management. It must be result oriented !

ANSWERS

1 (c) The action of managing.
Explanation : Action of managing means, the right action or positive action which produces results.

2(d) Having certain differences.
Explanation : Administration means organisation and running of an enterprise or system etc., whereas management means action of managing for getting the best results. Administration can be called as the top level management, which makes the policies, rules, regulations, etc., for running a system. Management deals with execution of work at all levels.

3(d) All the three above, viz.,
(a) conceptual skill,
(b) Human skill, and
(c) Technical skill.
Explanation : Conceptual skill means the power of thinking and execution, Human skill means man management skills and technical skills relate to professional skills of an individual.

4(d) It is an art as well as science.
Explanation : *Art* is a practical knowledge. It is the skill that an individual possesses. Creativity is the main constituent of an art. It has result oriented approach. Hence, management is an art. *Science* is a systematised knowledge. It relates to events and contains general truth. Science, normally has two aspects like Normative and Positive. Normative science deals with the aspect of what a particular aspect ought to be. Whereas Positive science relates to the aspect to provide answer to what a particular aspect is. Scientific principles are based on scientific experiments, analysis and observations. There is a cause and effect relationship of different factors. Genuineness of scientific factor can be tested and verified too. In view of the foregoing, management is an art, as well as science.

5(c) Effective way of practising basic functions of management.
Explanation : The concept of MBO is normally a logical application of basic management function-planning, control, motivation, etc. MBO introduces the manner in which planning and control to be carried out. The important feature, which distinguishes MBO from other planning and control system is its main emphasis on 'results rather than activities' or 'output rather than inputs'. MBO system was developed in USA and UK and thereafter came to India. Indian managers accept that MBO is a powerful means to achieve better individual and organisational performance.

6(c) Philosophy based on human behaviour and motivation.
Explanation : Peter Drucker's opinion is that MBO followed the development of behavioural approaches to management. It has adopted many of the concepts of the behavioural science for practical application. Some of the major findings of the behavioural science, which provide the base to MBO:
(i) Management's behaviour affects the economic results of the enterprise,
(ii) The authoritarian system of management has the most harmful effect on productivity and profitability,
(iii) Authoritarian system results from assumptions regarding the individual's will to work, etc., are not in accordance with the findings of behavoiural science,
(iv) The means to release untapped creativity in an organisation is to secure the commitment of the individual to identify himself in consonance with the organisation and to find that his work is the means of self-fulfilment.

7(d) F.W. Taylor.

8(b) An employee should receive orders from one superior.

9(c) A line of authority from superior to subordinate used for proper communication.

10(a) Capacity to make others act according to your wish.

11(b) Through formal sanction.
Explanation : According to 'French and Raven', a person who exerts power must possess legitimacy or formal sanction (official approval). In other words, the targets of influence understand that the power, a powerholder enjoys, is legitimate and his command should be complied with in order to meet their own goals.

12(d) Conducting without fear or favour.

13(c) Providing the advisory services to managers by the experts in the organisation.

14(b) A feeling of pride and loyalty, uniting members of a group.

15(d) Principles of division of work.

16(b) Man should not be treated as secondary and inferior to machine.
Explanation : Robert Owen was a social reformer. According to him, workers should be provided with incentives and motivation. They should not be treated as secondary and inferior to machine. He advocated fair wages and sense of security for workers. He also indicated cooperation among workers at the work place during the second half of eighteenth century.

17(b) Charles Babbage.

18(b) Henry Fayol.

19(b) One's ability to influence others.
Explanation : According to Wolfe, 'Power is a potential ability of a person to induce on other a change in his behaviour within a specific time and direction.'

20(c) Social rating of an individual in comparison with others.

21(c) The pattern of action expected of a person.

22(c) It is a social entity.
Explanation : According to Mc Farland, Davis, & Spriegal, "Orgnisation is a framework of relations. This group believes that organisation is an expression of mutual rights, relationship and responsibilities of personnel working in an enterprise."

23(a) Henry Fayol

24(c) Ensure the best overall performance.
Explanation : **Centralisation-** Set up authority is concentrated in a few hands at the top level of an organisation for decision making.
Decentralisation- In a decentralised organisation, there is delegation of authority to others in various departments for quick decision making and to carry out the work effectively. Decentralisation authorises greater power to persons away from the centre.

25(c) Application of social norms, values and goals in work culture.

26(a) Body of units, which are interdependent.

27(a) Interpersonal influence exercised in a situation and directed to achieve results.

28(c) Max Webber.

29(a) Directions to management activities.

30(c) Programme of action to achieve objectives.

31(b) Members of the organisation.

32(d) A framework of formal relationship that has been established.
Explanation : Structure is the established pattern of relationship among various components on the part of an

organisation. A formal structure refers to the pattern of formal relationship and duties. The task allotted to departments and personnel in the organisation, coordination and control of these activities. This behavioural relationship is within the organisation., Policies and procedures that regulate the functions and relationship in the organisation. As per the basis of authority there are three types of structure— (i) line, (ii) line and staff, and (iii) functional type.

33(c) Through men, money, materials, machines and methods.

34(c) Use of systems like telecommunication and computer for storing, retrieving and sending of information.

35(d) Louis Allen

36(c) Mary Parker Follet

37(c) Creates a strong social awareness about moral and social obligations of business in society.

38(b) Goal is achieved through certain fundamental management functions.
Explanation : Management process aims at achieving certain objectives or end results. The following are fundamental functions that are to be performed as per requirement of a manager— (i) Planning, (ii) Organising, (iii) Staffing, (iv) Motivating, and ((v) controlling.

39(d) Planning to bridge the gap from where we are and where we want to go.
Explanation : Planning is the basic management factor. It is selected from alternatives of future course of action, as a whole for the enterprise and each development within. In short, planning is the conscious determination of future course of action to achieve the desired result.

40(b) Interaction of available factors to an optimum relationship.

41(c) An attempt to select and develop right type of personnel as per requirement.

42(d) Instructions on how to do something, or how to reach the destination or a goal.

43(a) Ensure that activities are in accordance with the terms of the plan.

44(c) Departmentation, delegation and decentralisation.
Explanation : Departmentation- is grouping of organisational activities into jobs. In other words, it is a process of grouping activities of an organisation into a number of separate units for the purpose of efficient functioning.
According to Koontz and O'Donnell, a department designates distinct area duration or branch of an enterprise over which manager has authority for performance of specified activities.

Delegation- In centralised organisations, authority is concentrated in a limited number of top officials. Only a few are directly and fully involved in creative and problem solving aspects of the organisation. Other only carry out what has been told to them. It is felt that if the authority is highly centralised, the top executives will be deeply involved in routine matters and thereby important decisions will be delayed. Therefore, while delegating the authority the superior assigns duties to his subordinate and grants him certain rights necessary to fulfil them. He also obliges the subordinate to perform duties with the best of his ability.

45(b) The planner must be able to look into the future and visualise proposed activities for completion in time.

46(b) Developing alternative course of action to rectify the problem.

47(c) Selection of alternatives

48(a) Reaching at a proper conclusion after consideration.

49(d) All the above (a), (b), (c)
(a) Models, simulation, resource allocation technique.
(b) Waiting line problems and the queuing theory.
(c) Gaming and Game theory and Probability theory.

50(b) All quantitative decision making technique.

51(c) Human behaviour, motivation and performance.

52(c) Unemployment and poverty.

53(b) Interrelated physiological, psychological and socio-ethical aspects of human being.

54(b) According to the behaviour of people at work.

55(d) Kaith Davis.

56(c) Manager must have the ability to change his own behaviour according to the requirement of a certain situation.

57(c) A catalyst and facilitator.
Explanation : Catalyst- A substance that promotes the rate of a chemical reaction, while remaining unchanged. *Facilitator-* A person makes things easy.

58(c) Individual factors, informal group factors and formal organisational factors.

59(c) Pigors and Myers

60(d) All the above.
(a), (b), (c)
(a) It is the concept of development of human for better results.
(b) Men are valuable assets of the organisation. There must be efforts to realise the organisational goals by satisfying the needs of employees and also developing their potentials.
(c) Human resource development must aim to acquire competencies to perform the task efficiently.

61(a) Promotion of excellent growth opportunities for people, who will have to develop potentials.

62(b) It maximises the output and the satisfaction of employees.

63(c) Further research in behavioural science; new ideas in man management, and advances in the field of training and development.

64(a) Optimum productivity, group satisfaction and individual development.

65(b) Man is the only active factor of production, who engages all other factors of production to work.

66(d) All the above.
(a) Making the long-term and short-term planning.
(b) Planning the optimum level of man-power.
(c) Introducing training programmes to personnel.

67(a) Kaithi Davis

68(c) Peter Drucker and Douglas McGregor

69(c) Through commitments, competence, congruence and cost effectiveness.

70(b) Attitude and behaviour of management towards its work force.

71(b) Mechanical concept of a labour as a factor of production.

72(a) Employers realise that welfare of their employees has a direct effect on productivity.

73(a) The human relation and value of human assets.

74(c) Technical factors, awakening amongst workers, attitude of the government, cultural and social system.

75(b) A minimum; public intervention in economic activities.
Explanation : A minimum of public intervention means the minimum required intervention in the business by the government agencies.

76(c) They require intensified study in the nature of human resource at work.

77(c) Integration of people into a work situation that motivates them to work together to achieve productivity and also economic, psychological and social satisfaction.

78(c) Peter Drucker

79(d) It could change the attitude of management that an informal leader plays an important role in effecting workers' behaviour.

80(d) Provides work satisfaction by making further use of the capabilities of individuals.

81(b) Bureaucratic and participatory models.

82(c) Planning, organising, staffing, conducting and directing.

83(a) To help the management in securing, using and developing appropriate man-power to achieve objectives.

84(a) Sense of vocation, capacity for persuasion and leadership.

85(b) Managers belong to that group of rare men, who are aware of what is to be achieved.

86(b) Peter Drucker.

87(c) Emotionality.

88(c) In relation to others, during interaction.

89(b) Chris Agryris

90(b) Nature of every individual is attributed to his personality.

91(b) Psychologically the sum total of an individual.

92(b) It has the capability in shaping and delivering international corporate strategies with desired results.

93(c) Unions in most countries are considered as obstacles in the way to efficiency, competitiveness, introduction of new technology and labour flexibility.

94(a) Edwin B Flippo.

95(b) (c) and (d).
(b) Meet the increasing demand of companies and customers, final results or completed projects in record time.
(c) Undertake organisation and group development.
(d) Normal organisations may not be feasible forming a number of industries at a time.

96(b) A technique of appraising performance systematically against defined criteria.

97(b) Amartya Sen.

98(d) All the above.
(a) How do we induce group effort to produce synergy and effectiveness for better results.
(b) The method of motivation to achieve the targets.
(c) How do we make our organisation dynamic and vibrant in all respects.

99(b) It is basically proprietary in nature.

100(a) and (c)
(a) A set of fundamental assumptions and beliefs about reality which are shared by group of individuals to meet a common purpose.
(c) A system of thinking or behaving shared by the values, attitudes and sanctions in an organisation.

101(d) All the above.
(a) Globalisation, shifting of sectorial employment at international level and wide use of information technology.
(b) Change in organisational structure, change in social actions of collectivism to individualism.
(c) Society is moving from status to contract indicating the tendencies of individualism that can be seen in social process.

102(d) All the above.
(a) Recognise the talent and improve the same to achieve more productivity.

(b) Technological advancement, globalised competition, change in population and the trend towards a service oriented society have undergone drastic transformation that require utmost consideration.
(c) HR Manager is shifting from protector and scanner to a catalytic agent in the present scenario.

103(c) E.F.L. Brech

104(d) In the recent past, only management has become an integrated 'grasp' of various viewpoints of specialists and came up as a challenging subject.

105(c) It is a strategic fusion and development subject.

106(a) Beer and Spector

107(d) All the above
(a) Global decline in the population of employees in Trade Unions.
(b) More importance to individual's complaints than collective bargaining.
(c) Reduction in employment issues that is handled collectively and rise in short-term, part-time contract employments.

108(c) Unemployment and Poverty.

109(c) An organisation transforms its inputs into outputs according to the specific advancement of the time in its product and services.

110(b) When 70% of the work process in an organisation is evaluated and altered.

111(b) It integrates all demands for a proper functioning of an organisation.
Explanation : System approach- Organisations are social systems. Many variables exist in the system are interrelated and also interdependent. A manager must think over the effects of a particular action on the whole or a part of the whole system before taking any action; e.g., Organisation is a system and its departments are sub-systems.

112(b) HRM has been viewed as a tool for development of the people to achieve the global market.

113(b) Investment to develop people is an asset, it may not give immediate results; top management must visualise this factor carefully and act accordingly.

114(d) All the above (a), (b) and (c)
(a) Fair compensation, balance of work and co-determination in management decision making.
(b) Safe and healthy work environment and employees development.
(c) Congenial social integration and continued growth and security.

115(d) All the above (a), (b) and (c)
(a) United States created infrastructure for free trade and also the political scenario of the world was conducive especially to oil market.
(b) Institutions in Japan post- II World War made reforms for new dimensions for change.
(c) Japanese culture has high values, commitments, diligence, self-discipline and great respect for authority.

116 (a) and (d)
(a) Many of the Japanese management practices are not available in management books, whereas these features are found in personnel management as an integral part of Japanese style.
(d) The features of management practices have evolved as a result of the influence of cultural characteristics of Japanese society.

117(d) Japanese companies not only emphasize the price but also quality of the product.

118(a) Transcends achievements of

economic, technological growth and productivity during the post-II World War.

119(c) Japanese management being an organic organisation, encompasses the family and cultural norms, which are deeply rooted in Japanese society.

120(d) The problem of strikes by workers in UK enterprises and also lack of commitment, quality of management and team work not matching to increase the quality of production in USA (especially automobile industries).

121(c) Peter Drucker.

122(c) It is a system in contrast to American management system.

123(c) Harmony, respect and loyalty to authority are consistently seniority based rewards.

124(c) Under this a subordinate can make a suggestion to the top management for improvement in work procedure through appropriate channel for approval.

125(a) Richard Tanner, Pascale and Anthony G. Athos,

126(d) The 'genius' of turning adversity into advantage.

127(c) Result oriented and concerted efforts by employer and employees for a common goal.

128(a) Konosuke.

129(d) All the above (a), (b) and (c)

(a) Japan involved her traditions of community and human values to achieve a new industralised state after II World War.

(b) If one looks back, one can understand that Pre-Meiji or Tokugawa period actually paved the way to Japanese social progress.

(c) Japan had effectively borrowed the best of American management and translated it into their own organic management system to strengthen it.

130(a), (b) and (c)

(a) The company is referred to 'family' of the traditional family system.

(b) Company is not a mechanism of capital, it is considered as an organic human group.

(c) It is not the maximisation of profit alone, and pursuit of profit means not an end.

131(a) and (d)

(a) Employees have the responsibility for improvement of production, as they are part and parcel of the company.

(d) Whenever Japanese companies suffer losses, they are made good by reducing dividends and not penalising workers.

132(d) There is no class barrier in Japanese firms and the interaction between different classes induce strong faith and trust and also avoid difference of opinion among them.

133(d) An approach having integration with Japanese management and Western management.

134(d) Dr. Takamia

135(b) The employment is sponsored by 'Zaibatsu' a conglomerate trading company.

136(d) Individuals, who go faster to their upward designation are recognised for seniority and merit.

137(c) This process refers to delivery and use of components and supplies for manufacturing process, which are hold to a critical minimum to avoid excess holding of large quantity to avoid space problems of storage.

138(d) National

139(c) The task of generation and proper direction of human energy.

140(d) All the above (a), (b) and (c)
a) A transparent corporate culture.
(b) Involvement of employees' group in problem solving.
(c) Long-term human resource development and attractive compensation.

141(d) Matsushita recognises concepts of moral and social responsibility in business.

142(c) William Ouchi.

143(d) It brings out a complete change of motivational principles responsible for high performance in pursuit of management practices.

144(d) Trust intimacy and cordial relations amongst people in the organisation.

145(a) The model represents a simple but powerful insight, as to what makes an enterprise to succeed.

146(d) Use of the best Japanese technique adds to your own strength, benefiting both the cultures.

147(a) Traditions and social mores laid the impression for the evaluation of corporate culture.

148(c) The company culture encourages workers to offer suggestions on the productivity and other quality standards of the products to improve the quality to match international standards.

149(c) Japanese management system prefers to create capable workers to adapt organisational changes, as and when required.

150(c) Since there are no unhealthy practices of competitiveness, employees work in harmony, with trust and confidence .

◆◆◆◆◆

CHAPTER - 2

- ***RECRUITMENT AND SELECTION***
- ***PROMOTION AND TRANSFER***
- ***JOB ANALYSIS, JOB EVALUATION AND JOB DESIGN***
- ***MERIT RATING AND PERFORMANCE APPRAISAL***
- ***WAGE AND SALARY ADMINISTRATION***

FEATURES :

- Recruitment and selection process
- Method of recruitment and selection
- Types of test
- Principles of testing
- Interviewing methods
- Types of counselling for selection
- Induction
- Orientation
- Placement, promotion and transfer
- How to make induction effective?
- Productivity and efficiency
- Job evaluation and job design concepts, objectives and importance
- Merit rating and performance appraisal
- Essential features of an appraisal system
- Importance of merit rating
- What are the limitations of appraisals, wage and salary administration
- Employees' remuneration and wage legislation
- Principles and objectives of wage and salary administration
- Compensation to employees
- Wage differentials
- Wage determination
- Concept of minimum, fair and living wage
- Method of wage payment to employees
- Incentives and fringe benefits.

KEY NOTE

Recruitment and selection process : Recruitment is the procurement of required human resources. The need of man-power planning is to ensure that an organisation has the adequate number of right kind of personnel available for the work. When an organisation has decided the number and quality of personnel required, it should take appropriate action to procure them. In short, the recruitment is the process of procurement of human resource. Selection starts after the recruitment ends. According to Dale Yoder, "Selection is the process in which candidates for employment are divided into two classes- those who are to be offered employment and others who are not. The process might be called rejection since more candidates may be turned away than hired. For this reason selection is frequently described as negative process, in contrast with the positive programme of recruitment."

Promotion and transfer : Promotion is an upward movement or progress of an employee in the organisation to a higher position or rank. The promotions are decided according to seniority and merits of an individual. According to Pigors and Myers, "Management should stress ability above seniority in promotion. Seniority should be considered only when the qualifications of two candidates for a better job are for practical purposes substantially equal.

Transfer : Means movement of an individual from one place to another due to organisational needs. It is a change in assignment in which an employee remains in the same level of hierarchy. The purpose of transfer is to enhance the effectiveness of organisation, to acquire versatility and competence in profession, transfer on compassionate ground due to health and age factors, and also to train the employees for later advancement or promotion, etc.

Job analysis, job evaluation and job design :

Job analysis : This is a systematic study of the job in order to collect the information of a job holder, who carries it out under various circumstances and also what type of skills are required for performance of the job. According to Henry L. Wylie, job analysis deals with the anatomy of job. This is the complete study of the job (or position) embodying known and determinable factors including the duties and responsibilities involved in its performance, the conditions under which performance is progressed, the nature of the task, the qualifications required of a worker, and the conditions of the employment, such as pay, hours of work, opportunities and privileges.

Job evaluation : It is a process determining the worth of a job in relation to other jobs. The idea of this process is to assess the correct rate of pay. In this, the peculiarity is that it assesses and compares the demands with a normal performance of a particular job by a normal worker without taking into consideration the individual's abilities and performance. Concisely job evaluation appraises the job and not the man. Following are four basic methods of job evaluation— (i) Ranking method, (ii) Classification, (iii) Factor comparison, and (iv) Point method. Apart from the above, nowadays, market pricing method is also adopted for evaluation.

Job design : This can be named as a logical continuum or sequence of job analysis. Job analysis provides job related data and also the knowledge and skills expected of an individual to perform a particular job. Job design integrates work content like task, relationship, reward (monetary/non-monetary), qualifications like skill, ability and the knowledge for a certain job suitable to the employee.

Merit rating and performance appraisal :

Merit rating : This is a system followed in the early 19th century to evaluate the abilities, personal attributes of an employee. Robert Owen, the Scottish Millowner, who devised this system and made 'Character books' for his employees and displayed a colour block indicative of Merit at each worker's workplace. This system was known as 'Efficiency rating' and 'Employee rating' was also known as 'Performance rating',

According to Edwin B. Flippo, Merit rating is an employee's excellence in matters pertaining to his present job and to his potentialities for a better job. This process of merit rating is considered as equitable and just that weeds out inefficient employees and an aid to management.

Performance appraisal : This is a system evaluation of present performance and the potential capabilities of personnel by their immediate superiors in an organisation. It is a system, which analyses and evaluates the data related to job behaviour and also the output of individuals. This method is based on the principles of achievement of results. Organisations have to measure employee performance to establish whether acceptable standards of performance are being maintained. This system is considered vital to human resource management in all respects. The main objective of conducting the performance appraisals is to make practical approach to compensation decisions of management to create promotion avenues and conducting employee training and development programmes.

Wage and salary administration

Traditional wage principles state that wage and salary administration is a method through which wage and salary levels and structures are ascertained in an organisation. The initial purpose of wage administration is to ensure management and employees of suitable remuneration for services rendered.

A proper wage administration policy can be summarised as

- An effective wage administration must create a feeling that remuneration is fair and equitable.
- There must be consistency of wages between comparable jobs.
- Flexibility of wages in relation to changes in labour market.
- Rationality in solving wage problems.
- Wage administration should be adequately supervised by the management.
- Individual capability and excellence need proper recognition.

QUESTIONS

RECRUITMENT AND SELECTION PROCESS

1. **What is recruitment?**
   (a) A process by which people with requisite qualification, skills are recruited for functioning of organisations. It is only an informal persuade.
   (b) Recruitment is a method through which qualified applicants are recruited for organisational works.
   (c) Recruitment is not alone an activity of fulfilling an organisation's human resource needs, whereas it has a say over the future of the organsation.
   (d) Success of any organisation depends upon the people, who are recruited in the organisation for executing jobs.

2. **What is the purpose and significance of recruitment?**
   (a) To increase the number of workers in a cost effective method.
   (b) To determine the present and future requirements of any organisation in relation to human resource planning and subsequent job analysis.
   (c) To visualise the effectiveness of human resource in the short-term and long-term process.
   (d) All the above.

3. **Why do the recruitment needs arise in an organisation?**
   (a) Due to promotion, transfer, retirement, disability and death.
   (b) Expansion of business of the organisation.
   (c) When diversification of production and manufacture.
   (d) None of the above.

4. **What is the process of recruitment?**
   (a) An ideal recruitment process must attract a large number of candidates.
   (b) The process involve planning, evaluation of a particular strategy, screening and evaluation of applicants.
   (c) A recruitment programme must have the required standards specified for the candidates to enable the identification of the proper applicants.
   (d) Careful human resource planning process can avoid over estimation of cost.

5. **"Recruitment is the process of searching prospective employees and stimulating them to apply for jobs in the organisation", who said this?**
   (a) Robert Heller (b) E.B. Flippo
   (c) Keith Davis (d) A.C. Hamblin

6. **What are the sources of recruitment?**
   (a) Internal and external sources
   (b) Educational institutions like colleges, schools and technical training centres.
   (c) Labour market
   (d) Through agents.

7. **What procedure is followed in Government/Public sector undertakings, etc., for recruitment of non-technical and non-supervisory duties?**
   (a) Advertisement through media
   (b) Relations and friends of present employees.
   (c) Sponsored by Regional Employment Exchange

(d) All the above

8. What is known by recruitment under indigant circumstances?

(a) Recruitment under special circumstances.

(b) When breadwinner of the family becomes unfit or expires on duty, his eligible next of kin is offered the job by the employer.

(c) To support financially poor family of the worker, who becomes incapacitated or expires while in the service, his eligible next of kin is offered the job.

(d) None of the above.

9. What is the internal source of recruitment?

(a) It is the best method of recruiting upper and middle level managers.

(b) This is a process called 'Promotion from within.'

(c) Filling the vacancies within the organisation.

(d) It is advisable to take an inside employee, who already knows the company and have proved his ability and loyalty.

10. What are the Government guidelines for recruitment?

(a) While recruitment, SC and ST and other backward classes are given quota.

(b) Some of the government legislations bearing subjects like child labour, role of employment exchange are to be taken care of.

(c) Quota system is not followed in private sector.

(d) None of the above.

11. What are the different legislations governing policies of the government regarding recruitment?

(a) Factory Act, 1948

(b) Contract Act, 1970, Bonded labour system Abolition Act, 1976 and the Child labour Act, 1986.

(c) Minimum Wages Act, 1936, Industrial Disputes Act, 1947, Payment of Bonus Act, 1965.

(d) Payment of Wages Act, 1936, Trade unions Act, 1926, The workmen's Compensation Act, 1923.

12. What is selection?

(a) It is a process of matching a man with the job.

(b) The process of choosing individuals, who possess the necessary skills for successfully filling the specific vacancies in an organisation.

(c) A deliberate effort of an organisation to select a limited number of personnel from a large number of applicants.

(d) In short, right person for the right job.

13. What is meant by the scientific method of selection?

(a) It is one of the most important functions of HRM.

(b) It involves determining the nature of job to be executed, nature of personnel required, nature of sources of recruitment and the process of selection.

(c) Selection is to acquire such personnel, who are most likely to meet organisational standards of performance.

(d) It is matching the standards between person and the job.

14. What does the policy of selection process mean?

(a) This differs from organisation to organisation with regard to its function and type of jobs to be carried out.

(b) Selection procedure must take into consideration the public policy and operate within the framework of provisions laid down by the State or Central statutory controls.

(c) Public policy may not discriminate against any person on grounds of colour, race, caste, sex, etc., and at the same time prohibit through public policy employment of children in central industries or limit hours of work for women workers in a plant.

(d) None of the above.

15. What are the steps followed in selection procedure?

(a) Inviting applications, preliminary employment interviews (screening), employment tests, determining (final) interviews.

(b) Investigation of reference, Medical examination, short-listing and final approval (selection).

(c) Verification of individual's selection.

(d) All the above.

16. What are the prerequisites of a stable recruitment policy?

(a) It should have long term planning to give employment to personnel.

(b) It should highlight the necessity of job analysis.

(c) In conformity to general personnel policies, employment security, must be flexible to accomplish the changing needs of the orgsnisation.

(d) It should match qualities of the employees for work motivation.

17. What are the merits of internal source of recruitment?

(a) The incumbent will stay in the organisation for a longer period than the outside new entrants.

(b) "Known devils are preferable than unknown angels"— with better loyalty that can safely be relied upon.

(c) Improve the morale of employes, that they would be preferred over outsiders, when vacancies occur and also the employer is in a better position to evaluate the staff employed than a new entrant.

(d) It gives a sense of job security and opportunity for advancement of the staff already employed.

18. What is preliminary interview?

(a) Applications received from the job seekers are scrutinised and those who are not qualified are eliminated.

(b) Applications received are meticulously scrutinised and rejected, if they are not in accordance with the instructions.

(c) The applications, which are as per the requirements, are short-listed and the candidates are called for attending the selection process.

(d) None of the above.

19. What is the selection test?

(a) Test is generally used for selecting the candidates for various professions.

(b) Tests are used to determine the aptitude, personality and cognitive ability of the individual.

(c) Polygraph (test for reproducing writing/dictation) is also nowadays, used to find out correctness.

(d) All the above.

20. What are the criteria followed while using tests?

(a) The tests must provide correct data of information required.

(b) Test must possess certain amount of objectivity.

(c) The test must possess predictive validity.

(d) It must have reliability, validity, objectivity and necessary standardisation.

21. What do you mean by reference checks and recommendations?

(a) Employers make request in the application form to provide the address and telephone number/s of previous employers/respectable persons known to the applicant.

(b) This check is normally carried out

when an individual clears the final interview.

(c) Through this check the present employer of the individual can have a general idea of the candidate, whom he is going to offer the job.

(d) None of the above.

22. What is attitude measurement?

(a) A process of test usually carried out in business organisations to judge various characters of an individual.

(b) Attitude is an inclination of mind towards certain direction.

(c) Self-assessment and projective techniques are used to measure the attitude of an individual.

(d) Attitude measurement can provide guidelines to psychologist to know various character attributes of an individual.

23. What do you mean by personality measurement?

(a) Personality is measured through various tests.

(b) Measurement is carried out on three areas like personal adjustments, attributes and interests of an individual.

(c) Personality tests are used to find out the qualities possessed by an individual.

(d) All the above.

24. What is cognitive ability test?

(a) Test of intelligence is known as cognitive ability.

(b) This test is normally used for selection of jobs involving complex cognitive abilities.

(c) Used for selection of executives and certain categories of supervisors.

(d) All the above.

25. What does group discussion indicate?

(a) Nowadays, it is used as one of the most important tests and effective technique for personality and leadership evaluation.

(b) This test can bring out an individual's power of expression, sound reasoning, rich knowledge, confidence, fluency and delivery.

(c) It also brings out command over language, liveliness and sociability and ability to influence.

(d) None of the above.

26. What are the principles of testing?

(a) Which test to be used for a particular test is an important decision.

(b) Tests to be used only when there is exquisite need for them and also use the most appropriate one.

(c) Success of the tests depends on its correct use.

(d) All the above.

27. What does counselling refer to?

(a) Providing professional help and service, some are with psychological or personal problems.

(b) In industries employee counselling is conducted on various occasions.

(c) This is given by trained staff members.

(d) Many employers have introduced occupational health care for their employees.

28. What are different occasions on which counselling is required?

(a) Psychological or health counselling to employees with emotional or mental problem and vocational guidance by experts, who wish to advise on careers or vocation.

(b) Information given by a superior or other staff member concerning the organisation or the job.

(c) Information on community resources given by a trained staff member to assist employees with personal problems.

(d) All the above.

29. What is the manager's role as a counsellor?

(a) His role is very vital because he is the one, who interacts with employees in day-to-day work.

(b) His role can reduce stress situations at work, which is one of the methods for staff development.

(c) It improves organisational performance because people with less worries and stress will be more willing and innovative.

(d) None of the above.

30 What is meant by quality of work life?

(a) Proper and fair compensation, safe and healthy working conditions.

(b) Opportunities to use and develop human capacities with freedom at work place to develop skills and involvement in improving production standards.

(c) Future opportunity for continued growth and security of job.

(d) Constitutionalism at work place in all respects by intervention of Union and Management.

31. What do you mean by induction and placement?

(a) Action of introducing someone to a particular post.

(b) Appointing a person for a particular job.

(c) Introducing an individual to a temporary job undertaken to gain work experience.

(d) None of the above.

32. The selection procedure does not end once the selection is made. Why?

(a) After the selection induction is to be made for employees.

(b) In this process the individual is familiarised with most of the aspects of company like- history, product and major operations. The routine, leave, holidays, work time, welfare facilities, etc., by a senior person of the department.

(c) The purpose of induction is to educate the employee and make him oriented with the company and its various aspects like production, administration, discipline and welfare.

(d) During induction period an employee is familiarised with all aspects of the company and senior employees of his department.

33. What is follow-up?

(a) After induction, the new employee is directed to work under the supervision of the manager or supoervisor, who will be able to assess the employee's performance.

(b) It provides a scope for understanding whether the right man has been placed on the right job or there has been an omission.

(c) If a new employee is not carrying out his job properly; the reason for the same to be ascertained.

(d) Through interview, guidance and counselling need to be carried out to understand the problem of the employee and proper action to be suggested to overcome such issues.

34. What do you mean by placement?

(a) Placement is carried out after selection; a new employee is given a temporary placement to gain work experience.

(b) It involves assigning a specific position and responsibility to an employee.

(c) Placement is the actual posting of an employee to a specific job.

(d) Usually, the organisations place the new employees on 'Probation' for a specific period of time and after the followup and assessment, the employee is made permanent as per merit.

35. What is the purpose orientation?

(a) To make new employees-feel at home.

(b) Make the employees free from the anxiety.

(c) Make them get along with their work.

(d) Introduce the new employees to their coworkers and encourage them to interact.

36. What is the process followed for induction and orientation in Indian industries?

(a) Most of the industries conduct a comprehensive one-day programme. Company's HR Department normally initiate the programme.

(b) This includes the welcome to the organisation and giving a general idea of the industry and its functioning, by a responsible person designated for this purpose. New entrants are taken around the organisation to various departments for familiarisation. Audio-Visual programme featuring the various aspects of company and its policies are also shown, wherever such facilities are available.

(c) When the employees are detailed to their respective departments, the supervisor/foreman may educate them on their duties and responsibilities and work procedures, etc. Modern employers provide company's manual to new entrants to have a detail knowledge about the company as a whole.

(d) Induction and orientation are well defined procedures of every modern organisation to familiarise new employees.

37. What must be the inputs of induction and orientation programmes?

(a) It must inculcate confidence in workers so as to help them perform their duties in a comfortable manner.

(b) A new employee must feel that he is also a part and parcel of the company and have a sense of pride for the organisation.

(c) Induction must be a valuable source for information and interaction among coworkers to acquire special knowledge of the work ethos in general of the department and in particular one's assigned duties. This will place the individual at ease and will make himself to perform to the best of his abilities.

(d) In short, an induction programme must be pragmatic in all respects for the overall development of new employee.

38. How can induction be made effective?

(a) A new entrant be allowed to have adequate time to understand the work and organisational environment. Avoid overburdening the individual with many jobs in the initial stage.

(b) When individuals are new and require training for a particular job, place them 'on the job training' (OJT) under experienced supervisors so that they become perfect to handle the job independently and in the shortest possible time.

(c) Try to understand the capacity, ability, suitability and adaptability of the persons and then allot the job according to their standards. Do not compel them to do a work, which they do not know and have no confidence too.

(d) All the above.

39. What are the advantages of formal induction and orientation?

(a) It can improve organisational effectiveness.

(b) This will lead to match the workers properly with the job environment and create employees' effectiveness.

(c) It creates self-discipline amongst employees and also adjust to changes like technological and social aspects in business organisations.

(d) None of the above.

40. What is the purpose of interview?

(a) Much information can be obtained through the application of the candidate. During interview, the interviewer can ascertain correctness of the facts. It also enables the interviewer to make correct assessment of the individual.

(b) Through the interview the interviewee and the interviewer have face to face contact. It also measures the communication ability, sociability and the personality of the interviewee.

(c) It is the most common tool for any selection process.

(d) Usually the duration is not specified for interviews. It depends mostly on the interviewers and the number of candidates to be interviewed. Normally, the time for interviews range between 15 minutes and one hour.

41. What are the different types of interviews?

(a) Informal interview, formal interview and planned interview.

(b) Patterned interview, non-directive interview, depth interview.

(c) Stress interview, group interview.

(d) None of the above.

42. How a good interview is conducted?

(a) Let the candidate feel comfortable and attentive before asking any questions. Then tactfully ask personal questions. Allow the candidate talk freely throughout.

(b) Try to get relevant information during conversion. Do not express any displeasure through conversation or body language, i.e., gestures.

(c) Be dispassionate in your conclusion.

(d) All the above.

43. What is group discussion?

(a) It is a form of informal gathering in which normally, 8-10 members take part at a time.

(b) It is not a pre-planned exercise, whereas it is spontaneous conversation.

(c) It is an informal discussion on a subject.

(d) It is a democratic way of acquiring and examining knowledge.

44. What are the advantages of group discussion?

(a) In this discussion members learn how to communicate in a group and thus overcome their shyness.

(b) They learn many new things and it helps to improve their knowledge.

(c) The questions like self-confidence, alertness, manner of emphasising one's opinion, giving respect to others while talking, ability to discuss a subject without emotions, ability of reasoning.

(d) It provides entertainment to observers.

PROMOTION AND TRANSFER

45. What is promotion?

(a) This is a process carried out by the organisation for the employees advancement in the career.

(b) This is made according to vacancies of the more fresh posts.

(c) Organisation normally follows merit or seniority method or both for promotions.

(d) Promotion is an advancement in career of an employee in the organisation for the present position to a higher one with increase in pay or wage and higher status.

46. What is the purpose of promotion?

(a) Promotion is a recognition of employees capability and performance. It enhances the morale and loyalty of the employees.

(b) Promotions suggest the skills developed by employees.

(c) It is a means to retain and renewal for an employee for his long-standing association with the company.

(d) Promotion is as recognition of a worker's best performance.

47. What does transfer indicate?

(a) Movement of an employee from one place to another either on promotion or otherwise, as the case may be.

(b) It is a movement of an employee from one place to another.

(c) This is to deal with fluctuation in work requirement.

(d) This is to deal with an employee on the grounds of health or on personal or compassionate ground.

48. What are the salient features of a promotion policy?

(a) It should be within the organisation or may be as per the requirement. It should not deny promotion to qualified person within.

(b) The promotion be planned on a sound bases, either on performance appraisal or on confidential reports.

(c) The criteria for promotion need to be followed and stagnation point to be specified. Also organisations prepare their employees through training and short-list such personnel, who deserve higher grade promotion. This policy of promotion to be communicated to all personnel through official circulars.

(d) All the above.

49. What are the types of promotions?

(a) Promotion can be a multiple chain. This process provides clearly defined channel to higher stages in each position.

(b) Promotion without financial benefits are called 'dry promotions'. An individual's increments are stopped, when this type of promotion is offered.

(c) The procedure of promotion starts from the bottom level worker to the Managing director of a company.

(d) None of the above.

50. What do you mean by promotion, based on seniority vis-a-vis merit?

(a) Promotions are based on the ability, hardwork, honesty and merit, etc.

(b) Many informal influences are powerful determinants in promotion. A senior executive normally thinks that promotion is given to that person, who is loyal to himself and the organisation.

(c) Trade unions are of the opinion that promotion should be given on the basis of seniority, whereas management favours promotions on the basis of merit.

(d) Management prefers a known person with good performance in a higher position rather than any outsider.

51. What is the general policy of promotion followed in Govt. departments and public sector undertakings?

(a) Normally, the seniority is given weightage to avoid representations from the union.

(b) A middle path is selected largely in Govt. organisations taking into consideration the merit and seniority of the individual.

(c) Private sector, give importance to merit and ability of the individual.

(d) None of the above.

52. What is the main purpose of transfer?

(a) To fulfil the needs like reallocation and reduction of work force, etc., of an organisation

(b) To replace a new employee by an old one, who has been in the organisation for a long period.

(c) To meet an employees personal request due to domestic and other problems.

(d) All the above.

53. What do you mean by a resignation?

(a) A letter stating an intention of an individual to leave the job voluntarily.

(b) Leaving the job by an individual.

(c) Leaving the job or responsibility due to dissatisfaction.

(d) None of the above.

54. What is exit or separation?

(a) Cessation of service agreement with the organisation.

(b) This occurs due to resignation of the employee or discharge, dismissal, retirement or death.

(c) Separation due to temporary duty to other places and special assignment away from the organisation.

(d) None of the above.

55. What is the effect of a non-voluntary resignation?

(a) Resignation may be voluntary for better opportunities elsewhere (on personal grounds).

(b) It is compulsory resignation, when an employee is asked to resign on disciplinary grounds to avoid termination of service.

(c) This also occurs in case of severe dereliction of duties by the employee. In such a case, the employer asks the concerned employee to put-up his resignation to avoid disciplinary action.

(d) It is an acceptance of something undesirable but inevitable.

56. What is discharge?

(a) An employee is discharged means relieved of his duties and responsibilities.

(b) Discharge involves permanent separation of an employee from the pay roll of a company.

(c) In this process the employee forfeits his right to job.

(d) Discharge can take place due to non-availability of a suitable place to absorb the individual. This may also be a possible cause of individual's nature like laziness and also frequent absence without leave and lack of skill, etc.

57. What does dismissal refer to?

(a) A process of terminating the services of an employee on legal grounds.

(b) Termination of the services of an employee by way of punishment.

(c) Before terminating the services of an employee, he be given an opportunity to show cause why his services should not be dismissed.

(d) On dismissal there should not be any violation of the principles of natural justice by the employer.

58. What are the principles of retrenchment?

(a) Termination of the services of a workman for any reason whatsoever.

(b) If an employer wants to retrench any workman who is in his service for more then one year or so, the individual must be given one month's notice or one month's pay in lieu of such notice.

(c) The employer will also have to pay to the workman at the time of effecting retrenchment, compensation at the rate of 15 days average pay for every year of his service. Further, the employer is also required to inform the government by a notice in the manner prescribed.

(d) None of the above.

59. What do you mean by demotion?

(a) Lowering down of the status, salary and responsibilities of an employee.

(b) When demotion of an employee takes place, his prestige is adversely affected.

(c) It is carried out, when an individual is not performing his duties and responsibilities, as required.

(d) All the above.

60. "Demotion (down grading) refers to lowering down of the status, salary and responsibilities of an employee. It is used as a punitive measure, when there is serious breach of duty on the part of an employee. It is a reassignment of an individual to a job of a lower rank and pay usually involve lower level responsibility." Who said this?

(a) Yoder and Others (Haneman, Tumbull and Stones)

(b) Scott Clothier and Spriegal

(c) Mc Farland

(d) Likert, R.

61. What is the Concept of productivity?

(a) All types of economy like Socialist, Communist or Mixed productivity, play an important role.

(b) It is a key to prosperity in modern times.

(c) It is the ratio between the production of a given commodity measured by volume and one or more of the corresponding input factors also measured by volume.

(d) Modern concept of productivity evolved after World War II.

62. "Productivity means the balance between all factors of production that will give the greatest output for the smallest efforts." Who said this?

(a) Peter Drucker

(b) M. Banerjee

(c) Maya Deo and S.B. Karmarkar

(d) V.K.R. Menon.

63. What is production?

(a) Production relates to value, volume and quantum of goods and services produced during a specific period of time by workers.

(b) The quantity of goods produced by an enterprise for a particular period of time.

(c) The volume of goods produced in relation to the input or resources utilised in the process.

(d) Production is an absolute concept.

64. What does efficiency mean?

(a) The quality of working productivity with no waste or money or effort.

(b) Relates to inherent competence.

(c) Capacity of a given input or production unit to produce under given conditions of work.

(d) None of the above.

65. What are the important causes of inefficiency?

(a) Climatic conditions.

(b) Immigrant workers and lack of skills.

(c) Low wages and long hours of work.

(d) All the above.

66. What are the major factors affecting productivity?

(a) Development in science and technology, layout of plant, quality of raw materials used, equipment and machines, production process and managerial techniques.

(b) Performance and motivational factors.

(c) Availability of adequate finance.

(d) Environment and climatic factors.

67. Which methods increase the production?

(a) Motivation and incentives to workers, improved working conditions, standardisation of production methods, proper selection and job orientation to workers and efficient HR management.
(b) Strict supervision of cost, quality and production methods.
(c) Proper layout of enterprise to have smooth functioning of production process.
(d) Proper coordination of material handling in production units.

68. What are the benefits of productivity?
(a) Higher productivity leads to profit.
(b) Leads to higher per capita income.
(c) Reduces the price of goods thereby consumer satisfaction and increase in demand of goods.
(d) It also ensures utilisation of available resources.

69. What does productivity movement in India mean?
(a) Since independence, Government of India has been focusing this issue.
(b) India is a developing country, which needs to achieve the target in production for proper allocation and utilisation of available resources for increasing exports.
(c) Ensure higher standard of living and higher per capita income and decrease the production cost.
(d) Increase overall prosperity of economy and also developing the efficiency of the work force.

70. What is the importance of production planning and control?
(a) Production, planning and control are interrelated functions.
(b) This involves how much to produce, when, what and how.
(c) This requires proper planning and adequate control over the process of production.
(d) This process includes product engineering and process engineering.

71. How productivity can be measured?
(a) Physical output per man-hour and per rupee of working capital employed.
(b) Physical output per tonne of raw materials consumed to reveal waste and scrap reduction.
(c) Physical output as percentage of the rated capacity of the plant or radio of productive machine hours used in relation to total machine hours available.
(d) All the above.

JOB ANALYSIS, JOB EVALUATION AND JOB DESIGN

72. What is job analysis?
(a) It establishes job relation factor to identify what the job entails and also what a jobber must possess to carry out the job efficiently.
(b) Collecting the information of a particular job.
(c) Job analysis deals with determining the characteristics of each job.
(d) None of the above.

73. What does job study refer to?
(a) The study of job ingredients.
(b) The study helps individual for a particular job.
(c) Job ingredients are essential for developing the manual for job operations.
(d) The initial purpose of job study is to determine the proper way of doing the job, standardising the method and management of time.

74. What is the four-point job analysis formula?

(a) What the worker does and how he does it?

(b) Why he does it and the skill involve in doing.

(c) This formula to be used for accurate and useful study.

(d) All the above.

75. What do you mean by methods of job analysis?

(a) Sending out questionnaire to job-holders for answers.

(b) Conducting interviews of supervisors and job-holders.

(c) Observe the job-holder, while executing the job.

(d) All the above.

76. What is job specification?

(a) It is a product of job analysis and description.

(b) The name given to the part of the job study involving detailed statements of particulars of an employee necessary for performance of a particular job.

(c) With uniform mechanical methods and combination of specific human skills bring the required standard.

(d) None of the above.

77. What does job evaluation refer to?

(a) A job rating process.

(b) Represents the relative value of every job in a plant and determines the fair basic wage for such jobs.

(c) A process of analysing and assessing various jobs systematically to ascertain their relative worth in an organisation.

(d) In job evaluation, job is ranked and not the job-holder.

78. What is the purpose of job evaluation?

(a) To establish a definite plan of salary administration.

(b) Give proper emphasis on job factors.

(c) Solving wage controversies.

(d) To establish relative requirements of the job for the purpose of aptly rewarding the workers for their performance.

79. What do you mean by job evaluation objectives?

(a) Job analysis, job description and job specification.

(b) Process of evaluation for fixing the wage.

(c) Fixation of wage and salary and employees' classification.

(d) All the above.

80. What are the methods of job evaluation?

(a) At times, job evaluation may be subjective in nature, as the jobs are not separated into factors.

(b) Ranking and job classification methods are non-analytical ones.

(c) Analytical methods are point-ranking method and factor comparison.

(d) All the above.

81. What is job design?

(a) Importance of designing job goes back to the scientific management era.

(b) To redesign is a technique of enriching the job characteristics with a view to improving the quality of work life.

(c) The design is a process of deciding on the content of a job in respect of its duties and responsibilities.

(d) All the above.

82. What is the objective of job design?

(a) To satisfy the requirement of the organisation for productivity, operational efficiency and quality product or services.

(b) To satisfy motivational needs of the individual for interest and accomplishment.

(c) Overall objective of job design is to integrate the needs of the individual and organisation.

(d) All the above.

83. What are the techniques of design?

(a) Work specification, job rotation, job enlargement and job enrichment.

(b) Extend factors that affect the job design in many ways.

(c) Work simplification technique is an important factor in job design.

(d) It is the mental and physical skills of an employee to adopt the design.

84. What does work simplification mean?

(a) The job is simplified by dividing it into small subparts in stead of assigning the same to one individual.

(b) Work simplification follows, when job designers think that jobs are not rated as specialised.

(c) Over simplification can result into boredom amongst workers.

(d) Due to work simplification even the less trained employees can perform the jobs.

85. What is job rotation?

(a) When an activity of a job is no longer challenging, the employee is rotated to another job.

(b) This creates periodic assessment of an employee for his capability for the job to which he is rotated.

(c) Job rotation specially reduces boredom through diversifying the employee's activities.

(d) It is an effective system of developing multiple skills of employees.

86. What does job enlargement indicate?

(a) Jobs can be enlarged both horizontal and vertical dimensions.

(b) Job enlargement is the process by which organisation can utilise the entire abilities of employees.

(c) Job enlargement is a genetic term, which means adding more and difficult jobs.

(d) When additional simple tasks added to a job, the process is termed as horizontal job enlargement.

87. What does job enrichment refer to?

(a) Technique of job enrichment improves the quality of work, workers' involvement and motivation.

(b) It is one of the effective strategies against alienation.

(c) The worker needs to have the ability to take decision and exercise some discretion as to the way in which the work is to be performed.

(d) This method is also used as a motivational tool to satisfy higher order needs of the workers.

88. What is job description?

(a) It is an abstract of information gained from a report on job analysis.

(b) It describes the work performed, responsibility involved and skill required.

(c) Conditions under which the job is carried out.

(d) Type of personnel required for executing the job.

89. What is the purpose of job evaluation?

(a) Job evaluation is to establish the relative requirements of adequately rewarding the workers for their performance.

(b) Eliminating inequalities for solving wage controversies and removing personal prejudices.

(c) Faculty for comparison and survey.

(d) Standardization of job evaluation.

90. What are the important principles of job evaluation?

(a) Rate the job and not the man.

(b) Too many occupational wages should not be established.

(c) Success of job rating is dependent

on uniformity of understanding with regard to the definitions of elements and consistency in selection of these elements.
(d) All the above.

MERIT RATING AND PERFORMANCE APPRAISAL

91. What is merit rating?
(a) In olden days managers used to see the merits of an individual, therefore, the focus was on the merit of an individual.
(b) This process used to find what type of traits a person has than what he does.
(c) Merit rating focuses on merits than the performance of an individual. This type of rating was open to criticism because it did not give importance to performance.
(d) All the above.

92. "Merit rating is a systematic, periodic and so far as humanly possible, an impartial rating of an employee's excellence in matters pertaining to his present job and to his potentialities for better job." Who said this?
(a) Robert Owen,
(b) Edwin B. Flippo,
(c) E.F.L. Breach,
(d) Alford and Beatty.

93. What are the methods of merit rating?
(a) Ranking, man to man comparison, grading and graphic scales.
(b) Check-list, forced choice description, selection of critical incidents and descriptive evaluation.
(c) Method of merit rating means how a superior evaluate his subordinate's performance and merits.
(c) All the above.

94. What is critical incident method?
(a) This includes certain important acts of behaviour that make a difference between success and failure of an individual's performance.
(b) The rater selects critical events which occur in the performance of the individual.
(c) Critical incidents like refusal by an individual for the performance of a particular job.
(d) None of the above.

95. What is the importance of merit rating?
(a) It unifies the rating procedure which is more equitable and just.
(b) It is an appraisal of training needs, segregation of inefficient employees and an aid to management.
(c) Formal ratings are considered as superfluous in small organisations.
(d) In large organisations, it is recommended for personnel rating of their employees.

96. What is performance appraisal?
(a) It is a systematic and objective method of evaluating the potential usefulness of an employee to the organisation.
(b) Appraisal is a systematic evaluation of the performance of an employee.
(c) It helps to find out how an employee is performing his duties.
(d) It helps in acquiring an employee's job related strength and weakness.

97. What do you mean by objectives of performance appraisal?
(a) It helps the employer to gain a basis to identify the employee's merit and level of performance.

(b) Also leads to arrive at a decision to promote an employee according to his merit.
(c) It helps in understanding the training needs for a suitable employee, as to the increment in pay and promotion.
(d) All the above.

98. What is the periodicity of appraisal?
(a) Whenever the superior authority feels it necessary.
(b) Six monthly
(c) Annually
(d) All the above.

99. What are essential factors of the appraisal system?
(a) An appraisal system must be consistent and reliable, and should also be able to measure the performance area.
(b) The system should be practically easy to implement, economical to use continuously and must provide the feedback effectively.
(c) Appraisal must have the scope for recommending personnel for higher training if need be, for future promotions and transfers. It must be objective in nature and meant for improving employees' performance.
(d) All the above.

100. What are the limitations of appraisal?
(a) An appraisal is mostly a method of getting 'opinions' and not a method of measuring the performance. These opinions may have often error of judgement.
(b) Halo effect is the tendency to rate an individual 'high' and 'low;' according to the impression of the rater.
(c) There are possibility of having common error when a large number of personnel are to be rated. In such occasions, raters usually select a 'middle path', i.e., 'not high' or 'not low' to avoid the discontent of the employees and also to keep the raters safe so as not to invite criticism from any corner.
(d) Differences among raters in their rating ability.

101. What is annual confidential report (ACR)?
(a) ACRs are maintained by Govt. Departments and some of the public sector undertaking for the appraisal of their personnel for promotion and selection of career plans.
(b) It normally has 14 main areas, where a rater has to concentrate while assessing the individual.
(c Rating scales are fixed like Excellent, Good, Fair and Poor, as per the performance of an individual
(d) ACR contains the recommendation of the rater and the head of the department.

102. What are the performance evaluation criteria?
(a) Quality, quantity and the time consumed for the performance.
(b) Cost effectiveness, supervision and self-esteem with cohesive interaction.
(c) Criteria followed should be related to the job.
(d) None of the above.

103. What are the criteria for identifying good performance?
(a) The task to be completed and its possible outcome.
(b) When it is to be accomplished and its cost consideration.
(c) Performance skills of the individual.
(d) All the above.

104. How the performance is measured?
(a) Set the accepted performance standards.

(b) Be factual and report the critical behaviour that determine performance.
(c) Observe statistical, oral and written reports.
(d) None of the above.

105. What are key elements of MBO goal setting in an oranisation?
(a) In the MBO system top management formulate and inform the corporate goal to lower level.
(b) Lower level managers set their operational goals.
(c) In an organisation, individual performance goals, work group task goals and corporate goals are set in a systematic manner.
(d) All the above.

106. What is the need for post-appraisal interview?
(a) The appraiser gets an opportunity to explain the employee's strength and weakness what he had noted while making an appraisal.
(b) Help the employee to do better by understanding his weak points and rectifying them accordingly.
(c) This will create a better relationship between the superior and subordinate and both can create opportunities of development and growth in tandem.
(d) None of the above.

107 What is potential appraisal?
(a) Helps employees about their future prospects.
(b) It guides the employees on the improvement for future career prospects.
(c) It helps organisation to visualise a proper succession plan.
(d) All the above.

WAGE AND SALARY ADMINISTRATION

108. What is wage?
(a) The remuneration to which the person employed is entitled under the terms of employment.
(b) Reward for the work a person performed in terms of money.
(c) All remuneration including salary and allowance in terms of money for the employment.
(d) All the above.

109. What is the objective of a remuneration plan?
(a) To attract talented people to the organisation.
(b) Pay should be equal to the work of the individual; also, qualified people should get better wages. There must be equity in remuneration.
(c) If the compensation plan is below the expectation of the employees, they may leave the organisation in search of better remuneration.
(d) All the above.

110. Why wage administration has become an important factor in industry?
(a) Industrial disputes and labour unrest are quite often based on wage questions.
(b) Proper wage administration lie at the heart of industrial relation.
(c) Wage is regarded as an individual matter and a little difference in payment of weekly wage means

discontent and discord amongst workers.

(d) None of the above.

111. Which of the following payments come under the definition of Payment of Wages Act?

(a) Value of house accommodation, supply of light, water and medical attendance.

(b) Travelling allowance or the value of travelling concession.

(c) Any sum paid to defray special expenses entitled to him by nature of employment.

(d) Any additional remuneration payable under the terms of employment.

112. What are the permissible deductions from wages under Payment of Wages Act?

(a) Deduction of amount for company's welfare fund.

(b) Deduction of amount of employees' on sports meet.

(c) Deduction of wages, permissible under Section 7, Sub-section (2).

(d) All the above.

113. What are the important legislations for wage and salary administration?

(a) Industrial Disputes Act, 1947.

(b) Payment of Wage Act, 1936.

(c) Minimum Wages Act, 1947.

(d) Financial Regulations of the organisation.

114. Which are the institutions/legislation involved in fixing of wages?

(a) Employer, Wage Board, Pay Commission.

(b) Minimum Wage Act and Payment of Wages Act.

(c) State or Central Labour commission.

(d) Labour Court.

115. What are the Statutory Provisions regarding the payment of Wages?

(a) Payment to be disbursed on the last working day of every month.

(b) Period shall be fixed for payment of wages at intervals not exceeding one month and within first ten days after the last day of the wage period.

(c) Wages of a person by discharge or resignation must be paid not later than 2nd working day after his termination.

(d) Payment to be disbursed to employees every month before 5th and if the day happens to be Sunday or holiday, the next day.

116. What is the objective of compensation plan?

(a) Compensation or reward must encourage the employee to perform better.

(b) Different jobs must have different pay-scales according to the requirement of skills involved.

(c) It must be able to satisfy the internal, external, and individual equity.

(d) All the above.

117. The compensation function contributes to the organisational effectiveness in four basic ways like-

- **Allocation of Human Resources,**
- **Exercising adequate control over wages and salaries,**
- **Maintain satisfaction amongst employees,**
- **Motivate employees to perform better- Who said this?**

(a) Ewing, David, W.

(b) Beach, D.S.

(c) Kogelman Richard, D.

(d) Cummings, Paul, W.

118. What is the minimum wage to be paid?

(a) A wage suitable to employer paid to the employee.

(b) The quantum of payment prescribed by the 15th Labour Conference to a worker.

(c) The wage to be paid whether the company is big or small, makes profit or not. It is the barest minimum that a worker can expect to get for his service rendered by him.
(d) All the above.

119. What is known as method of wage payments?

(a) It is the oldest system of compensating labour.
(b) The employee can expect compensation for the work executed either based on the length of time at work or the production of work.
(c) The methods are usually named as day work (per diem) and piece work (compensation paid or the price of job).
(d) None of the above.

120. Which are the factors that influence wage and salary administration?

(a) Capacity of the organisation to pay, supply, and demand of labour and ongoing market rate.
(b) Cost of living, living wage, productivity and psychological and sociological factors.
(c) Trade Unions interference and bargaining.
(d) Approach of management.

121. What are the principles of wage and salary administration?

(a) They must be in accordance with the wage policies of the organisation.
(b) Salary plans must be flexible, wage fixation to be carried out after proper job evaluation and must be consistent with organisational plans and programmes.
(c) They must be in conformity to equity and social and economic objectives of the nation.
(d) All the above.

122. Why wage surveys are carried out?

(a) These surveys are carried out to gather information on bench mark jobs.
(b) They seek to answer questions like what are the payment rates of other companies? What they do by way of social insurance? What is the level of pay offered by other firms for same type of jobs etc.
(c) Most of the firms adopt results of package surveys available from research organisations.
(d) Wage survey must be useful and satisfy the frequency, scope and accuracy of the results obtained.

123. What are the components of wage structure of a company?

(a) Pay structure depends on several factors such as labour, market conditions, paying capacity of the company, and the legal provisions.
(b) Wage, dearness allowance (DA linked with Indian Consumer Price Index).
(c) Fair and equitable remuneration offering similar pay for similar work.
(d) All the above.

124. What is the wage differential?

(a) Wage differs in different employment or in industries and localities and also between in some employment and grade.
(b) The differential can be interindustry, inter-area, geographical and personal.
(c) Difference in technological advancement of companies.
(d) None of the above.

125. What is the importance of wage differential?

(a) Differential has a great economic and social significance.
(b) It is directly related to the allocation of economic resources of a country including human resource, growth natural income and the pace of economic development.

(c) Differential wages show differences in the physical and mental abilities of workers.

(d) It facilitates the most desirable rate of economic progress.

126. What are the differential wages in India?

(a) They depict a characteristic of the unorganised labour market.

(b) Personal differential because of job selling.

(c) Individual bargaining and wage discrimination in organised and unorganised sectors in industry.

(d) Interference of Wage Boards and Government in fixation of minimum wages and pressure of Trade Unions try to eliminate the conditions.

127. What is the minimum Wages Act, 1948?

(a) The Act prescribes minimum rate of wages to certain categories of workers. This can be fixed by hours, day, week, month or any other longer period.

(b) The Act provides for setting up of a tripartite body consisting of employees, union and government to advise on fixing and revising minimum wage rates. The rate could be for a period of five years and subject to revision thereafter.

(c) The Act could not prevent fully the exploitation of labour due to various inconsistencies. The Act also did not define minimum wages nor specified any guidelines for its determination.

(d) All the above.

128. What is the payment of Wage Act, 1936?

(a) It provides for regular payment of wages without any unauthorised deduction by the employer.

(b) Deductions are only permissible under Section 7 (ii) of the Act, which are called authorised deductions.

(c) This Act covers all industrial establishments, factories, railways and contractors, where monthly wages of workers are less than Rs. 1,600/- (to be revised).

(d) None of the above.

129. What criteria are followed to determine basic wages?

(a) Report of Fair Wage Committee, 1948 and the recommendations of Indian Labour Conference, 1957.

(b) Various awards by Wage Tribunals, Wage Boards and reports of Pay Commission.

(c) The skills required for execution of the job, experience of the individual, requirement of mental and physical work, training needed, responsibilities involved in and the hazardous nature of work are the determinant factors of basic wage.

(d) None of the above.

130. What is the mandatory requirement of wage to be followed by an employer?

(a) Fair wage.

(b) Living wage.

(c) Minimum wage.

(d) None of the above.

131. What are the constituents of a good wage plan?

(a) Plan should be easily understood, capable of easy computation and effectively motivating the employees.

(b) It should be stable and also provide remuneration to employees.

(c) In wage plan, remuneration does not vary with quality of output.

(d) All the above.

**132. "Residual claimant wage theory constitutes four factors of production/ business activity, viz.,
(i) land, (ii) labour, (iii) capital, and (iv) entrepreneurship. Wages represent the amount of value created**

in production, which remains after payment has been made for all these factors of production. In other words, labour is the residual claimant." Who said this?

(a) John Bates Clark
(b) Francis A. Walker,
(c) Marsh and Simon,
(d) Karl Mark

133. What is the procedure of fixing minimum rate of wage?

(a) According to Section 4 of Minimum Wages Act, any minimum rate of wages are fixed by the appropriate government (State/Central) for the scheduled employment under Section 3 of Minimum Wages Act.
(b) A basic rate of wage and a special allowance at the rate to be adjusted at intervals as directed by the government and also in the variation in the cost of living index applicable to such workers.
(c) A basic rate of wage with or without the cost of living allowance and the cash value of concessions in supply essential commodities at concessional rates so authorised.
(d) An all inclusive rate allowing for the basic rate, the cost of living allowance and the cash value of the concessions, if any.

134 "What Bargaining theory of wages is determined by the relative bargaining power of workers or trade unions and of employers. When a trade union is involved, basic wages, fringe benefits, job differential and individual differences tend to be determined by the relative strength of organisation and trade union." Who said this?

(a) John Davidson (b) Adam Smith.
(c) Ricardo, D. (d) Beach, D.S.

135 'Subsistence Theory' of wages was propounded by David Ricardo during 1817. It states that labourers are paid to enable them to subsist and perpetuate the race without increase or diminution. This theory is known as some other theory of wages. What is it?

(a) Wage fund theory,
(b) Surplus value theory of wages.
(c) Iron law of wages.
(d) Marginal productivity theory.

136. What is fair wage?

(a) It is the wage that is above the minimum wage.
(b) The prevailing rate of wages in the similar occupation, it stands at the level of natural income and also depends on the place of industry and employer's capacity to pay.
(c) This wage is considered below the living wage.
(d) All the above.

137. What does living wage indicate?

(a) It substantiates the living standard of an employee to a certain extent.
(b) It is the highest among three wages of the Wage Policy of India.
(c) It provides basic amenities of life, efficiency of worker and satisfy the social needs of the worker like medical, education, retirement, etc.
(d) None of the above.

138. What is Wage Boards?

(a) Important institutions set up by Government of India for fixation and revision of wages.
(b) The Wage Board studies various aspects of wage related subjects and submit the recommendations to the government for approval. They are at times accepted or modified by the government or reject all together. Recommendations approved are to be enforced by the concerned parties.
(c) Wage Board fix and revise various aspects of wages like basic pay, DA,

incentives, over-time and other allowances, etc.

(d) All the above.

139. What does bonus mean?

(a) Bonus is an ex gratia payment to the workers beyond their normal wages.

(b) Bonus to workers is governed by the Bonus Act, 1965.

(c) Bonus is a share of the workers in the profit of an organisation.

(d) It is treated as a source of supplementing the actual wage and the need-based wage.

140. What is an incentive?

(a) An incentive or reward, which attracts a worker and motivates him to perform better.

(b) An incentive plan may consist of monetary and non-monetary elements.

(c) Time and correctness, and frequency are the basis for success of the incentive plan.

(d) The plan needs to be correctly communicated to employee for its effectiveness.

141. "Incentive system has a limited meaning that it excludes many kinds of inducements offered to employees to perform work or to work up to or beyond acceptable standards. It does not include:
(i) wage and salary payments and merit pay, (ii) overtime payments, pay for holidays, work or differentials according to shifts, i.e., all payments which could be considered for incentives to perform work as undesirable times, and (iii) premium pay for performing dangerous tasks. It is related wage payment plans which tie wages directly or indirectly to standards of productivity to profitability of the organisation or to both criteria." Who said this?

(a) French,

(b) David Ricardo,

(c) Adam Smith

(d) Francis A. Walker.

142. What are the objectives of wage incentive schemes?

(a) To improve the profit of the company, reducing labour and material cost.

(b) To implement incentives as a useful method for utilisation of man-power.

(c) Increasing workers' income without making higher wage rates.

(d) Enhance the morale to increase productivity.

143. What is the need of wage incentive system in India?

(a) In a country like India, the role of financial incentives has become the primary tool for motivating workers.

(b) The necessity of improving the productivity of Indian labour is also a great concern for industries. This can be only achieved by need-based financial incentive system.

(c) First, second and third Five Year Plans have adequately supported incentive system, earning beyond minimum wages, higher productivity and reduction in cost of production, respectively to the need of incentive system.

(d) None of the above.

144. What are the types of wage incentive plans?

(a) Plan for white-collar workers, plan for blue-collar workers and plan for managerial staff.

(b) Different category people have different needs, as such the plan to be designed accordingly for accomplishing their needs.

(c) All the incentive plans have two factors like- (i) they get a standard time for completion of a definite output or piece of work for a fixed wage,

(ii) the fixing of a rate of percentage by which bonus would be earned by a worker over and above his set wage, if the standard time is saved or the standard output is exceeded.

(d) None of the above.

145 What are different kinds of incentive schemes?

(a) Personal or individual incentive bonus.

(b) Group incentive bonus scheme.

(c) General incentive bonus scheme.

(d) All the above.

146. Under what category the Halsey and Rowan plan does come?

(a) Group incentive bonus scheme.

(b) Personal or individual incentive bonus scheme.

(c) General incentive scheme.

(d) Personal incentive time- or production-based incentive scheme.

147. "In production-based incentive bonus scheme, differential wage plan was one of the earliest incentive plans. In short, it is a piece rate method of wage payment, where the rate of payment increases as the worker speeds up his rate of working. In this respect, it is vitally different time-based incentive bonus schemes under which the rate falls the more quickly the work is completed." Who made this differential wage plan?

(a) Gantt, (b) F.W. Taylor,

(c) Merrick (d) Hasley.

148. What are the characteristics of an incentive plan?

(a) Minimum wages are guaranteed to all workers.

(b) Incentives are given to workers, who saved the performance time.

(c) For every work standard time is specified for its completion.

(d) All the above.

149. Where the group incentive scheme is most suitable?

(a) Where it is not possible to measure the performance of individual worker.

(b) Where the number of workers in a group is not very large.

(c) Who among the workers' group has equal skills and abilities.

(d) All the above.

150. What are the essentials of good incentive plan?

(a) Suitable environment of relation between management and workers.

(b) Workers must be informed the general idea of the plan going to be introduced.

(c) Plan must have simplicity and must be equitable having flexibility and attractive payments, over and above the plan must be economical.

(d) All the above.

151. Identify the following incentive plans, Priestman plan, Scailon plan, Productive bargaining, Copartnership, Profit sharing.

(a) Individual incentive plans.

(b) Group incentive plans.

(c) Personal incentive plans.

(d) None of the above.

152. What are fringe benefits?

(a) Fringe benefits mean extra benefits given to employees in addition to their pay.

(b) Fringe benefits got this name because they were insignificant components of compensation.

(c) They are supplementary form of compensation.

(d) They help raise the living conditions of employees.

INTROSPECTION

Managers belong to that group of rare men, who are aware of what is to be achieved.

ANSWERS

1 (a) A process by which people with requisite qualification, skills are recruited for functioning of organisations. It is only an informal persuade.

2 (b) To determine the present and future requirements of any organisation in relation to human resource planning and subsequent job analysis.

3 (a) and (b)
(a) Due to promotion, transfer, retirement, disability and death.
(b) Expansion of business of the organisation.

4 (b) The process involve planning, evaluation of a particular strategy, screening a n d evaluation of applicants.

5 (a) Robert Heller

6 (a) Internal and external sources.
Explanation : *Intrnal source*- Within the organisation means general man-power policy declares the intention to give present employees first chance at all employment opportunities in the organisation. Promotion within the employees and transfers. *External Source*- Advertisements, man-power consultants, contracts, present employee's friends and relations, employment exchanges, company's recruitments in educational institutions, etc.

7 (c) Sponsored by Regional Employment Exchange.

8 (c) To support financially poor family of the worker, who becomes incapacitated or expires while in the service, his eligible next of kin is offered the job.

9 (c) Filling the vacancies within the organisation.

10 (a) and (b)
(a) While recruitment, SC and ST and other backward classes are given quota.
(b) Some of the government legislations bearing subjects like child labour, role of employment exchange are to be taken care of.

11 (a), (b), (c), and (d)
(a) Factory Act, 1948
(b) Contract Act, 1970, Bonded labour system Abolition Act, 1976 and the Child labour Act, 1986.
(c) Minimum Wages Act, 1936, Industrial Disputes Act, 1947, Payment of Bonus Act, 1965.
(d) Payment of Wages Act, 1936, Trade unions Act, 1926, The workmen's Compensation Act, 1923.

12 (b) The process of choosing individuals, who possess the necessary skills for successfully filling the specific vacancies in an organisation.

13 (b) It involves determining the nature of job to be executed, nature of personnel required, nature of sources of recruitment and the process of selection.

14 (a), (b) and (c)
(a) This differs from organisation to organisation with regard to its function and type of jobs to be carried out.
(b) Selection procedure must take into consideration the public policy and operate within the framework of provisions laid down by the State or Central statutory controls.
(c) Public policy my not discriminate against any person on grounds such as colour, race, caste, sex, etc., and at the same time prohibit through public policy employment of children in central industries or limit hours of work for women workers in a plant.

15 (a) and (b)

(a) Inviting applications, preliminary employment interviews (screening), employment tests, determining (final) interviews.
(b) Investigation of reference, Medical examination, short-listing and final approval (selection).

16 (c) In conformity to general personnel policies, employment security, must be flexible to accomplish the changing needs of the organisation.

17 (c) Improve the morale of employees, that they would be preferred over outsiders, when vacancies occur and also the employer is in a better position to evaluate the staff employed than a new entrant.

18 (c) The applications, which are as per the requirements, are short-listed and the candidates are called for attending the selection process.

19 (b) Tests are used to determine the aptitude, personality and cognitive ability of the individual.

20 (d) It must have reliability, validity, objectivity and necessary standardisation.

21 (c) Through this check the present employer of the individual can have a general idea of the candidate, whom he is going to offer the job.

22 (c) Self-assessment and projective techniques are used to measure the attitude of an individual.

23 (b) Measurement is carried out on three areas like personal adjustments, attributes and interests of an individual.

24 (a) Test of intelligence is known as cognitive ability.

25 (a), (b) and (c)
(a) Nowadays, it is used as one of the most important tests and effective technique for personality and leadership evaluation.
(b) This test can bring out an individual's power of expression, sound reasoning, rich knowledge, confidence, fluency and delivery.
(c) It also brings out command over language, liveliness and sociability and ability to influence.

26 (b) Tests to be used only when there is exquisite need for them and also use the most appropriate one.

27 (a) Providing professional help and service, some are with psychological or personal problems.

28 (a) Psychological or health counselling to employees with emotional or mental problem and vocational guidance by experts, who wish to advise on careers or vocation.

29 (a), (b) and (c)
(a) His role is very vital because he is the one, who interacts with employees in day-to-day work.
(b) His role can reduce stress situations at work, which is one of the methods for staff development.
(c) It improves organisational performance because people with less worries and stress will be more willing and innovative.

30 (a), (b) and (c)
(a) Proper and fair compensation, safe and healthy working conditions.
(b) Opportunities to use and develop human capacities with freedom at work place to develop skills and involvement in improving production standards.
(c) Future opportunity for continued growth and security of job.

31 (c) Introducing an individual to a temporary job undertaken to gain work experience.

32 (c) The purpose of induction is to educate the employee and make him oriented with the company and its various aspects like production, administration, discipline and welfare.

33 (b) It provides a scope for understanding whether the right man has been placed on the right job or there has been an omission.

34 (c) Placement is the actual posting of an employee to a specific job.

35 (a) To make new employees-feel at home.

36 (b) and (c)

(b) This includes the welcome to the organisation and giving a general idea of the industry and its functioning, by a responsible person designated for this purpose. New entrants are taken around the organisation to various departments for familiarisation. Audio-Visual programme featuring the various aspects of company and its policies are also shown, whereever such facilities are available.

(c) When the employees are detailed to their respective departments, the supervisor/foreman may educate them on their duties and responsibilities and work procedures, etc. Modern employers provide company's manual to new entrants to have a detail knowledge about the company as a whole.

37 (a), (b) and (c)

(a) It must inculcate confidence in workers so as to help them perform their duties in a comfortable manner.

(b) A new employee must feel that he is also a part and parcel of the company and have a sense of pride for the organisation.

(c) Induction must be a valuable source for information and interaction among coworkers to acquire special knowledge of the work ethos in general of the department and in particular one's assigned duties. This will place the individual at ease and will make himself to perform to the best of his abilities.

38 (a) A new entrant be allowed to have adequate time to understand the work and organisational environment. Avoid overburdening the individual with many jobs in the initial stage.

39 (c) It creates self-discipline amongst employees and also adjust to changes like technological and social aspects in business organisations.

40 (a) Much information can be obtained through the application of the candidate. During interview, the interviewer can ascertain correctness of the facts. It also enables the interviewer to make correct assessment of the individual.

41 (a), (b) and (c)

(a) Informal interview, formal interview and planned interview.

(b) Patterned interview, non-directive interview, depth interview.

(c) Stress interview, group interview.

42 (d) All the above

(a) Let the candidate feel comfortable and attentive before asking any questions. Then tactfully ask personal questions. Allow the candidate talk freely throughout.

(b) Try to get relevant information during conversion. Do not express any displeasure through conversation or body language, i.e., gestures.

(c) Be dispassionate in your conclusion.

43 (a), (b) and (c)

(a) It is a form of informal gathering in which normally, 8-10 members take part at a time.

(b) It is not a pre-planned exercise, whereas it is spontaneous conversation.

(c) It is an informal discussion on a subject.

44 (a) and (c)

(a) In this discussion members learn how to communicate in a group and thus overcome their shyness.

(c) The questions like self-confidence, alertness, manner of emphasising one's opinion, giving respect to others while talking, ability to discuss a subject without emotions, ability of reasoning.

45 (d) Promotion is an advancement in career of an employee in the organisation for the present position to a higher one with increase in pay or wage and higher status

46 (a) Promotion is a recognition of employees' capability and performance. It enhances the morale and loyalty of the employees.

47 (a) It is a movement of an employee from one place to another either on promotion or otherwise, as the case may be.

48 (d) All the above.
(a) It should be within the organisation or may be as per the requirement. It should not deny promotion to qualified person within.
(b) The promotion be planned on a sound bases, either on performance appraisal or on confidential reports.
(c) The criteria for promotion need to be followed and stagnation point to be specified. Also organisations prepare their employees through training and short-list such personnel, who deserve higher grade promotion. This policy of promotion to be communicated to all personnel through official circulars.

49 (a) and (b)
(a) Promotion can be a multiple chain. This process provides clearly defined channel to higher stages in each position.
(b) Promotion without financial benefits are called 'dry promotions'. An individual's increments are stopped, when this type of promotion is offered.

50 (c) Trade unions are of the opinion that promotion should be given on the basis of seniority, whereas management favours promotions on the basis of merit.

51 (b) A middle path is selected largely in Govt. organisations taking into consideration the merit and seniority of the individual.

52 (d) All the above.
(a) To fulfil the needs like reallocation and reduction of work force, etc., of an organisation
(b) To replace a new employee by an old one, who has been in the organisation for a long period.
(c) To meet an employees personal request due to domestic and other problems.

53 (a) A letter stating an intention of an individual to leave the job voluntarily.

54 (a) Cessation of service agreement with the organisation.
Explanation : This cessation can be due to resignation or discharge, dismissal, retirement and death of an employee.

55 (d) It is an acceptance of something undesirable but inevitable.
Explanation : Resignation may be voluntarily like employee's better prospects elsewhere (on personal grounds). Compulsory resignation is asked for on disciplinary grounds to avoid termination of his services. This also occurs, in case of severe dereliction of duties; the employer may ask the concerned employee to tender his resignation so as to help avoid disciplinary action.

56 (a) An employee is discharged means relieved of his duties and responsibilities.
Explanation : Expelled from the organisation without any liability. It is an administrative action.

57 (b) Termination of the services of an employee by way of punishment.
Explanation : An order to leave the job on disciplinary grounds; normally after domestic inquiry.

58 (a), (b) and (c)
(a) Termination of the services of a workman for any reason whatsoever.
(b) If an employer wants to retrench any workman who is in his service for more then one year or so, the individual must be given one month's notice or one month's pay in lieu of such notice.
(c) The employer will also have to pay to

the workman at the time of effecting retrenchment, compensation at the rate of 15 days average pay for every year of his service. Further, the employer is also required to inform the government by a notice in the manner prescribed.

59 (a) Lowering down of the status, salary and responsibilities of an employee.

60 (a) Yoder and Others (Haneman, H.G.; Tumbull, J.G.and Stones).

61 (c) It is the ratio between the production of a given commodity measured by volume and one or more of the corresponding input factors also measured by volume.

62 (a) Peter Drucker

63 (a) Production relates to value, volume and quantum of goods and services produced during a specific period of time by workers.
Explanation : The volume of goods in relation to the inputs produced by an enterprise for a particular period of time.

64 (a) The quality of working productivity with no waste or money or effort.
Explanation : It relates to inherent competence, the capacity of a given output or a production unit to produce under a particular condition of work situation.

65 (d) All the above. (a) (b) (c).
(a) Climatic conditions.
(b) Immigrant workers and lack of skills.
(c) Low wages and long hours of work.

66 (a) Development in science and technology, layout of plant, quality of raw materials used, equipment and machines, production process and managerial techniques.

67 (a) Motivation and incentives to workers, improved working conditions, standardisation of production methods, proper selection and job orientation to workers and efficient HR management.

68 (a) and (c)
(a) Higher productivity leads to profit.
(c) Reduces the price of goods thereby consumer satisfaction and increase in demand of goods.

69 (c) Ensure higher standard of living and higher per capita income and decrease the production cost.

70 (b) This involves how much to produce, when, what and how.

71 (d) All the above.
(a) Physical output per man-hour and per rupee of working capital employed.
(b) Physical output per tonne of raw materials consumed to reveal waste and scrap reduction.
(c) Physical output as percentage of the rated capacity of the plant or radio of productive machine hours used in relation to total machine hours available.

72 (c) Job analysis deals with determining the characteristics of each job.
Explanation : There are three main aspects of job analysis —
(i) Determination of each job in terms of duties and responsibilities,
(ii) Identification of the nature of work and working conditions,
(iii) Evaluation of the requirements as to abilities and skills that are prescribed for the worker, who performs the job.

73 (a) The study of job ingredients.

74 (a) and (b)
(a) What the worker does and how he does it?
(b) Why he does it and the skill involve in doing.

75 (d) All the above
(a) Sending out questionnaire to job-holders for answers.
(b) Conducting interviews of supervisors and job-holders.
(c) Observe the job-holder, while executing the job.

76 (b) The name given to the part of the job study involving detailed statements of particulars of an employee necessary for performance of a particular job.

77 (c) A process of analysing and assessing various jobs systematically to ascertain their relative worth in an organisation.

78 (d) To establish relative requirements of the job for the purpose of aptly rewarding the workers for their performance.

79 (d) All the above
(a) Job analysis, job description and job specification.
(b) Process of evaluation for fixing the wage.
(c) Fixation of wage and salary and employees' classification.

80 (b) and (c)
(b) Ranking and job classification methods are (non-analytical ones).
(c) Analytical methods are point-ranking and factor comparison.

81 (c) The design is a process of deciding on the content of a job in respect of its duties and responsibilities.

82 (a) To satisfy the requirement of the organisation for productivity, operational efficiency and quality product or services.

83 (a) Work specification, job rotation, job enlargement and job enrichment.

84 (a) The job is simplified by dividing it into small subparts in stead of assigning the same to one individual.

85 (a) When an activity of a job is no longer challenging, the employee is rotated to another job.

86 (c) Job enlargement is a genetic term, which means adding more and difficult jobs.

87 (a) Technique of job enrichment improves the quality of work, workers' involvement and motivation.

88 (a) It is an abstract of information gained from a report on job analysis.

89 (a) Job evaluation is to establish the relative requirements of adequately rewarding the workers for their performance.

90 (d) All the above.
(a) Rate the job and not the man.
(b) Too many occupational wages should not be established.
(c) Success of job rating is dependent on uniformity of understanding with regard to the definitions of elements and consistency in selection of these elements.

91 (d) All the above.
(a) In olden days managers used to see the merits of an individual, therefore, the focus was on the merit of an individual.
(b) This process used to find what type of traits a person has than what he does.
(c) Merit rating focuses on merits than the performance of an individual. This type of rating was open to criticism because it did not give importance to performance.

92 (b) Edwin B. Flippo

93 (a) and (b)
(a) Ranking, man to man comparison, grading and graphic scales.
(b) Check-list, forced choice description, selection of critical incidents and descriptive evaluation.

94 (a) This includes certain important acts of behaviour that make a difference between success and failure of an individual's performance.

95 (a) and (b)
(a) It unifies the rating procedure which is more equitable and just.
(b) It is an appraisal of training needs, segregation of inefficient employees and an aid to management.

96 (a) It is a systematic and objective method of evaluating the potential usefulness of an employee to the organisation.

97 (d) All the above.
(a) It helps the employer to gain a basis to identify the employee's merit and level of performance.
(b) Also leads to arrive at a decision to promote an employee according to his merit.
(c) It helps in understanding the training needs for a suitable employee, as to the increment in pay and promotion.

98 (d) All the above.
(a) Whenever the superior authority feels it necessary.
(b) Six monthly
(c) Annually.

99 (a) An appraisal system must be consistent and reliable, and should also be able to measure the performance area.

100(a) An appraisal is mostly a method of getting 'opinions' and not a method of measuring the performance. These opinions may have often error of judgement.
Explanation : When performance appraisals are made, appraiser at times may commit error of judgement, as given below :
Primary effect- The initial impression of a candidate may lead to evaluation error. The first impression whether it is 'positive' or 'negative' that may have a say over the subsequent behaviours. The next is the 'halo-effect', in this the appraiser makes an impression on one of the good qualities of the individual, he ignores all bad qualities and rate him blindly. This may be due to personal attachment or the individual has the power to influence the appraiser.
Leniency effect- This takes place due to the mental make up at the time of the appraisal. The appraiser may not feel to give very less rating to a candidate even though the individual is below standard. This is a sort of psychological instability of the rater.
Central tendency- In this an appraiser makes the report on a 'middle path' i.e., neither high nor low so that he can play safe. Since the appraisals are not made objectively.

101(a) Annual Confidential Reports (ACRs) are maintained by Govt. Departments and some of the public sector undertaking for the appraisal of their personnel for promotion and selection of career plans.

102 (a), (b) and (c)
(a) Quality, quantity and the time consumed for the performance.
(b) Cost effectiveness, supervision and self-esteem with cohesive interaction.
(c) Criteria followed should be related to the job.

103(a) and (b)
(a) The task to be completed and its possible outcome.
(b) When it is to be accomplished and its cost consideration.

104(a), (b) and (c)
(a) Set the accepted performance standards.
(b) Be factual and report the critical behaviour that determine performance.
(c) Observe statistical, oral and written reports.

105(d) All the above
(a) In the MBO system top management formulate and inform the corporate goal to lower level.
(b) Lower level managers set their operational goals.
(c) In an organisation, individual performance goals, work group task goals and corporate goals are set in a systematic manner.

106(a), (b) and (c)
(a) The appraiser gets an opportunity to explain the employee's strength and weakness what he had noted while making an appraisal.
(b) Help the employee to do better by

understanding his weak points and rectifying them accordingly.
(c) This will create a better relationship between the superior and subordinate and both can create opportunities of development and growth in tandem.

107(b) It guides the employees on the improvement for future career prospects.

108(a) The remuneration to which the person employed is entitled under the terms of employment.
Explanation : Wages mean all remuneration capable of being expressed in terms of money, which would, if the terms of contract of employment express or imply be payable to a person employed in respect of his employment or the work executed in such an employment, which includes House Rent (HR) allowance, as per Minimum Wages Act, 1948.

109(b) Pay should be equal to the work of the individual; also, qualified people should get better wages. There must be equity in remuneration.
Explanation : Equity in remuneration means, it must have 'Internal equity'. This indicates more difficult jobs are paid more. 'External equity' denotes that jobs are fairly compensated in comparison to similar jobs in the labour market. Lastly, the 'Individual equity' ensures equal pay for equal work - each individual's pay is fair in comparison to others executing similar jobs.

110(c) Wage is regarded as an individual matter and a little difference in payment of weekly wage means discontent and discord amongst workers.

111(d) Any additional remuneration payable under the terms of employment.

112(c) Deduction of wages, permissible under Section 7, Sub-section (2).

113(b) and (c)
(b) Payment of Wage Act, 1936.
(c) Minimum Wages Act, 1947.

114(a) and (b)
(a) Employer, Wage Board, Pay Commission.
(b) Minimum Wage Act and Payment of Wages Act.

115(b) and (c)
(b) Period shall be fixed for payment of wages at intervals not exceeding one month and within first ten days after the last day of the wage period.
(c) Wages of a person by discharge or resignation must be paid not later than 2nd working day after his termination.

116(c) It must be able to satisfy the internal, external, and individual equity.

117(b) Beach, D.S.

118(c) The wage to be paid whether the company is big or small, makes profit or not. It is the barest minimum that a worker can expect to get for his services rendered by him.

119(c) The methods are usually named as day work (per diem) and piece work (compensation paid or the price of job).

120(b) and (d)
(b) Cost of living, living wage, productivity and psychological and sociological factors.
(d) Approach of management.

121(b) and (c)
(b) Salary plans must be flexible, wage fixation to be carried out after proper job evaluation and must be consistent with organisational plans and programmes.
(c) They must be in conformity to equity and social and economic objectives of the nation.

122(a) and (b)

(a) These surveys are carried out to gather information on bench mark jobs.
(b) They seek to answer questions like what are the payment rates of other companies? What they do by way of social insurance? What is the level of pay offered by other firms for same type of jobs? etc.

123(a) and (b)
(a) Pay structure depends on several factors such as labour, market conditions, paying capacity of the company, and the legal provisions.
(b) Wage, dearness allowance (DA linked with Indian Consumer Price Index).

124(a) and (b)
(a) Wage differs in different employment or in industries and localities and also between in some employment and grade.
(b) The differential can be interindustry, inter-area, geographical and personal.

125(b) It is directly related to the allocation of economic resources of a country including human resource, growth natural income and the pace of economic development.

126(a), (b), (c) and (d)
(a) They depict a characteristic of the unorganised labour market.
(b) Personal differential because of job selling.
(c) Individual bargaining and wage discrimination in organised and unorganised sectors in industry.
(d) Interference of Wage Boards and Government in fixation of minimum wages and pressure of Trade Unions try to eliminate the conditions.

127(a) and (b)
(a) The Act prescribes minimum rate of wages to certain categories of workers. This can be fixed by hours, day, week, month or any other longer period.
(b) The Act provides for setting up of a tripartite body consisting of employees, union and government to advise on fixing and revising minimum wage rates. The rate could be for a period of five years and subject to revision thereafter.

128 (a), (b) and (c)
(a) It provides for regular payment of wages without any unauthorised deduction by the employer.
(b) Deductions are only permissible under Section 7(ii) of the Act, which are called authorised deductions.
(c) This Act covers all industrial establishments, factories, railways and contractors, where monthly wages of workers are less than Rs. 1,600/-.

129(c) The skills required for execution of the job, experience of the individual, requirement of mental and physical work, training needed, responsibilities involved in and the hazardous nature of work are the determinant factors of basic wage.

130(c) Minimum Wage

131(a) and (b)
(a) Plan should be easily understood, capable of easy computation and effectively motivating the employees.
(b) It should be stable and also provide remuneration to employees.

132(b) Francis A. Walker.

133(a), (b), (c) and (d)
(a) According to Section 4 of Minimum Wages Act, any minimum rate of wages are fixed by the appropriate government (State/Central) for the scheduled employment under Section 3 of Minimum Wages Act.
(b) A basic rate of wage and a special allowance at the rate to be adjusted at intervals as directed by the government and also in the variation in the cost of living index applicable to such workers.

(c) A basic rate of wage with or without the cost of living allowance and the cash value of concessions in supply essential commodities at concessional rates so authorised.
(d) An all inclusive rate allowing for the basic rate, the cost of living allowance and the cash value of the concessions, if any.

134(d) Beach, D.S.

135(c) Iron law of wages

136(b) The prevailing rate of wages in the similar occupation, it stands at the level of natural income and also depends on the place of industry and employer's capacity to pay.

137(c) It provides basic amenities of life efficiency of worker and satisfy the social needs of the worker like medical, education, retirement, etc.

138(d) All the above
(a) Important institutions set up by Government of India for fixation and revision of wages.
(b) The Wage Board studies various aspects of wage related subjects and submit the recommendations to the government for approval. They are at times accepted or modified by the government or reject all together. Recommendations approved are to be enforced by the concerned parties.
(c) Wage Board fix and revise various aspects of wages like basic pay, DA, incentives, over-time and other allowances, etc.

139(a) and (b)
(a) Bonus is an ex gratia payment to the workers beyond their normal wages.
(b) Bonus to workers is governed by the Bonus Act, 1965.

140(a) and (b)
(a) An incentive or reward, which attracts a worker and motivates him to perform better.
(b) An incentive plan may consist of monetary and non-monetary elements.

141(a) French

142(a) and (b)
(a) To improve the profit of the company, reducing labour and material cost.
(b) to implement incentives as a useful method for utilisation of man-power.

143(a) and (b)
(a) In a country like India, the role of financial incentives has become the primary tool for motivating workers.
(b) The necessity of improving the productivity of Indian labour is also a great concern for industries. This can be only achieved by need-based financial incentive system.

144(a) and (b)
(a) Plan for white-collar workers, plan for blue-collar workers and plan for managerial staff.
(b) Different category people have different needs, as such the plan to be designed accordingly for accomplishing their needs.

145(a) and (b)
(a) Personal or individual incentive bonus.
(b) Group incentive bonus scheme.

146(d) Personal or individual incentive bonus scheme.

147(b) F.W. Taylor.

148(d) All the above
(a) Minimum wages are guaranteed to all workers.
(b) Incentives are given to workers, who saved the performance time.
(c) For every work standard time is specified for its completion.

149 (d) All the above
(a) Where it is not possible to measure the performance of individual worker.

(b) Where the number of workers in a group is not very large.
(c) Who among the workers' group has equal skills and abilities.

150(d) All the above
(a) Suitable environment of relation between management and workers.
(b) Workers must be informed the general idea of the plan going to be introduced.
(c) Plan must have simplicity and must be equitable having flexibility and attractive payments, over and above the plan must be economical.

151(b) Group incentive plans.

152(a) Fringe benefits mean extra benefits given to employees in addition to their pay.

◆◆◆◆◆

CHAPTER - 3

- *TRAINING AND DEVELOPMENT*
- *WELFARE AND SOCIAL SECURITY*
- PERSONNEL *RECORDS, RESEARCH AND AUDIT*
- GRIEVANCE *AND DISCIPLINE*
- COLLECTIVE *BARGAINING, SETTLEMENT OF INDUSTRIAL DISPUTES*
- *INDUSTRIAL DEMOCRACY*

FEATURES :

- Training and development
- Concepts
- Importance of training
- Types of training
- Objectives
- Evaluation of training
- Managerial development
- Stages of development
- Welfare and social security
- Concepts
- Meaning of labour welfare
- Need for labour welfare
- Provisions of labour welfare
- Industrial hygiene
- Safety measures in industry
- Social security
- Role of social insurance
- Personnel records
- Research and audit
- Meaning of personnel records
- Importance of personnel records
- Maintenance of records
- Meaning of management audit
- Advantages of audit
- Areas of audit
- Meaning of personnel research
- Grievance and discipline
- Grievance policy
- Types of grievances
- How to detect grievance
- Negative and positive discipline
- Self-discipline
- Meaning of misconduct
- Objectives of good discipline
- Major causes of indiscipline
- Domestic inquiry
- Chargesheet framing
- Principles of natural justice
- Collective bargaining
- Settlement of industrial disputes
- Meaning of collective bargaining
- Characteristics
- Important Issues relating to collective bargaining
- Meaning of labour problem
- Meaning of industrial disputes
- Conciliation
- Board of conciliation
- Court of inquiry, Labour court
- Tribunal National tribunal
- Meaning of strike
- Causes and Ingredients of strike
- Meaning of lockout
- Illegal strike
- Lay off meaning
- Retrenchment
- Unfair labour practice
- Industrial democracy
- Meaning and objectives of workers' participation in management
- Types of participation
- Forms of workers' participation
- Works committee
- Joint council
- Shop council
- Quality circle
- Autonomous work group
- Co-determination

KEY NOTE

Training and development

Training : It is an organisationally planned programme to change the behaviour or attitudes of personnel so as to enable them to perform their jobs to the required standards. Training is the important management action in achieving the change in the organisation.

Development : It is focused with more thrust on communicating organisational pattern and values for particular roles. In development of human resource, training and developing functions are applied together to develop attitudes and skills. This programme of training and development play a vital role in organisational development activities that contribute the strategic direction of the organisation.

Welfare and social security

Welfare : It has been defined as a concept totally related to physical, mental, moral and emotional well-being. Labour welfare play a vital role today in establishments in development of human resources. It is expressly a corporate commitment for the care of employees at all levels. Proper implementation of welfare measures in an organisation requires the support of management, employees, trade unions, shareholders and the government.

Social security : It is a society that provides help and assistance to sick, disabled, aged and those who are temporarily incapacitated and need others' help. It is a planned commitment of a society to enable bright future for the posterity, an active development of present generation and also to relieve the discomforts of the retired personnel in helping them live in peace and tranquility. Under the social security scheme in India benefits like medical care, sickness help, old age pension, invalidity pension, maternity, accident benefits, etc., are usually provided. Also, we have adequate legislations for payment of compensation to the affected workers working in industries and other establishments.

Personnel records, research and audit

Personnel records : These are maintained by the establishment with regard to personnel. These include service record containing full particulars of the employee, his leave record, his professional qualifications, any punishment through disciplinary action, promotions, training carried out in foreign countries, rating on performance appraisals, awards and certificates of meritorious services, etc. In short, personal record is the 'Career record' of an employee from entrance to exit of his service life.

Research : This deals with investigation, examination and re-examination of the facts ascertained for proper evaluation. The research is required to understand the Human Resource Management (HRM). HRM today confronts with assumptions to the fact that theory and practice of employment relationship rests upon certain assumptions. The need of HR research is to add more knowledge to present assumptions and pursue the study on various dimensions like- Does HRM pose special problems for trade unions? What issues should managers bear in mind while dealing with HRM culture and so on.

Audit : Personnel audit is a review of transactions with regard to human resource, which include records of human resource accounts, evaluation of policies and procedures to ascertain the effectiveness and efficiency to human resource management.

Grievance and discipline

Grievance : According to Beach, grievance means any dissatisfaction or feeling of injustice in connection with one's employment situation that is brought to the notice of the management. Jucius defines grievance as any discontent or dissatisfaction whether exposed or not, whether valid or not, arising out of anything connected with the company which an employ thinks, behaves or even feels to be unfair, unjust or inequitable.

Discipline : It is an intellectual awareness to one's rights and responsibilities; in other words, training or a way of life aimed at self-control and obedience observed among people. Discipline exercise control over the members of an organisation. Punishment is given to correct a person or enforce obedience. In short, discipline can be just like two sides of a coin - rights and responsibilities.

Collective bargaining, settlement of industrial disputes

Collective bargaining : It is a process in which representatives of management and union together solve problems. It was introduced in India after World War II in 1950, when Indian industry felt certain problems of modernisation. It involves the process of negotiation, intrerpretation and administration of the collective agreement of management and union in respect of wages, working hours and other conditions of employment for a particular period. Normally, collective bargaining occurs as and when one party's goal perspective diffe rs from the other party.

Settlement of disputes : Promotion of industrial relation through collective bargaining and cooperation between management and employees is always the focal point of the industrial relation policy of the Government. Differences arising from management and employees should be settled by the parties themselves. In case disputes are not settled, the methods of negotiation, conciliation and arbitration are resorted to resolve the industrial disputes. If this machinery is unable to settle the dispute, the only option left is of adjudication and this can be used as the last resort.

Industrial democracy

Industrial democracy is an approach on the part of employer to give freedom to his employees in realisation of common goals. The concept of workers' participation in management is a part of industrial democracy. According to Clegg, there are three principles of industrial democracy-(i) full independence to trade unions from state and the management, (ii) only union will represent the industrial interest of workers, and (iii) ownership of industry is irrelevant term in industrial democracy. Workers' participation is a socio-psychological scheme that can be directed towards satisfying urge of workers in their self-expression and improving their association with decision making.

QUESTIONS

TRAINING AND DEVELOPMENT

1. What is training?

(a) Training provides increased knowledge and skill in performing a particular job.

(b) Training is an organised procedure by which people learn the knowledge and skill.

(c) In an industrial situation the trainees shall acquire new techniques, problem solving abilities and also develop the required work behaviour.

(d) All the above

2. "The act of increasing the knowledge and skill of an employee for doing a particular job." Thus, the training refers to the process of increasing knowledge, skill, attitude and potentials of an employee to increase his performance. Who said this?

(a) Dale S. Beach

(b) Baron, Robert A.

(c) Henri Fayol

(d) Edwin B. Flippo.

3. What is the importance of training?

(a) It reduces the need of supervision.

(b) Improve the performance of workers.

(c) It reduces wastage of men, materials and time.

(d) It increases the productivity.

4. What are the different types of training programme?

(a) Self-training programme

(b) On the job method

(c) Off the job method

(d) All the above.

5. What are the methods followed on a specific job training?

(a) Learning by experience

(b) Coaching

(c) Under study

(d) None of the above.

6. What does position rotation indicate?

(a) Position rotation broadens the knowledge of trainee on various jobs.

(b) It provides a general background of various jobs to an individual.

(c) This training takes place in actual situations.

(d) The productive work can suffer because of the obvious disruption caused by rotation.

7. What are the special projects on the job training?

(a) This is a very flexible training device.

(b) A trainee is assigned to perform a special task, so as to enable him to understand the work procedure.

(c) At times a task force is created consisting of a number of trainees representing different functions in an organisation.

(d) In a project different people work in a cooperative manner.

8. Is selective reading a training programme?

(a) In this individuals can gather knowledge and advance in their particular field of profession.

(b) Various business organisations have large number of collection of books for acquiring the advanced knowledge for their personnel.

(c) This is a good method of assimilating knowledge.

(d) All the above.

9. How does apprenticeship help in advancement of professional skills?

(a) In olden days trade skills were taught by a master craftsman to the aspirants who worked under guidance.

(b) At present industrial establishments require a large number of skilled craftsmen, who can be trained by the system for better output.

(c) This particular training is normally imparted by industrial organisations or imparted by government agencies.

(d) At present there is Apprenticeship Act that governs the procedure of training of various craftsmen.

10. What are vestibule schools?

(a) Large organisations frequently provide vestibule schools. This is a primary training based on actual shop experience.

(b) This is normally imparted by special instructors.

(c) It is widely used in providing training for clerical, as well as factory production jobs.

(d) This type of training being rather expensive is normally used for training a large number of people.

11. What is multiple management?

(a) This system emphasizes the use of committee to increase the flow of ideas from less experienced managers to train them for positions of greater responsibility.

(b) Initially this technique was developed in USA.

(c) In this, junior managers are authorised to discuss the major problems normally dealt with by senior executives of the company.

(d) All the above.

12. What do you understand by off the job training methods?

(a) In this, the trainees have to leave their work place and devote their entire time in developmental objectives.

(b) In this, theoretical training to people is given.

(c) There are many modern techniques used in this type of programme.

(d) All the above.

13. What do you mean by the special course and lectures?

(a) Lecturing is the most traditional form of formal training method.

(b) Special lectures and workshops, etc., are conducted in this type of training.

(c) Normally, a large number of organisations have their own course programme conducted by their trained instructors.

(d) Trainees are sponsored by the organisation to undergo training programmes, organised by universities and foreign management institutes.

14. What type of training does a conference provide?

(a) In order to avoid limitations of classroom lectures, many organisations include guided discussions and conferences in their training programmes.

(b) In this participants put-forth their ideas and discuss and arrive at an improved way of solving problems.

(c) Conferences may include 'buzz sessions'.

(d) Conference sessions are to be directed to the needs of participants, otherwise it will not serve the purpose.

15. How are case studies useful in training?

(a) This technique was developed by the Harvard Business School, USA.

(b) A case study is a written account of a

trained analyst seeking to describe an actual situation. Some cases are merely illustrative, while others are detailed facts demanding extensive analytical ability to solve it.

(c) Case studies are widely used in a number of programmes.

(d) This method increases the trainees' power of observation and problem solving capability.

16. What is brainstorming method of training?

(a) This is the method of simulating the participant to creative thinking.

(b) This method was developed by Alex Osborn

(c) This method seeks to reduce inhibiting forces by providing a maximum group participation and a minimum of criticism.

(d) In this, ideas are encouraged and criticism of any idea is discouraged, chain reaction to idea to idea is often developed. The ideas are critically examined.

17. What does the laboratory training indicate?

(a) This training provides situations in which the participants experience through interaction and some of the conditions as to what they are discussing about.

(b) It is more concerned about changing individual behaviour and attitude.

(c) It is found successful in changing job performance than conventional training methods.

(d) There are two methods of laboratory training (i) simulation and (ii) sensitivity training.

18. What does simulation refers to?

(a) An increasingly popular technique of management development.

(b) In this method participants are not taken to the actual situation. This situation can be simulated in the training session itself.

(c) It is the presentation of a real situation of the organisation in the training session. In this, participants involve themselves and deal with the situations they encounter in real life.

(d) There are two simulation methods of training (i) role playing and business game.

19. What is role playing?

(a) It can be used as a supplement to conventional training methods. Its purpose is to increase the treasure of skills in dealing with other people.

(b) It is greatly used in human relations training and also in sales training programmes, etc.

(c) It is a spontaneous creation of realistic situation involving two or more persons under classroom situations.

(d) In this some play the role of a manager and other act according to his directions; so through the interaction of a manager and his subordinates, the role awareness is created in the classroom situation. In this, trainees can broaden their experience through different approaches.

20. What is the role of gaming in off the job training?

(a) Gaming has been devised to simulate the problem of an industry or department.

(b) Role playing tends to emphasize feelings and the reaction between people. Gaming is a laboratory method in which role playing exists; it focuses on administrative problems.

(c) In gaming each team makes discussion on various matters such as fixation of price, level of production and so on.

(d) All the above.

21. What are the various levels of personnel, who require to undergo training programme in an organisation?

(a) Rank and file employees
(b) Supervisory level
(c) Managerial level
(d) All the above.

22. Who are to be governed by the job training, apprenticeship, pre-employment training?

(a) Middle management
(b) Executives
(c) Rank and file employees
(d) Temporary employees

23. Which level of personnel in an organisation requires supervisory skill training, coaching, special course and classroom, conferences, job rotation, brain-storming session, special projects, simulation and role playing?

(a) Top executive level
(b) Supervisory level
(c) The ones promoted to higher level
(d) None of the above.

24. Which categories of personnel do require coaching, special courses and classes, conference, job rotation, brain-storming session, selective reading, understudy, multiple management, simulation and sensitivity training?

(a) Employees skilled and unskilled
(b) Personnel of managerial level
(c) Foreman
(d) Executive trainees.

25. What are the criteria of a good training programme?

(a) It must have the allowance for individual differences.
(b) Relevance to job requirements and training needs.
(c) Suitable incentives, management support and simultaneous teaching of theory and practical.
(d) All the above.

26. What are the criteria of better performance for all level personnel?

(a) Job experience
(b) Knowledge of the work
(c) Induction and orientation programmes
(d) Selective reading

27. "Training need exists, when there is a gap between the present performance of an employee or group of employees and the desired performance. The existence of this gap can be determined on the basis of skill analysis." Who said this?

(a) Price (b) Mc Ferland
(c) Varoom, Y.H. (c) Flippo, E.B.

28. What are the common objectives of a training programme?

(a) To enhance effectiveness in the present position.
(b) Keep updating development in technical and administrative fields.
(c) To create capabilities and competence to assume higher responsibilities.
(d) Develop value systems and behavioural practices and commitment to excellence in organisational activities.

29. How to design a proper training programme?

(a) Area of training content.
(b) Key learning principles
(c) Trainees' characteristics and cost factor
(d) All the above

30. What is the process of evaluating training methods?

(a) Do trainees like the programme? Do they think it worthwhile? Reaction of trainees about the training programme.

(b) Learning

(c) Behaviour

(d) Results.

31. **What does education mean?**

(a) Training differs from education. It is concerned with increase in knowledge skills and abilities of the employees doing a particular job.

(b) Education has a broader aim and its purpose is to develop the individual.

(c) Education is connected with improving general knowledge and motivating a person to understand the total environment.

(d) Education is imparted at all schools and colleges, whereas training is of vocational and oriental nature.

32. **What are the objects of managerial training?**

(a) To impart the knowledge of basic principles of management.

(b) Training the future executives to act according to the new situations and methods.

(c) Acquiring knowledge of general industrial and managerial values.

(d) Developing the skills of managers to analyse and take decisions relating to the various problems of day to day management of industrial and other organisations.

33. **"Management development is a systematic process of training and growth by which individuals gain and apply knowledge, skills, insights and attitudes to manage orientation effectively." Who said this?**

(a) Dale S. Beach

(b) Likert, R.

(c) Koontz, H. and O'Donnel, C.

(d) Herzberg, F.

34. **What is the need of executive development?**

(a) Technological, social changes and professionally managed enterprises.

(b) Management as an important profession.

(c) Recognition of social and public responsibilities and research orientation.

(d) All the above.

35. **What are the stages of management development programme?**

(a) Planning and programme targeting.

(b) Ascertaining key position requirements and managerial appraisals.

(c) Replacement of skill inventory.

(d) Appraising the programme by top management.

36. **What is the importance of behaviour modelling in managerial (executive) development programme?**

(a) It is a new method of teaching personal skills and change in attitude.

(b) It teaches specific supervisory skills by providing a model of good behaviour to be learned.

(c) This is an expensive training method through video system for a limited group of 10-12 trainees at a time.

(d) It can provide feedback and reinforcement on practice attempts.

37. **What are the techniques normally used for development of executives on-the-job method?**

(a) Coaching

(b) Job rotation

(c) Understudy

(d) Multiple management.

38. **What are off the job methods for development of executive?**

(a) Sensitivity training, case study, simulation programmes and management games.

(b) Managerial grid, role playing, incident method, in-basket method,

conference, lectures programme by academic institutions.
(c) Transactional analysis
(d) All the above.

WELFARE AND SOCIAL SECURITY

39. "Welfare is fundamentally an attitude of management, influencing the method by which management activities are undertaken." Who said this?
(a) E.S. Pounds
(b) ILO
(c) Aurther James Todd
(d) R.R. Hopkins.

40. What is labour welfare?
(a) Sincere efforts made by employers for the benefit of their employees' well-being.
(b) Make the workers free from personal and family worries.
(c) Welfare means able to combat the sense of frustration.
(d) All the above.

41. What does welfare of labour aim at?
(a) It is a humanitarian activity.
(b) To improve the efficiency of the workers.
(c) To fulfil the future needs and aspirations of the work force in an industry.
(d) Make the workers lead a happier life.

42. What is the necessity of labour welfare?
(a) Organisation of economic life in a country must conform to principles of justice and a decent standard of living.
(b) It is the responsibility of the state to safeguard the interest of industrial workers and secure them through suitable legislation.
(c) They need to be protected against exploitation and governed by legislations like living wage, healthy working conditions, specified working hours, suitable provisions of settlement of disputes, protection of economic aspects, old age, sickness and unemployment.
(d) None of the above.

43. What are the labour welfare provisions that have been given by the constitution?
(a) Right to adequate means of livelihood.
(b) Effective provisions for right to work.
(c) Maternity relief and provisions of human conditions.
(d) Directive principles of state policy providing adequate security provisions under Articles 41, 42 and 43 of labour welfare.

44. What are the important labour welfare movements in post-independent India?
(a) It was accepted that labour welfare have a positive role to play in increasing productivity and reducing industrial tension.
(b) State began to realise its social responsibility towards weaker sections of the society.
(c) Emergence of different trade unions gave boost to the growth of labour welfare movement.
(d) All the above.

45. What are the statutory welfare provisions?

(a) Washing facilities, facilities for storing and drying clothes, facilities for sitting at the work place.
(b) Provisions of first aid, shelter, rest-room, canteen, creche, etc.
(c) Welfare officer
(d) All the above.

46. What are the enactments covering statutory welfare provisions?
(a) Workmen's Compensation Act, 1923
(b) Payment of Wages Act, 1936.
(c) Factories' Act, 1948, Plantation Labour Act, 1961.
(d) Contract labour (Regulation & Abolition) act, 1970.

47. What are the voluntary welfare measures?
(a) All other welfare measures, that do not come under statutory welfare provisions.
(b) Educational, medical and transport facilities.
(c) Recreational and housing facilities
(d) Welfare works by workers' organisations.

48. "After the Ahmedabad model in industrial relation a constructive programme was formulated and called upon all organisations including trade unions to adopt and implement the same. The programme included activities to promote communal unity, removal of untouchability, prohibition, education, health and hygiene, upliftment of women, harijans and the tribal communities for elevation of their living standard." Who made this proposal.
(a) Vinoba Bhave
(b) Mulkraj Anand
(c) M.K. Gandhi
(d) INTUC

49. What is industrial hygiene?
(a) Hygienic working environment is the main factor in maintenance of good health of workers.
(b) Practice of keeping oneself and the industrial area clean in order to prevent illness or disease.
(c) Importance of personal hygiene should be constantly told to individual employees to comply at the work place.
(d) Cleanliness at the work place is necessary to prevent indifferent health, as the adage goes- "Cleanliness is next to Godliness."

50. What are the various necessary precautions to be followed to keep the industry/factory away from health hazards?
(a) Cleanliness, disposal of wastes and effluents, ventilation and temperature, dust and fume, artificial humidification, and over crowding.
(b) Lighting, drinking water, cooling water in hot wether, toilets and spittoons.
(c) Sections 11 to 20 of Factories Act, 1948, speak on health provisions.
(d) All the above.

51. What does industrial safety mean?
(a) Industrial conditions of being safe and prevent causing injury or damage.
(b) No accidents or injuries to personnel at the work place.
(c) Taking adequate preventive measures against causing injury or loss of limb or life in the industry or organisation.
(d) All the above.

52. What are the safety measures taken to protect the personnel in an industry?
(a) Fencing of machinery, working on or near machinery in motion. No women or young person be allowed to clean and lubricate machinery.
(b) Young persons are not to be employed on dangerous or moving

machines, prohibition of employment of women and children near cotton openers.

(c) Hoists and lifts to be in good condition, all floor area of the factory to be properly maintained, no person to be employed in any factory to lift or carry heavy load as it is likely to cause injury.

(d) Special care to be taken to protect eyes from all types of foreign object, precaution to be taken against dangerous fumes, inflammable dust and gas.

53 How are safety measures of plant and machinery carried out?

(a) Section 40 of the Factories' Act provides measures for the safety of buildings and machinery.

(b) If the factory inspector feels that any machinery or plant is in a condition dangerous to human life or safety, he may serve an order on the manager of the factory specifying the measures to be taken within a specified date.

(c) If the Inspector of Factories feels that the use of any building, plant and machinery involves immediate danger. He may serve order to Factory Manager for prohibiting its use till it is property repaired.

(d) All the above.

54. What is social security?

(a) Protect against want, squalor, disease, ignorance and unemployment.

(b) Social security benefits are admissible to all.

(c) It provides benefits according to economic needs of the person.

(d) It is a complete institution. Social assistance, a part of social security, is completely government operated.

55. "In order to fully understand the meaning of social security one needs to examine certain elements of social security. Social security is an attack on five giants, namely, Want, Disease, Ignorance, Squalor and Idleness." Who said this?

(a) Clow, A.G.

(b) Giri, V.V.

(c) Beverridge, H.W.

(d) Oza and Kotlawal

56. "Social security is a controversial and dynamic subject with various facets-Philosophical, theoretical, humanitarian, financial, administrative, social, economic, political, statistical, medical and legal." Who said this?

(a) Weber and Cohen

(b) Singh, M.M.

(c) Mongia, J.N.

(d) Saxena, R.C.

57. What is the role of social insurance?

(a) It is operated jointly by the workers, industrialists and government.

(b) Social insurance makes the social security possible, i.e., it creates and initiates a mechanism, which is 'Sine qua non' of the realisation of social security.

(c) Provides benefits without reference to economic needs.

(d) It protects wants only.

58. What are the social security measures taken by the Government?

(a) Provide social security to workers during the contingencies as ill health.

(b) Contingencies against industrial accidents.

(c) Contingencies against maternity.

(d) Financial contingencies.

PERSONNEL RECORDS RESEARCH AND AUDIT

59. What is known as personnel records?

(a) Permanent account of personal information that is kept as evidence for future reference.

(b) Records are stored in files, computer CDs and/or in any other form.

(c) Personnel records are the complete information of our individuals' entry in the service book till their exit. This is usually of personal and family particulars, examination passed, pay and increments, promotions and other aspects connected to the service.

(d) All the above.

60. What are the types of record?

(a) Records store the information in files, documents, magnetic diskettes.

(b) Records are prepared from reports, orders, minutes, etc.

(c) These records contain information about employees, employer, trade union, Government, Employment bodies, etc.

(d) All the above.

61. What is the significance of records?

(a) Records help in arriving at right decisions on various matters.

(b) It provides the documentary proof to support any action.

(c) Records are the information containing the past and it can be used in the future.

(d) None of the above.

62. What are essential attributes of maintaining good record?

(a) The records and its objectives to be clear and consistent in all respects.

(b) Records to be up-dated from time to time.

(c) The information contained in the records should not be of classified nature and easily accessible.

(d) A proper procedural manual should be maintained for following the maintenance of records.

63. What are the criteria of good record keeping?

(a) Records to contain requisite information in a concised form.

(b) They should be classified according to the importance of subject it dealt with, viz., Top Secret, Secret, Confidential, Restricted, etc.

(c) Records need to be verified for its authenticity.

(d) They be maintained according to the subjectwise for easy reference.

64. What does management audit refer to?

(a) A review of the performance of management team of any organisation.

(b) It focuses on a systematic search of effectiveness and efficiency of management performance on various fields in an organisation.

(c) Audit is a review of verification of completed transactions to find out whether they represent a true state of affairs of the business or not.

(d) All the above.

65. What are the advantages of management audit?

(a) It should evaluate the performance of control mechanisms.

(b) Check on overall plans and objectives of business.

(c) It brings out the cases in which

organisational policies and procedures are not complied with.

(d) It should determine whether the enterprise is operating as efficiently as it should be.

66. What are the areas of HR audit?

(a) Accomplishment

(b) Practices, procedures and HR development

(c) Methods of conflict management and morale of personnel

(d) None of the above.

67. What are the indicators of personnel audit?

(a) Major functions of quantitative and qualitative indicators.

(b) Audit of personnel inventory and replacement table and turnover rates, selection rates, retrenchment, dismissal, lay off and recruitment rates.

(c) Training programmes, managerial and supervisory personnel, time taken in training, apprentice ratio, material waste, increased productivity.

(d) Employees voluntary participation in various activities, morale, ratio of communication, absenteeism, turnover, number of grievances and settlement, accident rate and arbitration cost, etc.

68. "Personnel research is a shortcut to knowledge and understudy, which can replace the slower, more precarious road to trial and error in experience. It implies search, investigation, reexamination, reassessment and revaluation. It is a purposive and systematic investigation designed to test carefully considered hypotheses or thoroughly framed questions." Who said this?

(a) Peter Dracker (b) Kaith Davis

(c) Flippo (d) Dale Yoder

69. What does HR research indicate?

(a) It is a study of material and sources connected with human resources in an effort to establish facts and arrive at new conclusions.

(b) Human resource research is to investigate into the ongoing practices and activities against HR objectives.

(c) Improve the possibilities to strengthen the skills, and behavioural standards of personnel in an organisation to achieve better results.

(d) All the above.

70. What does attendance mean?

(a) Any employed person must report to his duty as per the time specified by the organisation.

(b) Attendance is normally marked for the employees by the in charge of the employees under whom they work.

(c) Attendance register is maintained by in charge of the employees and concerned employee must sign against his name and the date for his personal presence for duty.

(d) If an individual reports for duty later than 15 minutes, the individual is considered absent for half a day on the day of his late reporting.

71. What does the entitlement of weekly holiday for workers imply?

(a) Section 52 of Factories Act prescribes that 1st day of the week shall be a rest day for all workers.

(b) The Act stipulates that no worker should be required to work on Sunday, unless the worker has or will have a substituted holiday on one of the three days immediately before or after the Sunday.

(c) The substitution should not result in any worker working for more than 10 days consecutively without holiday.

(d) None of the above.

72. What does leave record indicate?

(a) Leave record is an important part of the service book of an employee, kept along with his service record. Various types of leave, the individual availed during his service career is entered in this record book at the allotted place for the same with proper authentication.

(b) Leave facilities are- privileges leave, sick leave, casual leave, leave without pay, National and festival holidays, quarantine leave and accident leave.

(c) All the leave availed are periodically audited by the concerned audit personnel for its correctness.

(d) None of the above.

73. What does absenteeism refer to?

(a) Absenteeism refers to unauthorised absence of worker from his job.

(b) In India the problem of absenteeism is greater than any other country.

(c) Absenteeism means, when an employee remains absent himself without permission from his duty or it is a willful absence without leave.

(d) Absenteeism is higher amongst women workers and among workers who live away from the place of work.

74. What are the main causes of absenteeism?

(a) Long hours of work, bad working conditions, boredom, lack of cooperation between workers and management, sickness.

(b) Accidents, occupational diseases, fatigue, problem of transport facilities to reach the work place and low wages.

(c) Lack of proper medical aid and health care, lack of canteen services, rest room, bad housing conditions, evils of drinking, lack of social or religious facilities, domestic problems and consequent worries.

(d) All the above.

75 How does absenteeism affect the industry?

(a) It is an important problem of labour welfare.

(b) It is the main cause of labour unrest.

(c) It affects earning of workers.

(d) It affects the production and output, and also morale and efficiency of workers.

76 How can the management reduce absenteeism of employees?

(a) Introduction of attendance bonus to employees.

(b) Good leave record of employees is an important factor to consider them for more responsible positions.

(c) Habitual absenteeism must be treated as a misconduct and so stated in standing orders that it will lead to disciplinary action.

(d) None of the above.

GRIEVANCE AND DISCIPLINE

77. What is grievance?

(a) It is a cause for a complaint.

(b) When an employee feels something unfair has been done to him.

(c) When an employee finds everybody is unkind to him, he becomes aggrieved.

(d) Any discontent or dissatisfaction can create a grievance.

78. "Any dissatisfaction or feeling of injustice in connection with one's employment situation that is brought to the notice of management." Who said this?

(a) Flippo (b) Jucius

(c) Beach (d) None of the above.

79. What should be the aim of a good grievance policy?

(a) Every organisation should have fair and impartial grievance policy.

(b) Promote healthy labour relations, a good grievance policy that can bring better understanding amongst management and workers.

(c) There should not be any room for favouritism and injustice.

(d) All the above.

80. What is the need of grievance procedure?

(a) Keep the employees' morale high and thereby increase the production.

(b) It serves as a check on the arbitrary action of the management.

(c) It enables employees to be free from discontent and frustration.

(d) All the above.

81. What are the types of grievances?

(a) Factual (b) Imaginary

(c) Disguised (d) Aggressive

82. What are the causes of grievances?

(a) Economic dissatisfaction

(b) Due to work environment.

(c) The attitude of supervisors

(d) Miscellaneous causes.

83. How do grievances affect the organisation?

(a) They affect the quality and quantity of production.

(b) Increase the rate of absenteeism and turnover.

(c) They strain superior-subordinate good relations.

(d) All the above.

84. What methods are used to understand grievance amongst employees?

(a) Observing employees for unusual behaviour.

(b) Systematic grievance procedure.

(c) Complaint box

(d) 'Walk-in-meeting' with top manager (Open door policy).

85. What does discipline refer to?

(a) Intellectual awareness of one's rights and responsibilities.

(b) Obedience to supervisors.

(c) Implicit obedience

(d) None of the above.

86. What is negative discipline?

(a) It is the discipline that restrains freedom of a person.

(b) This is a method of imposing penalties for improper behaviour.

(c) It creates compulsion for an individual to observe rules and regulations.

(d) None of the above.

87. What does positive discipline refer to?

(a) Positive discipline enables an individual to have greater freedom of expression.

(b) In this, organisation is marked with two-way communication and effective cooperation.

(c) It can enable an organisation to have better climate and inherent desire for result oriented work.

(d) Employees adhere to rules not because of fear or coercion.

88. "Self-discipline means the training that corrects, moulds and strengthens. It refers to one's efforts to self-control for the purpose of adjusting oneself to certain needs and demands. This form of discipline is raised on two psychological principles. First, punishment seldom produces the desired results. Often it

produces undesirable results and second, a self-respecting person tends to be a better worker than one, who is not." Who said this?

(a) Peter Drucker (b) Megginson
(c) Das, R.K. (d) Hilton, J.

89. **What does misconduct or indiscipline indicate?**

(a) One does not obey order.
(b) One violates rules and regulations.
(c) One resorts to wilful damage of the property or violates disciplinary norms.
(d) All the above.

90. **What are the objectives of good discipline?**

(a) An employee should understand his duties to the organisation and the organisation should recognise his right as an employer.
(b) Create a spirit of tolerance amongst employees and make requisite adjustments.
(c) Increase the working efficiency and morale of the employees.
(d) All the above.

91. **What is 'Red hot stove' rule in imposing discipline?**

(a) This draws an analogy between touching the hot stove and understanding the heat.
(b) Disciplinary action under this rule should have the following consequences-burns immediately, provides warning, imposes constant punishment and burns impersonally.
(c) Disciplinary action should be impersonal. There cannot be any favouritism in dealing with any violation of disciplinary norms.
(d) None of the above.

92. **Who initiated the procedure of 'Red hot stove rule' in imposing discipline?**

(a) Henry Fayol (b) Peter Drucker
(c) Keith Davis (d) Douglas McGregor

93. **What are the major causes of indiscipline?**

(a) Lack of proper behaviour, unfair labour practices, barriers of organisational communication.
(b) Arbitrary disciplinary actions, disunity among management and work groups, lack of proper attention to welfare problems of personnel, victimisation of personnel without any reasons.
(c) Frustration amongst employees.
(d) None of the above.

94. **What does domestic inquiry refer to?**

(a) Inquiry is conducted to find out the facts of the misconduct committed by an employee.
(b) When the management of an organisation finds that an act of omission has been committed by the employee that warrants disciplinary procedure to be followed to arrive at a conclusion whether the act or omission is a misconduct or not.
(c) Disciplinary procedure from within the organisation or by the personnel constituted from outside the organisation.
(d) All the above.

95. **How is a chargesheet framed against an employee, who is alleged to have committed an offence?**

(a) It must be found out whether the offence committed is under the standing orders or service rules or under common law.
(b) The foreman or supervisor or the manager in charge of the employee should make a report to the departmental head indicating the action recommended.
(c) If the department head considers the preliminary inquiry necessary, he must depute a department manager

or a manager from personnel department to conduct the same. At all times, it is advisable to keep the disciplinary authority (normally the head of the organisation) informed about the progress of the case. If the preliminary inquiry states that there is no *prima facie* case; the individual may be exempted of the charges, the individual may be suitably warned orally or in writing. If there is a *prima facie* case of raising chargesheet, the same be got prepared and signed by disciplinary authority.

(d) All the above.

96. What does domestic inquiry mean?

(a) Calling for explanation of the employee by the disciplinary authority.

(b) Considering the explanation of the employee the disciplinary authority may proceed to next action.

(c) Issuance of Show cause notice by the disciplinary authority if disagreeing with the explanation submitted by the employee.

(d) Issue orders for a domestic enquiry.

97. What are the principles of natural justice?

(a) Justice is normally given to the accused person.

(b) Principles of natural justice are-that no man should be held guilty without giving him an opportunity to explain his point of view.

(c) Present evidence of his choice without any fear.

(d) Cross-examine the evidence of management.

98. What are the types of punishment?

(a) Oral warning, written warning, suspension.

(b) Withholding of increment.

(c) Termination of services.

(d) Sentence to civil prison.

COLLECTIVE BARGAINING AND INDUSTRIAL DISPUTES

99. What is collective bargaining?

(a) Bargain collectively for the rights and privileges by employees.

(b) A method by which trade unions safeguard and improve the conditions of the working life of the union members (workers).

(c) It is procedure by which employers and a group of employees agree upon the conditions of the work.

(d) None of the above.

100. What are the characteristics of collective bargaining?

(a) It is an individual action.

(b) It is a group actin and intended through the representatives of workers.

(c) It is a continuous process of organisational relationship between employers and trade unions.

(d) It is a two party process.

101. Who originated collective bargaining?

(a) V.V. Giri

(b) George R. Terry

(c) Austin David

(d) Sydney and Beatrice Webb

102. Is the collective bargaining a competitive process?

(a) Yes, it is a collective process.

(b) It is a democratic process.

(c) Yes, a competitive process.

(d) Yes, it is a complementary process

103. What is the importance of collective bargaining?

(a) It highly increases the economic stand of unions and management's disagreement.

(b) It avoids industrial disputes and maintains stability and peace in the organisation.

(c) It also maintains consistency of fair wages and conducive working conditions, when the bargain concludes.

(d) All the above.

104. "Collective bargaining is essentially a rule-making process whereby the terms and conditions of employment of labour are determined." Who said this?

(a) N.F. Dufty

(b) A.Flanders

(c) J.Henry Richardson

(d) John T.Dunlop.

105. What are the prerequisites of collective bargaining?

(a) Cordial relations between labour and management.

(b) Parties going to have collective bargaining must organise themselves.

(c) Parties should be ready to enter into agreement in-between.

(d) The agreement of bargaining need to be implemented by the concerned parties.

106. How the collective bargaining agreement made?

(a) Backed by compulsion.

(b) Voluntary agreement.

(c) Settlement

(d) Consent award.

107. When was the collective bargaining introduced in India?

(a) Before Second World War.

(b) After India's independence in 1948.

(c) In the year 1950.

(d) After adoption of the code of conduct by the industry in 1958.

108. What are the issues related to collective bargaining in India?

(a) Inadequate arrangements of recognition by majority of unions, as sole bargaining agent.

(b) The threat of confrontation and work stoppage associated with relatively free collective bargaining.

(c) Reasonable degree of involvement by government as a third party in bipartite decision making.

(d) None of the above.

109. What do you mean by labour problem?

(a) When a man hires another man for wage, the relation between them is of master and servant.

(b) This relationship is governed by implicit understanding about the terms and conditions of work.

(c) Terms and conditions of work, such as wages, allowances, quantum of work, hours of work. Any violation of terms and condition may create a problem.

(d) All the above.

110. What are the important causes of labour problem?

(a) Always the desire of the employers to get the maximum profit from the industry with minimum input.

(b) Changing of the industry from the domestic system of manufacturing to modern large scale production unit.

(c) Migration of most labourers from rural to urban areas due to industrialisation.

(d) Unskilled labourers, who migrate, face economic, social and psychological problems, which are migratory ones.

111. What is industrial dispute?

(a) A dispute or difference between workmen and the employer.
(b) The dispute to be connected with the employment or non-employment.
(c) It must be of the terms of employment or the condition of labour of any person.
(d) All the above.

112. When does an individual dispute become an industrial dispute?

(a) Ordinarily a dispute between employees is not termed as an industrial dispute.
(b) When the dispute is supported by the union of which the workman is a member.
(c) Individual dispute, when supported by a group of workmen.
(d) An individual dispute connected with dismissal, discharge, retrenchment or termination of service of any workman.

113. Who is a workman? Does designation of a person decide the status?

(a) An individual's status is decided.
(b) Nature of work performed by a person.
(c) Designation that decides whether he is a workman.
(d) None of the above.

114. What is 'Giri Formula' for settlement of disputes?

(a) Adjudication (b) Conciliation
(c) Negotiation (d) Arbitration.

115. What are the statutory provisions for settlement of industrial disputes?

(a) Works committee, Conciliation Officer.
(b) Board of Conciliation, Court of Inquiry.
(c) Labour Court, Industrial Tribunal and National Tribunal.
(d) All the above.

116. What is the appropriate time for referring a dispute to Labour Court, Industrial Tribunal or National Tribunal

(a) When negotiations fail.
(b) No useful result has been achieved through arbitration.
(c) When conciliation does fail.
(d) Immediately after accomplishment of the Inquiry.

117 What is the main purpose of settlement of disputes through negotiation?

(a) No doubt, it is the most ideal one.
(b) Employers and workers' unions, as far as possible, try to settle their differences and disputes by a round table approach.
(c) Due to unwise actions, uncompromising attitude of the management and workers, minor disputes lead to adjudication. This can be avoided.
(d) None of the above.

118. Is a dismissed worker covered by the Industrial Disputes Act, 1947?

(a) A workman who has been dismissed, discharged or retrenched or terminated is covered by the Act.
(b) Any dismissal connected with or arising out of such dismissal, discharge, retrenchment or termination is also an industrial dispute.
(c) Irrespective of the fact, no other workman or any union of workmen is a party to the dispute (Sec. 2(s) and 2A of Industrial Disputes Act) give protection to dismissed workman.
(d) Non of the above.

119. What is the role of arbitration in settlement of disputes?

(a) Parties to the dispute can settle their dispute by appointing an arbitrator.
(b) Both parties can appoint an arbitrator in agreement to settle the dispute.
(c) After appointment of the arbitrator, arbitration award, which has become

enforceable shall be binding on the parties to the industrial dispute.

(d) All the above.

120. What is conciliation?

(a) Section 12 of Industrial Disputes Act deals with the duties of the Conciliation Officer.

(b) If settlement is arrived at as a result of conciliation, he must make a report to the Government within 14 days, along with memorandum of settlement.

(c) Conciliation officer has no power to give final decision in the matter of disputes. His role is of a mediator between the parties to settle the dispute.

(d) The role of a conciliation officer is difficult and delicate one, which requires extraordinary virtues.

121. What is Board of Conciliation?

(a) The Board of Conciliation appointed by the Government will have an independent Chairman and two or four members representing the parties in equal number.

(b) They investigate into all matters affecting the case and induce the parties to come to a fair and amicable settlement.

(c) If any agreement is reached, the board sends a report to the Government together with memorandum of settlement.

(d) If negotiations fail, a report, along with recommendations, is sent, not later than two months.

122. What is meant by Court of Inquiry?

(a) It may consist of one independent person or such members or persons as the government may decide.

(b) If Court consists of two or more members, one of them will be appointed as a chairman.

(c) It will inquire into matters referred to and submit to government the report within a period of six months.

(d) All the above.

123. What are the functions of Labour Court?

(a) Legality of an order passed by an employer and application and interpretation of standing orders.

(b) Discharge or dismissal of workmen and reinstatement of workmen wrongfully dismissed.

(c) Withdrawal of concessions, illegality of a strike or lockout.

(d) It has the power to adjudicate all matters rather than those coming under the jurisdiction of tribunal.

124. What does Tribunal refer to?

(a) It consists of one independent person or such number of persons that may be decided by Government. If there are two or more members, one will be the Chairman. He must be a judge of High Court or having equal qualification.

(b) Jurisdiction or wages and the payment, allowances, hours of work, rest, leave with wage and holidays, bonus, profit sharing, PF and gratuity, shift working other than standing orders, classification grade, discipline, rationalisation, retrenchment of workmen and closure of establishment.

(c) Any matter that may be prescribed by the government

(d) None of the above

125. What are the functions of National Tribunal?

(a) National tribunal is appointed by the Central Government.

(b) Industrial disputes having national importance or of such nature that industrial establishment situated in more than one state.

(c) National Tribunal shall consist of one

person not below the rank of a High Court Judge and not below sixty-five years of age.

(d) All the above.

126. What is the binding effect of an award on the settlement of a dispute of conciliation?

(a) It is binding on all parties to dispute.

(b) The heirs, successors, or assigns of the employer in respect of his establishment

(c) All persons in the establishment whether employed on the date on which the dispute arose or subsequent to that.

(d) All the above.

127. What is strike?

(a) When persons employed in any industry or in any establishment stop their work acting in combination is said to be a strike.

(b) Strike is the stoppage of work.

(c) A concerted refusal of work under common understanding of group of people.

(d) None of the above.

128. What are the causes of strike?

(a) Strike is a measure of industrial unrest.

(b) Fatigue and frustration at the place of work and bad social conditions of workmen.

(c) Demand of wages and the desire to raise them.

(d) Multiple immediate issues.

129. How do you distinguish strike? What are its ingredients?

(a) Plurality of workmen.

(b) Cessation of work or refusal to do work.

(c) Combination and concerted action.

(d) None of the above.

130. What is lock-out?

(a) Closing the place of employment or refusal of the employer to continue work by the employees of his organisation.

(b) There must be closure, suspension of work or refusal to employees.

(c) It must be the consequence of an industrial dispute or in anticipation of an altercation.

(d) It should be intended to compel the employees to accept certain terms and conditions of employment.

131. What is meant by illegal strike?

(a) A strike resorted to during the pendency of proceedings before a Board of Conciliation.

(b) A strike resorted to during the pendency of proceedings before the Labour Court, Industrial Tribunal, National Tribunal for adjudication.

(c) A strike resorted to during the pendency of proceedings before the arbitration.

(d) Settlement of an award is binding on workmen and they are not supposed to make any demand inconsistent with the settlement of an award while it is in operation.

132. What are the special provisions covering a strike in public utility establishment other than the normal establishment, for it is termed as 'illegal?'

(a) If workers do not give notice of strike to the employer within six weeks before commencement of the strike.

(b) If workers go on strike within 14 days of giving such a notice.

(c) If they go on strike before the expiry of the specified date in the notice for commencing the strike.

(d) If they go on strike during the pendency of any conciliation proceedings before a Conciliation and during 7 days after the conclusion of such proceedings.

133. What is lay-off?

(a) Failure, refusal or inability of an employer to give employment to a worker, whose name is currently on the muster roll of the industry.

(b) Failure to give job to the employee on account of shortage of coal, power or raw material.

(c) Breakdown of machinery or any other reason to give employment.

(d) All the above.

134. Which of the following options are included in 'retrenchment'?

(a) Termination as a result of non-renewal of contract.

(b) Termination on the ground of continued ill-health.

(c) Termination as a punishment or voluntary retirement.

(d) Termination of service of a workman for any reason whatsoever.

135. What are unfair labour practices?

(a) The expression of victimisation is included in that practice.

(b) Arbitrary actions of management against labour.

(c) A practice or an act of employer that causes loss to workmen in matters of wages or results in retrenchment or any loss for that matter.

(d) Industrial Disputes Act prohibits the commission of any unfair practices.

INDUSTRIAL DEMOCRACY

136. What is meant by industrial democracy?

(a) The idea of involving workers in those aspects affected them more and providing them autonomy and control over their work-life.

(b) An ideal way of promoting self-management.

(c) A process increasing cooperation between management and workers by giving the workers more powers in managing the activities for efficiency.

(d) All the above.

137. What are the objectives of workers' participation in management (WPM)?

(a) An attempt of employer to make his employees into an effective team for realisation of common goal.

(b) To motivate the workers to satisfy their esteemed needs.

(c) Development of self-management in industry.

(d) Involvement of employees in decision making process.

138. What are Mhetra's different participative views?

(a) Informative participation and consultative participation.

(b) Associated and administrative participation.

(c) Decisive participation.

(d) All the above.

139. How does workers' participation made effective?

(a) Need of proper managerial attitude.

(b) Cooperation of trade unions.

(c) It should be consultative and purposeful.

(d) Workers need to have faith in the system.

140. J.H. Dobbs discussed necessary conditions for empowerment of workers. What are they ?

(a) Participation

(b) Innovation

(c) Information and accountability

(d) None of the above

141. What are the forms of workers' participation in management?

(a) Works committee, Joint Management council.

(b) Joint Council, Shop Council.

(c) Participative decision making.

(d) All the above.

142. What is meant by works committee?

(a) Works committee is provided under the Industrial Disputes Act, 1948.

(b) It consists of representatives of employer and employees.

(c) The aim of this committee is to promote harmony at the work place and sort out differences in respect of common interest.

(d) None of the above.

143. What is Joint Management Council (JMC)?

(a) Second Five Year Plan recommended setting up of these councils.

(b) This consists of representatives of both management and workers.

(c) Its aim is to improve the efficiency of the workers and provide adequate welfare facilities to them.

(d) Educate workers so as to enable them to participate in such schemes and also to satisfy their psychological needs.

144. What is the purpose of Joint Councils?

(a) Joint Councils are for the entire organisation and its members are confined to same organisation.

(b) Tenure of the Joint Council is for two years.

(c) The Chief Executive Officer of the organisation becomes its Chairman.

(d) Joint Council appoints a Secretary, who conducts the activities of the Council.

145. What does Shop Council refer to?

(a) It represents each department or a shop in a unit.

(b) The council represents equal number of employers and employees.

(c) Employer's representatives are nominated by the management and consist of persons from the entire unit. Workers' representatives are from various departments or shops concerned.

(d) The number of members of each Council is determined by the employers in consultation with recognised union. Total number, generally, is limited to twelve.

146. What is a quality circle?

(a) A group of personnel which exercises the quality control of products in an organisation.

(b) Employees from different work areas join voluntarily and form a group.

(c) They analyse and solve problems of quality. The purpose is to improve the quality of product and work life too.

(d) It has its own programme and normally the members meet once a week to discuss the problems and recommend solutions.

147. What are the advantages of a Quality Circle?

(a) Better productivity, profitability and better quality of worklife.

(b) Improvement in job performance and job satisfaction.

(c) Attitude for development of proper solution to quality standards.

(d) None of the above.

148. What are the measures that lead to successful participation of workers in the management?

(a) There should not be too many forms of schemes overlapping.

(b) Schemes of participation to be created on the basis of realistic expectations.

(c) Participation should emerge out of the need felt by the parties involved so as to ensure higher commitment.

(d) It has to be an integrated process of collective bargaining so that it may lead to stable and workable bipartite relations.

149. What is autonomous work group?

(a) A group of workers working in a department having complete authority and responsibility to carry out the task assigned to it.

(b) It provides freedom of decision making to members.

(c) Each work group decides its work schedule and target.

(d) It manages work independently in the unit, where they work.

150. What is coditermination?

(a) Taking decisions relating to various issues by managers and workers jointly.

(b) This promotes involvement of workers in every aspect and feel that they do play a vital role in organisational efficiency.

(c) This creates a feeling that management and workers are 'part and parcel' of the organisation.

(d) None of the above.

INTROSPECTION

"People are social capital capable of development."

ANSWERS

1 (a) Training provides increased knowledge and skill in performing a particular job.

2 (d) Edwin B. Flippo

3 (a), (b), (c) and (d)
- (a) It reduces the need of supervision.
- (b) Improve the performance of workers.
- (c) It reduces wastage of men, materials and time.
- (d) It increases the productivity.

4 (b) and (c)
- (b) On the job method
- (c) Off the job method

5 (a), (b) and (c)
- (a) Learning by experience
- (b) Coaching
- (c) Under study

6 (a), (b) and (c)
- (a) Position rotation broadens the knowledge of trainee on various jobs.
- (b) It provides a general background of various jobs to an individual.
- (c) This training takes place in actual situations.

7 (b) A trainee is assigned to perform a special task, so as to enable him to understand the work procedure.

8 (a) In this individuals can gather knowledge and advance in their particular field of profession.

9 (a) and (b)
- (a) In olden days trade skills were taught by a master craftsman to the aspirants who worked under guidance.
- (b) At present industrial establishments require a large number of skilled craftsmen, who can be trained by the system for better output.

10 (a) and (d)
- (a) Large organisations frequently provide vestibule schools. This is a primary training based on actual shop experience.
- (d) This type of training being rather expensive is normally used for training a large number of people.

11 (a) This system emphasizes the use of committee to increase the flow of ideas from less experienced managers to train them for positions of greater responsibility.

12 (a) and (b)
- (a) In this, the trainees have to leave their work place and devote their entire time in developmental objectives.
- (b) In this, theoretical training to people is given.

13 (a) and (c)
- (a) Lecturing is the most traditional form of formal training method.
- (c) Normally, a large number of organisations have their own course programme conducted by their trained instructors.

14 (a), (b), (c) and (d)
- (a) In order to avoid limitations of classroom lectures, many organisations include guided discussions and conferences in their training programmes.
- (b) In this participants put-forth their ideas and discuss and arrive at an improved way of solving problems.
- (c) Conferences may include 'buzz sessions'.
- (d) Conference sessions are to be directed to the needs of participants, otherwise it will not serve the purpose.

15 (b) and (d)
- (b) A case study is a written account of a trained analyst seeking to describe an actual situation. Some cases are merely illustrative, while others are detailed facts demanding extensive analytical ability to solve it.

(d) This method increases the trainees' power of observation and problem solving capability.

16 (a), (c) and (d)

(a) This is the method of simulating the participant to creative thinking.

(c) This method seeks to reduce inhibiting forces by providing a maximum group participation and a minimum of criticism.

(d) In this, ideas are encouraged and criticism of any idea is discouraged, chain reaction to idea to idea is often developed. The ideas are critically examined.

17 (a) This training provides situations in which the participants experience through interaction and some of the conditions as to what they are discussing about.

18 (b) and (c)

(b) In this method participants are not taken to the actual situation. This situation can be simulated in the training session itself.

(c) It is the presentation of a real situation of the organisation in the training session. In this, participants involve themselves and deal with the situations they encounter in real life.

19 (a), (b), (c) and (d)

(a) It can be used as a supplement to conventional training methods. Its purpose is to increase the treasure of skills in dealing with other people.

(b) It is greatly used in human relations training and also in sales training programmes, etc.

(c) It is a spontaneous creation of realistic situation involving two or more persons under classroom situations.

(d) In this some play the role of a manager and others act accordingly to his directions; so through the interaction of a manager and his subordinates, the role awareness is created in the classroom situation. In this, trainees can broaden their experience through different approaches.

20 (a) and (b)

(a) Gaming has been devised to simulate the problem of an industry or department.

(b) Role playing tends to emphasize feelings and the reaction between people. Gaming is a laboratory method in which role playing exists; it focuses on administrative problems.

21 (d) All the above

(a) Rank and file employees

(b) Supervisory level

(c) Managerial level

22 (c) Rank and file employees

23 (b) Supervisory level

24 (d) Executive trainees.

25 (d) All the above

(a) It must have the allowance for individual differences.

(b) Relevance to job requirements and training needs.

(c) Suitable incentives, management support and simultaneous teaching of theory and practical.

26 (a) and (c)

(a) Job experience

(c) Induction and orientation programmes

27 (a) Price

28 (a), (b), (c) and (d)

(a) To enhance effectiveness in the present position.

(b) Keep updating development in technical and administrative fields.

(c) To create capabilities and competence to assume higher responsibilities.

(d) Develop value systems and behavioural practices and commitment to excellence in organisational activities.

29 (d) All the above
- (a) Area of training content.
- (b) Key learning principles
- (c) Trainees' characteristics and cost factor

30 (a), (b), (c) and (d)
- (a) Do trainees like the programme? Do they think it worthwhile? Reaction of trainees about the training programme.
- (b) Learning
- (c) Behaviour
- (d) Results.

31 (b) and (c)
- (b) Education has a broader aim and its purpose is to develop the individual.
- (c) Education is connected with improving general knowledge and motivating a person to understand the total environment.

32 (b) and (c)
- (b) Training the future executives to act according to the new situations and methods.
- (d) Developing the skills of managers to analyse and take decisions relating to the various problems of day to day management of industrial and other organisations.

33 (a) Dale S. Beach

34 (d) All the above
- (a) Technological, social changes and professionally managed enterprises.
- (b) Management as an important profession.
- (c) Recognition of social and public responsibilities and research orientation.

35 (a), (b), (c) and (d)
- (a) Planning and programme targeting.
- (b) Ascertaining key position requirements and managerial appraisals.
- (c) Replacement of skill inventory.
- (d) Appraising the programme by top management.

36 (a), (b).
- (a) It is a new method of teaching personal skills and change in attitude.
- (b) It teaches specific supervisory skills by providing a model of good behaviour to be learned.

37 (a), (b), (c) and (d)
- (a) Coaching
- (b) Job rotation
- (c) Understudy
- (d) Multiple management.

38 (d) All the above
- (a) Sensitivity training, case study, simulation programmes and management games.
- (b) Managerial grid, role playing, incident method, in-basket method, conference, lectures programme by academic institutions.
- (c) Transactional analysis

39 (d) R.R. Hopkins.

40 (a) Sincere efforts made by employers for the benefit of their employees' well-being.

41 (b) and (d)
- (b) To improve the efficiency of the workers.
- (d) Make the workers lead a happier life.

42 (a), (b) and (c)
- (a) Organisation of economic life in a country must conform to principles of justice and a decent standard of living.
- (b) It is the responsibility of the state to safeguard the interest of industrial workers and secure them through suitable legislation.
- (c) They need to be protected against exploitation and governed by legislations like living wage, healthy working conditions, specified working hours, suitable provisions of settlement of disputes, protection of economic aspects, old age, sickness and unemployment.

43 (d) Directive principles of state policy providing adequate security

provisions under Articles 41, 42 and 43 of labour welfare.

<u>*Explanation :*</u> Articles 41, 42 and 43 - *Article 41 :* The State shall within the limits of its economic capacity and development make effective provision for securing the right to work, to education and to public assistance in case of unemployment, old-age, sickness and disablement and in other cases of deserved wants. *Article 42:* The State shall make provision for securing just and human conditions of work and for maternity relief. *Article 43:* The State shall endeavour to secure by suitable legislation or economic organisation or in any other way to all workers, agricultural, industrial or otherwise work, a living wage, conditions of work ensuring a decent standard of living and full employment, leisure and social and cultural opportunities, in particular, the Sate shall endeavour to promote cottage industries on an individual or cooperative basis in rural areas.

44 (d) All the above

(a) It was accepted that labour welfare have a positive role to play in increasing productivity and reducing industrial tension.

(b) State began to realise its social responsibility towards weaker sections of the society.

(c) Emergence of different trade unions gave boost to the growth of labour welfare movement.

45 (a) All the above

(a) Washing facilities, facilities for storing and drying clothes, facilities for sitting at the work place.

(b) Provisions of first aid, shelter, rest-room, canteen, creche, etc.

(c) Welfare officer

46 (c) and (d)

(c) Factories' Act, 1948, Plantation Labour Act, 1961.

(d) Contract labour (Regulation & Abolition) act, 1970.

47 (b), (c) and (d)

(b) Educational, medical and transport facilities.

(c) Recreational and housing facilities

(d) Welfare works by workers' organisations.

48 (c) M.K. Gandhi

49 (b) Practice of keeping oneself and the industrial area clean in order to prevent illness or disease.

50 (d) All the above

(a) Cleanliness, disposal of wastes and effluents, ventilation and temperature, dust and fume, artificial humidification, and over crowding.

(b) Lighting, drinking water, cooling water in hot wether, toilets and spittoons.

(c) Sections 11 to 20 of Factories Act, 1948, speak on health provisions.

51 (a) and (c)

(a) Industrial conditions of being safe and prevent causing injury or damage.

(c) Taking adequate preventive measures against causing injury or loss of limb or life in the industry or organisation.

52 (a), (b), (c) and (d)

(a) Fencing of machinery, working on or near machinery in motion. No women or young person be allowed to clean and lubricate machinery.

(b) Young persons are not to be employed on dangerous or moving machines, prohibition of employment of women and children near cotton openers.

(c) Hoists and lifts to be in good condition, all floor area of the factory to be properly maintained, no person to be employed in any factory to lift or carry heavy load as it is likely to cause injury.

(d) Special care to be taken to protect eyes from all types of foreign object, precaution to be taken against dangerous fumes, inflammable dust and gas.

53 (a) and (c)

(a) Section 40 of the Factories' Act provides measures for the safety of buildings and machinery.

(c) If the Inspector of Factories feels that the use of any building, plant and machinery involves immediate danger. He may serve order to Factory Manager for prohibiting its use till it is property repaired.

54 (a), (b), (c), and (d)

(a) Protect against want, squalor, disease, ignorance and unemployment.

(b) Social security benefits are admissible to all.

(c) It provides benefits according to economic needs of the person.

(d) It is a complete institution. Social assistance, a part of social security, is completely government operated.

55 (c) Beverridge, H.W.

56 (a) Weber and Cohen

57 (b) Social insurance makes the social security possible, i.e., it creates and initiates a mechanism, which is 'Sine qua non' of the realisation of social security.

Explanation: 'Sine qua non' means indespensible condition.

58 (a), (b) and (c)

(a) Provide social security to workers during the contingencies as ill health.

(b) Contingencies against industrial accidents.

(c) Contingencies against maternity.

59 (a) Permanent account of personal information that is kept as evidence for future reference.

60 (d) All the above. (a), (b) and (c).

(a) Records stored the information in files, documents, magnetic diskettes.

(b) Records are prepared from reports, orders, minutes, etc.

(c) These records contain information about employees, employer, trade union, Government, Employment bodies, etc.

61 (a), (b) and (c)

(a) Records help in arriving at right decisions on various matters.

(b) It provides the documentary proof to support any action.

(c) Records are the information containing the past and it can be used in the future.

62 (a), (b), (c) and (d)

(a) The records and its objectives to be clear and consistent in all respects.

(b) Records to be up-dated from time to time.

(c) The information contained in the records should not be of classified nature and easily accessible.

(d) A proper procedural manual should be maintained for following the maintenance of records.

63 (a), (b), (c), and (d)

(a) Records to contain requisite information in a concised form.

(b) They should be classified according to the importance of subject it dealt with, viz., Top Secret, Secret, Confidential, Restricted, etc.

(c) Records need to be verified for its authenticity.

(d) They be maintained according to the subjectwise for easy reference.

64 (b) It focuses on a systematic search of effectiveness and efficiency of management performance on various fields in an organisation.

65 (a), (b) and (c)

(a) It should evaluate the performance of control mechanisms.

(b) Check on overall plans and objectives of business.

(c) It brings out the cases in which organisational policies and procedures are not complied with.

66 (a), (b) and (c)
(a) Accomplishment
(b) Practices, procedures and HR development
(c) Methods of conflict management and morale of personnel

67 (b), (c) and (d)
(b) Audit of personnel inventory and replacement table and turnover rates, selection rates, retrenchment, dismissal, lay off and recruitment rates.
(c) Training programmes, managerial and supervisory personnel, time taken in training, apprentice ratio, material waste, increased productivity.
(d) Employees voluntary participation in various activities, morale, ratio of communication, absenteeism, turnover, number of grievances and settlement, accident rate and arbitration cost, etc.

68 (d) Dale Yoder

69 (a) and (c)
(a) It is a study of material and sources connected with human resources in an effort to establish facts and arrive at new conclusions.
(c) Improve the possibilities to strengthen the skills, and behavioural standards of personnel in an organisation to achieve better results.

70 (a) Any employed person must report to his duty as per the time specified by the organisation.

71 (a) and (b)
(a) Section 52 of Factories Act prescribes that 1st day of the week shall be a rest day for all workers.
(b) The Act stipulates that no worker should be required to work on Sunday, unless the worker has or will have a substituted holiday on one of the three days immediately before or after the Sunday.

72 (a) Leave record is an important part of the service book of an employee, kept along with his service record. Various types of leave, the individual availed during his service career is entered in this record book at the allotted place for the same with proper authentication.

73 (c) Absenteeism means, when an employee remains absent himself without permission from his duty or it is a willful absence without leave.

74 (d) All the above
(a) Long hours of work, bad working conditions, boredom, lack of cooperation between workers and management, sickness.
(b) Accidents, occupational diseases, fatigue, problem of transport facilities to reach the work place and low wages.
(c) Lack of proper medical aid and health care, lack of canteen services, rest room, bad housing conditions, evils of drinking, lack of social or religious facilities, domestic problems and consequent worries.

75 (c) and (d)
(c) It affects earning of workers.
(d) It affects the production and output, and also morale and efficiency of workers.

76 (a) and (c)
(a) Introduction of attendance bonus to employees.
(c) Habitual absenteeism must be treated as a misconduct and so stated in standing orders that it will lead to disciplinary action.

77 (b) When an employee feels something unfair has been done to him.

78 (c) Beach

79 (a) Every organisation should have fair and impartial grievance policy.

80 (a) Keep the employees' morale high and thereby increase the production.

81 (a), (b) and (c)
(a) Factual
(b) Imaginary
(c) Disguised

Explanation: (a) *Factual:* Grievance surfaces, when a rightful need of an employee is not looked after; (b) *Imaginary:* When an employee's dissatisfaction does not have any proper reason; (c) *Disguised:* When an employee's dissatisfaction is under false pretext.

82 (a), (b), and (c)
(a) Economic dissatisfaction
(b) Due to work environment.
(c) The attitude of supervisors

83 (d) All the above
(a) They affect the quality and quantity of production.
(b) Increase the rate of absenteeism and turnover.
(c) They strain superior-subordinate good relations.

84 (a), (b), (c) and (d)
(a) Observing employees for unusual behaviour.
(b) Systematic grievance procedure.
(c) Complaint box
(d) 'Walk-in-meeting' with top manager (Open door policy).

85 (a) Intellectual awareness of one's rights and responsibilities.

86 (a) and (b)
(a) It is the discipline that restrains freedom of a person.
(b) This is a method of imposing penalties for improper behaviour.

87 (a) Positive discipline enables an individual to have greater freedom of expression.

88 (b) Megginson

89 (c) One resorts to wilful damage of the property or violates disciplinary norms.

90 (d) All the above
(a) An employee should understand his duties to the organisation and the organisation should recognise his right as an employer.
(b) Create a spirit of tolerance amongst employees and make requisite adjustments.
(c) Increase the working efficiency and morale of the employees.

91 (a) and (c)
(a) This draws an analogy between touching the hot stove and understanding the heat.
Explanation : If you violate the discipline, you are bound to be punished.
(c) Disciplinary action should be impersonal. There can be any favouritism in dealing with any violation of disciplinary norms.

92 (d) Douglas McGregor.

93 (a) and (b)
a) Lack of proper behaviour, unfair labour practices, barriers of organisational communication.
(b) Arbitrary disciplinary actions, disunity among management and work groups, ack of proper attention to welfare problems of personnel, victimisation of personnel without any reasons.

94 (b) When the management of an organisation finds that an act of omission has been committed by the employee that warrants disciplinary procedure to be followed to arrive at a conclusion whether the act or omission is a misconduct or not.

95 (d) All the above
(a) It must be found out whether the offence committed is under the

standing orders or service rules or under common law.

(b) The foreman or supervisor or the manager in charge of the employee should make a report to the departmental head indicating the action recommended.

(c) If the department head considers the preliminary inquiry necessary, he must depute a department manager or a manager from personnel department to conduct the same. At all times, it is advisable to keep the disciplinary authority (normally the head of the organisation) informed about the progress of the case. If the preliminary inquiry states that there is no *prima facie* case; the individual may be exempted of the charges, the individual may be suitably warned orally or in writing. If there is a *prima facie* case of raising chargesheet, the same be got prepared and signed by disciplinary authority.

96 (a), (b), (c) and (d)

(a) Calling for explanation of the employee by the disciplinary authority.

(b) Considering the explanation of the employee the disciplinary authority may proceed to next action.

(c) Issuance of Show cause notice by the disciplinary authority if disagreeing with the explanation submitted by the employee.

(d) Issue orders for a domestic enquiry.

97 (b) Principles of natural justice are-that no man should be held guilty without giving him an opportunity to explain his point of view.

98 (a), (b), and (c)

(a) Oral warning, written warning, suspension.

(b) Withholding of increment.

(c) Termination of services.

99 (a) Bargain collectively for the rights and privileges by employees.

100 (b) It is a group actin and intended through the representatives of workers.

101 (d) Sydney and Beatrice Webb

102 (d) Yes, it is a complementary process

103 (d) All the above

(a) It highly increases the economic stand of unions and management's disagreement.

(b) It avoids industrial disputes and maintains stability and peace in the organisation.

(c) It also maintains consistency of fair wages and conducive working conditions, when the bargain concludes.

104 (c) J. Henry Richardson

105 (b), (c) and (d)

(b) Parties going to have collective bargaining must organise themselves.

(c) Parties should be ready to enter into agreement in-between

(d) The agreement of bargaining need to be implemented by the concerned parties.

106 (b), (c) and (d)

(b) Voluntary agreement.

(c) Settlement

(d) Consent award.

107 (c) In the year 1950.

108 (a), (b), and (c)

(a) Inadequate arrangements of recognition by majority of unions, as sole bargaining agent.

(b) The threat of confrontation and work stoppage associated with relatively free collective bargaining.

(c) Reasonable degree of involvement by government as a third party in bipartite decision making.

109 (d) All the above

(a) When a man hires another man for

wage, the relation between them is of master and servant.

(b) This relationship is governed by implicit understanding about the terms and conditions of work.

(c) Terms and conditions of work, such as wages, allowances, quantum of work, hours of work. Any violation of terms and condition may create a problem.

110 (a), (b), (c), and (d)

(a) Always the desire of the employers to get the maximum profit from the industry with minimum input.

(b) Changing of the industry from the domestic system of manufacturing to modern large scale production unit.

(c) Migration of most labourers from rural to urban areas due to industrialisation.

(d) Unskilled labourers, who migrate, face economic, social and psychological problems, which are migratory ones.

111 (d) All the above

(a) A dispute or difference between workmen and the employer.

(b) The dispute to be connected with the employment or non-employment.

(c) It must be of the terms of employment or the condition of labour of any person.

112 (b), (c) and (d)

(b) When the dispute is supported by the union of which the workman is a member.

(c) Individual dispute, when supported by a group of workmen.

(d) An individual dispute connected with dismissal, discharge, retrenchment of termination of service of any workman.

113 (b) and (c)

(b) Nature of work performed by a person.

(c) Designation that decides whether he is a workman.

114 (c) Negotiation

115 (d) All the above

(a) Works committee, Conciliation Officer.

(b) Board of Conciliation, Court of Inquiry.

(c) Labour Court, Industrial Tribunal and National Tribunal.

116 (a), (b) and (c)

(a) When negotiations fail.

(b) No useful result has been achieved through arbitration.

(c) When conciliation does fail.

117 (c) Due to unwise actions, uncompromising attitude of the management and workers, minor disputes lead to adjudication. This can be avoided.

118 (a) and (c)

(a) A workman who has been dismissed, discharged or retrenched or terminated is covered by the Act.

(c) Irrespective of the fact, no other workman or any union of workmen is a party to the dispute (Sec. 2(s) and 2A of Industrial Disputes Act) give protection to dismissed workman.

119 (d) All the above

(a) Parties to the dispute can settle their dispute by appointing an arbitrator.

(b) Both parties can appoint an arbitrator in agreement to settle the dispute.

(c) After appointment of the arbitrator, arbitration award, which has become enforceable shall be binding on the parties to the industrial dispute.

120 (a), (b), (c) and (d)

(a) Section 12 of Industrial Disputes Act deals with the duties of the Conciliation Officer.

(b) If settlement is arrived at as a result of conciliation, he must make a report to the Government within 14 days, along with memorandum of settlement.

(c) Conciliation officer has no power to give final decision in the matter of disputes. His role is of a mediator between the parties to settle the dispute.

(d) The role of a conciliation officer is

difficult and delicate one, which requires extraordinary virtues.

121 (b), (c) and (d)

(b) They investigate into all matters affecting the case and induce the parties to come to a fair and amicable settlement.

(c) If any agreement is reached, the board sends a report to the Government together with memorandum of settlement.

d) If negotiations fail, a report, along with recommendations, is sent, not later than two months,

122 (d) All the above

(a) It may consist of one independent person or such members or persons as the government may decide.

(b) If Court consists of two or more members, one of them will be appointed as a chairman.

(c) It will inquire into matters referred to and submit to government the report within a period of six months.

123 (a), (b), (c) and (d)

(a) Legality of an order passed by an employer and application and interpretation of standing orders.

(b) Discharge or dismissal of workmen and reinstatement of workmen wrongfully dismissed.

(c) Withdrawal of concessions, illegality of a strike or lockout.

(d) It has the power to adjudicate all matters rather than those coming under the jurisdiction of tribunal.

124 (a), (b) and (c)

(a) It consists of one independent person or such number of persons that may be decided by Government. If there are two or more members, one will be the Chairman. He must be a judge of High Court or having equal qualification.

(b) Jurisdiction or wages and the payment, allowances, hours of work, rest, leave with wage and holidays, bonus, profit sharing, PF and gratuity, shift working other than standing orders, classification grade, discipline, rationalisation, retrenchment of workmen and closure of establishment.

(c) Any matter that may be prescribed by the government.

125 (d) All the above.

(a) National tribunal is appointed by the Central Government.

(b) Industrial disputes having national importance or of such nature that industrial establishment situated in more than one state.

(c) National Tribunal shall consist of one person not below the rank of a High Court Judge and not below sixty-five years of age.

126 (d) All the above

(a) It is binding on all parties to dispute.

(b) The heirs, successors, or assigns of the employer in respect of his establishment

(c) All persons in the establishment whether employed on the date on which the dispute arose or subsequent to that.

127(a) When persons employed in any industry or in any establishment stop their work acting in combination is said to be a strike.

128 (b), (c) and (d)

(b) Fatigue and frustration at the place of work and bad social conditions of workmen.

(c) Demand of wages and the desire to raise them.

(d) Multiple immediate issues.

129 (a), (b), and (c)

(a) Plurality of workmen.

(b) Cessation of work or refusal to do work.

(c) Combination and concerted action.

130 (a), (b), (c) and (d)

(a) Closing the place of employment or refusal of the employer to continue work by the employees of his organisation.

(b) There must be closure, suspension of work or refusal to employees.

(c) It must be the consequence of an industrial dispute or in anticipation of an altercation.

(d) It should be intended to compel the employees to accept certain terms and conditions of employment.

131(a), (b), (c) and (d)

(a) A strike resorted to during the pendency of proceedings before a Board of Conciliation.

(b) A strike resorted to during the pendency of proceedings before the Labour Court, Industrial Tribunal, National Tribunal for adjudication.

(c) A strike resorted to during the pendency of proceedings before the arbitration.

(d) Settlement of an award is binding on workmen and they are not supposed to make any demand inconsistent with the settlement of an award while it is in operation.

132 (a), (b), (c), and (d)

(a) If workers do not give notice of strike to the employer within six weeks before commencement of the strike.

(b) If workers go on strike within 14 days of giving such a notice.

(c) If they go on strike before the expiry of the specified date in the notice for commencing the strike.

(d) If they go on strike during the pendency of any conciliation proceedings before a Conciliation and during 7 days after the conclusion of such proceedings.

133(a) Failure, refusal or inability of an employer to give employment to a worker, whose name is currently on the muster roll of the industry.

134(d) Termination of service of a workman for any reason whatsoever.

135(a) The expression of victimisation is included in that practice.

136 (a) The idea of involving workers in those aspects affected them more and providing them autonomy and control over their work-life.

137 (c) and (d)

(c) Development of self-management in industry.

(d) Involvement of employees in decision making process.

138 (d) All the above

(a) Informative participation and consultative participation.

(b) Associated and administrative participation.

(c) Decisive participation.

139 (a), (b), (c), and (d)

(a) Need of proper managerial attitude.

(b) Cooperation of trade unions.

(c) It should be consultative and purposeful.

(d) Workers need to have faith in the system.

140 (a), (b) and (c)

(a) Participation

(b) Innovation

(c) Information and accountability

141(a), (b) and (c)

(a) Works committee, Joint Management council.

(b) Joint Council, Shop Council.

(c) Participative decision making.

142 (b) and (c)

(b) It consists of representatives of employer and employees.

(c) The aim of this committee is to promote harmony at the work place and sort out differences in respect of common interest.

143 (b), (c) and (d)

(b) This consists of representatives of

both management and workers.

(c) Its aim is to improve the efficiency of the workers and provide adequate welfare facilities to them.

(d) Educate workers so as to enable them to participate in such schemes and also to satisfy their psychological needs.

144 (a), (b), (c) and (d)

(a) Joint Councils are for the entire organisation and its members are confined to same organisation.

(b) Tenure of the Joint Council is for two years.

(c) The Chief Executive Officer of the organisation becomes its Chairman.

(d) Joint Council appoints a Secretary, who conducts the activities of the Council.

145 (a), (b), (c) and (d)

(a) It represents each department or a shop in a unit.

(b) The council represents equal number of employers and employees.

(c) Employer's representatives are nominated by the management and consist of persons from the entire unit. Workers' representatives are from various departments or shops concerned.

(d) The number of members of each Council is determined by the employers in consultation with recognised union. Total number, generally, is limited to twelve.

146 (b), (c), and (d)

(b) Employees from different work areas join voluntarily and form a group.

(c) They analyse and solve problems of quality. The purpose is to improve the quality of product and work life too.

(d) It has its own programme and normally the members meet once a week to discuss the problems and recommend solutions.

147 (a), (b), and (c)

(a) Better productivity, profitability and better quality of worklife.

(b) Improvement in job performance and job satisfaction.

(c) Attitude for development of proper solution to quality standards.

148 (a), (b), (c) and (d)

(a) There should not be too many forms of schemes overlapping.

(b) Schemes of participation to be created on the basis of realistic expectations.

(c) Participation should emerge out of the need felt by the parties involved so as to ensure higher commitment.

(d) It has to be an integrated process of collective bargaining so that it may lead to stable and workable bipartite relations.

149 (a) A group of workers working in a department having complete authority and responsibility to carry out the task assigned to it.

150 (a) Taking decisions relating to various issues by managers and workers jointly.

◆◆◆◆◆

CHAPTER - 4

- ➢ HUMAN RESOURCE PLANNING AND LABOUR MARKET
- ➢ CONCEPTS OF MOTIVATION
- ➢ ORGANISATIONAL DYNAMICS
- ➢ ORGANISATIONAL DEVELOPMENT (OD)

FEATURES :

- Human resource planning and labour market
- Human resource planning
- Technique of human resource planning
- Basics of human resource planning
- Estimation of human resource
- Human resource forecasting labour market
- Features of labour market
- Wage rigidity
- Organised labour market
- Bounded labour
- Motivational variables
- Nature of motivation
- Types of motivation
- Techniques of motivation
- Theories of motivation
- Determinants of motivation
- Morale
- Evaluation of morale
- Role
- Importance
- Organisation dynamics
- Objectives
- Approaches
- Principles
- Corporate culture
- Types of goals
- Organisation theories
- Organisational development (OD)
- Process
- Training methods of OD
- Conflict
- Types
- Levels of conflict
- Causes
- Resolution of conflict
- Methods of conflict
- Organisation change
- Hawthrone effect
- Resistance of change
- Dimensions of change
- Levels of change
- Types of change
- Total quality management (TQM)
- Re-engineering
- External causes of change

KEY NOTE

Human Resource Planning and Labour Market

It is a part of overall corporate planning. This is a process of ensuring the right number of employees at the right place and right time. The requirement of man-power depends upon factors like economic factors, sales, forecast, expansion programmes and the employees market forecast. Dimensions of man-power planning in India is based on sheer number involved. There is misconception that India with considerably a large population does have a large number of man-power available for any specific requirement of skill. Specific man-power shortage will prevent fulfilment of expansion, diversification or technological change. The management of enterprise has at times to cope up with the shortage of certain skilled personnel and excess of unskilled ones. Therefore, an effective human resource planning is needed for growth and advancement.

Labour market : According to Bhogaliwal labour market is a process by which supply of particular type of labour and demand for that type of labour to obtain a balance. Labour has been termed as a quasi fixed factor of production. Normally labour cost vary directly with production in both levels for short and long periods. It clearly indicates that it is responsible for forming the capital. It also shows that the amount does not vary in a short span, since there is variation in the production level. The organisations have to incur lot of expenditure during recruitment and selection of skilled man-power. There are certain factors like terms and conditions of employment, wage differentials, monopoly, incoming and outgoing migratory labour force, etc., that influence the labour market.

Concepts of motivation : Motivation is an act of stimulating specific course of action. It has relation with the behaviour of an individual, who is at work. The main purpose of motivation is to create a condition in which the employees/people are willing to work whole-heartedly. In a nut-shell, we can say that motivation has two significant variables that a manager should understand correctly. They are- (i) willingness to work, and (ii) the capacity to work. These variables are identified in a person prior to motivation. If they are correctly identified, the motivation will be effective. This is possible only by an astute manager in an organisation.

Organisational dynamics : Organisations are entities of social nature. The modern organisations are too large in size and also in terms of investment. Speciality of modern organisation is that it forms a suitable coordination of a large number of people for attaining individual as well as group goals. A systematic chain of division of labour is carried out by assigning authority and responsibility. Every organisation has certain objectives to achieve and the same are structured in the form of hierarchy. Peter Drucker has suggested certain key areas of needs like innovation, productivity, physical and financial resources, market standing, performance of the manager and department, workers' performance profitability and public responsibility etc., for effective functioning of an organisation.

Organisational development (OD) : Organisation development is an intervention strategy used to change the benefits, attitude, values and structure of organisation so as to bring about a planned change. When we talk about the origin of organisational development, we mean- reward structure of the job, fast development of technology and urge for new innovations and experimental learning process, in which aspects like action research, problem solving, uses of group process, are involved. They are contingency oriented and also use the change agent. Organisational development focuses on the entire organisation and not any part of it.

QUESTIONS

HUMAN RESOURCE PLANNING AND LABOUR MARKET

1. What is human resource planning?

(a) Deciding the number and type of people required for each job.

(b) Ensuring right number and kind of employees.

(c) Human resource planning aims at procuring the right type of personnel.

(d) All the above.

2. What are the key elements in human resource planning?

(a) Recruiting the right personnel for right jobs.

(b) Assessing future skill requirements

(c) Necessary resources are made available on time.

(d) Work force forecast, man-power assessment and staffing programme.

3. What are the corporate level strategies normally affecting human resource planning?

(a) Expansion and diversification

(b) Acquisition and merger

(c) Retrenchment

(d) Organisation experiencing the effect of technological change.

4. What are the objectives of human resource planning?

(a) Ensure optimum utilisation of working personnel.

(b) Assess the requirement of future skills.

(c) Improve the standard of skill, knowledge and ability.

(d) Minimising turn over and filling up turn over vacancies.

5. "Human resource planning is an integrated approach to perform the planning aspects of personnel function in order to have a sufficient supply of adequately developed and motivated people to perform the duties and tasks required to meet organisational objectives and satisfy the individual needs and goals of organisational members." Who said this?

(a) Stainer, G.

(b) E.W. Vetter

(c) C.B. MacKey

(d) Leon C. Megginson

6. How to organise human resource planning?

(a) Every line manager has to perform certain human resource planning in his department.

(b) Specialist of the department may assist the line manager for planning.

(c) A line manager to be adequately supported by central HR planning department.

(d) Mainly line managers furnish the required information on the basis of estimates of operating levels, the staff furnish supplementary data like turn over rates and then final estimates are made.

7. What are the different techniques of Human Resource Planning (HRP)?

(a) Managerial judgement

(b) Ratio trend analysis and work study techniques.

(c) Delfi techniques and others

(d) None of the above.

8. What are the internal factors affecting HRP?

(a) Company strategies, human resource planning and formal and informal groups.

(b) Job analysis, time horizons and type of information.

(c) Company's production policies and trade unions.

(d) Factors of business environment.

9. What does the basis of Human Resource Planning mean?

(a) Economic forecast.

(b) Sales forecast.

(c) Expansion programme and employee market forecast.

(d) All the above.

10. What is the human resource planning process?

(a) Forecasting future needs.

(b) Projecting Human Resource supply.

(c) Comparison of forecast needs and projection supply.

(d) Planning policies and progarammes.

11. How can we place the right man on the right job?

(a) Finding out the capabilities of the individual.

(b) What is the job like to be performed.

(c) Matching the individual with the job.

(d) Through a scientific selection process.

12. How are the future needs of human resource projected by plann« rs?

(a) Judgement and exp.rience; budgetary planning.

(b) Data of work standards and key procedure factors

(c) Analysis of future needs.

(d) All the above.

13. How the human resource planning is estimated at various levels?

(a) Macro level (National).

(b) Micro level (Industry).

(c) State level (Including all).

(d) All the above.

14. What is the periodicity of human resource planning?

(a) Short period (one year).

(b) Medium period (five years).

(c) Long period (ten-fifteen years).

(d) None of the above.

15. "Human resource planning is the process including forecasting, developing and controlling by which a firm ensures that it has the right number of people and the right kind of the people at the right places doing work for which they are economically most useful." Who said this?

(a) E.B. Geisler (b) C.B. Mackey

(c) J.F. De Santo (d) J.W. Walker

16. What are the activities of Human Resource Planning?

(a) Forecasting and man-power inventory.

(b) Anticipating man-power problem.

(c) Planning.

(d) None of the above.

17. What are the organisational objectives based on the human resource forecasting?

(a) Own competitive position, market opportunities and Government policies.

(b) Import/Export policies/opportunities

(c) Technological change, labour market and audit of existing man-power.

(d) All the above.

18. What is human resource inventory?

(a) Total number of various types of skilled personnel on the strength of the organisation.

(b) Total number of man-power available at a particular time.

(c) Total number of skilled and unskilled personnel

(d) All the above.

19. What is human resource forecast?

(a) Forecasting the requirement of personnel.

(b) Forecasting the future needs of human resource.

(c) A prediction of future demands of employees of an organisation.

(d) None of the above.

20. What is labour market?

(a) A specialised or a large number of small independent employers competing for labour in the market and also a large number of workers competing for jobs.

(b) Competitive theory of the labour market derived from neoclassical economics.

(c) In a labour market, supplies of a particular type of labour and demands for that type of labour seek to obtain a balance.

(d) All the above.

21. What are the main features of labour market?

(a) The relationship between the buyer and a seller in labour market (except casual labour) is not a temporary one and it lasts for a longer period.

(b) Labour markets are local.

(c) The utilisation of labour markets is for the buyers and sellers, who are in contact with each other for the purchase and sale of workers' services.

(d) All the above.

22. Does the labour market affect development of economy?

(a) In India there is a great surplus of all type of workers for all available jobs.

(b) Workers are vocationally and psychologically unprepared for industrial work.

(c) There is acute shortage of skilled workers for many jobs, such imbalance usually cause hindrance to the development of economy.

(d) None of the above.

23. Is there any possibility of unemployment, where labour market is in practice?

(a) All those seeking work cannot find the job in an existing wage rate of the market.

(b) Unemployment can prevail with unfilled vacancies and rising wages for those who are already working.

(c) The wage adjustment process either does not work or works inaccurately.

(d) All the above.

24. What do you mean by wage rigidity?

(a) Employers do not immediately reduce wages, as the demand of labour falls.

(b) The employers, instead of adjusting the wage, normally resort to reduction in recruitment and overtime; also introduce short time work schedules and lay off the workers, if necessary.

(c) At the time of demand for increase of labour, employers do not immediately reduce the wages, but increase overtime and recruitment.

(d) It is seen that wages do not move flexibly in response to demand and supply of labour.

25. What are the important features of Indian Labour market?

(a) Relationship between the employer and employee is long-standing.

(b) Existence of unstable labour force.

(c) Indian labour market is mostly favourable to employer than employee.

(d) Labour market is imperfect therefore, workers do not get proper wages.

26. What is organised labour market?

(a) In the organised labour market, employment generation is the main object of the government both for private and public sectors.

(b) Creation of employment exchange has been a great help for the organised labour market in providing employment opportunities to the local people for certain type of jobs both in private and public sectors.

(c) Organised labour markets are standardised and they operate in a systematic manner.

(d) All the above.

27. What is a bonded labour?

(a) Employers like mine owners, tobacco processing companies, etc., employ people on very low wages.

(b) Those, who live below the poverty line, need money to celebrate marriages of their children, hospital expenses etc., and they take loan from their land lords or money lenders, who levy heavy interest on the loan amount. Ultimately the poor man fails to pay back the amount of loan. Such people become bonded labours to the landlords/money lenders.

(c) Government of India abolished the bonded labour.

(d) All the above.

28. What does unorganised labour market mean?

(a) This includes small industries, cottage industries, shops and establishments, hotels, mobile business and agriculture, etc.

(b) In this labour market, there is no particular design of job and also no man power planning.

(c) Unsystematic business dealings.

(d) All the above.

29. How can the unorganised sector labour be identified?

(a) Employees possess no bargaining power.

(b) No special place of employment.

(c) They are mostly of contract labours.

(d) They are mobile (moving from one place to another).

CONCEPTS OF HUMAN MOTIVATION

30. What is motivation?

(a) Inspire a person to act in a particular way.

(b) Motivation is a function that a manager performs in order to get his subordinates achieve the goal.

(c) Motivation is required by all; it can be of various kinds and varying degrees.

(d) Inspiring a person to perform a job by some incentive (monetary or other).

31. What are the variables that a manager must understand in motivating an individual or an employee?

(a) Selecting and applying motivation.

(b) Willingness and capacity to work.

(c) Understanding the fundamental urges of the people.

(d) None of the above.

32. "Carrot of material rewards has not, like the stick of fear lost its potency." Who said this?

(a) George R. Terry

(b) Peter F. Drucker

(c) Michael J. Jucins

(d) Edwin B. Flippo.

33. What is the nature of motivation?

(a) An unending process, by which an individual is motivated.

(b) A psychological factor; a frustrated individual cannot be motivated easily.

(c) Goals are the motivators.
(d) All the above.

34. What are the principles of motivation?

(a) People are of selfish nature, if that is satisfied, put their best to achieve organisational goal.
(b) Attainable goals give an employee satisfaction.
(c) An executive, who has capabilities to motivate his subordinates, is a successful one.
(d) All the above.

35. What are type types of motivation?

(a) Positive motivation.
(b) Negative motivation.
(c) Extrinsic and intrinsic motivation.
(d) None of the above.

36. What is Maslow's theory of motivation?

(a) Intrinsic motivation.
(b) Hierarchy of needs.
(c) Financial motivation.
(d) Social needs.

37. The problem of motivation is the key to management actions in executive form, it is among chief tasks of General Manager. We may safely lay it down that the tone of an organisation is the reflection of the motivation from top." Who said this?

(a) E.F.L. Brech (b) Jucius, M.J.
(c) Dubin Robert (d) Viteles Morris

38. What do you understand by the concept of motivation

(a) It is derived from motive, means idea, need and emotion.
(b) An organic state prompts man to an action.
(c) It is a psychological concept.
(d) It is an organic state of mind.

39. What is the importance of motivation in an organisation?

(a) Organisational objectives are achieved through motivation.
(b) It is a key to management actions in its executive form.
(c) It infuses the willingness to work.
(d) Proper utilisation of human resource.

40. Which are the techniques of motivation?

(a) An important function of management.
(b) Normally human being works only 70-75% of his capacity; one can utilise his full capacity.
(c) Financial incentives.
(d) Non-financial incentives.

41. What does Prof. A.H. Maslow's self-actualisation need indicate?

(a) Maslow's theory speaks five types of needs like physiological, safety, social, self-esteem and self-actualisation .
(b) It is the last need of an individual
(c) People, who attained self-actualisation are self-satisfied people.
(d) Self-actualisation is the transformation of one's perception into reality.

42. How does Frederick Herzberg's Two-factor theory distinguish in motivation?

(a) Distinction between motivation and maintenance factors in work situation.
(b) Maintenance factors are like company policies, supervision, interpersonal relations, work conditions, pay, job security, status, etc.
(c) Motivational factors are achievement, recognition, advancement and work itself.
(d) All the above.

43. "McGregor has propounded two theories of human behaviour based on the theme of dual nature of human being." What are they?

(a) Theory 'Z'
(b) Expectancy and valence
(c) 'X' and 'Y' theory
(d) None of the above.

44. What is Mc Clelland's contribution in his theory of motivation?

(a) According to him, two motives are innate or natural, striving for pleasure and seeking to avoid displeasure.
(b) According to him, people can be classified into two groups, one small and the other large.
(c) Achievement oriented people have certain qualities, they prefer a moderate degree of risk, and they feel their efforts and abilities will bring the outcome.
(d) All the above.

45. What theory Vector H. Varoom devised in motivation?

(a) Behaviour theory.
(b) Contingency theory.
(c) Human relation theory.
(d) Expectancy theory.

46. What is the importance of expectancy theory?

(a) The theory denotes that employees' is as driving force to achieve certain level of performance.
(b) Motivation is a product of the values one seeks and one's expectation of the probability that a particular action will lead to those values.
(c) The outcome of the theory is that an employee performs certain cost-benefit analysis to find out that the estimated benefit is enough to justify the cost of greater effort, he is likely to perform.
(d) All the above.

47. Who originated behaviourist theory?

(a) Cambell and Hakel (b) R.Likert
(c) Herzberg (d) Skinner

48. What is the importance of behaviour theory?

(a) Prof. Skinner has contributed a new way of motivating people.
(b) The concept is called behaviour modification or positive reinforcement.
(c) Psychological satisfaction of employees on the job largely depends upon the appreciation and recognition of their good work.
(d) None of the above.

49. What was the motivational approach made by Renis Likert in his theory?

(a) Employee centered
(b) Employer centered
(c) Work centered
(d) None of the above.

50. How does the behaviour modification occur in an individual?

(a) Behaviour of a person is modified through conditioning.
(b) Behaviour depends on its consequences, therefore it is an external motivation process, unlike internal motivation process of other theories of motivation.
(c) Modification occurs through positive reinforcement (motivation) and negative reinforcement (motivation).
(d) All the above.

51. What does Alderfer's ERG theory refer to?

(a) The analysis of work motivation tends to support Alderfer's theory over Maslow's and Herzberg.
(b) The ERG theory stands for existence and growth.
(c) ERG means 'Existence', 'Relatedness' and 'Growth'. These three sets of needs are the main force of alternative theory of human needs.
(d) All the above.

52. What is Stancy Adam's Equity Theory?

(a) The theory mainly deals in motivating people to have good relations with others.

(b) Equity Theory is a process that does comparison with inequity in organisation.

(c) The main features of Equity Theory are inputs, outputs and comparison.

(d) All the above

53. What are the determinants of motivation?

(a) Motivation is personal and internal urge that arises from needs.

(b) Human needs are multifarious and complex.

(c) Worker is an individual and he is the whole person having both his pleasures and problems.

(d) Management must understand the 'Whole person' and not the 'Part person' for work alone.

54. What is morale?

(a) Mental status or attitude of an individual or a group willing to cooperate.

(b) Emotion affecting the attitude to work.

(c) Employees' enthusiasm that voluntarily conform to regulations.

(d) Higher degree of cohesiveness that leads to effectiveness of a group.

55. "Morale is a feeling somewhat related 'esprit de corps', enthusiasm or zeal" Who said this?

(a) Mc Farland (b) Haimann

(c) Yoder (d) None of the above

56. How can morale be evaluated?

(a) It can be estimated according to individual's attribute.

(b) Through observation.

(c) Prediction of behavioural data.

(d) Interviews.

57. How is the morale survey conducted?

(a) Using questionnaire and interview technique.

(b) Observation.

(c) Objective survey.

(d) None of the above.

58. What is the indication of low morale among the employees?

(a) Lack of interest in work.

(b) Low productivity.

(c) Absenteeism, indiscipline problems, employees unrest and increased grievances.

(d) All the above.

59. "The extend to which individual needs are satisfied and the extent to which the individual perceives that satisfaction, stemming from has total job satisfaction in morale." Who said this?

(a) S.W. Gellarman.

(b) S.M. Robbins.

(c) Robert M. Guion.

(d) Koontz O' Donnel.

60. What is the importance of morale?

(a) Morale keeps the employees happy.

(b) It is a state of mind for an individual to have a team spirit.

(c) Production and productivity are directly affected by high morale.

(d) It is the requirement of management to keep high morale among employees.

61. What role does morale play to improve productivity?

(a) Morale refers to total satisfaction of a person from his job, work group and superiors.

(b) Where the morale is high, its output is also high.

(c) Low morale tends to low productivity.

(d) None of the above.

62. What factors are responsible for high morale?

(a) Confidence of an individual member in achievement of the goal of a group.
(b) Confidence of the members in their leader.
(c) Organisational environment.
(d) All the above.

63. What are the measures that promote morale?

(a) Proper wage structure based on efficiency.
(b) Security of job and recognition of efforts of people.
(c) Delegation of authority and foolproof grievance system.
(d) All the above.

ORGANISATIONAL DYNAMICS

64. What are the types of social organisations?

(a) Private, profit making organisations.
(b) Public service organisations.
(c) Organisations that are neither private nor public, but they do provide services which are not provided by the business or government.
(d) All the above.

65. How can the organisation be distinguished?

(a) It is the rational coordination of the activities of a certain number of people.
(b) Its activities are governed by a structure.
(c) In an organisation people involve in interaction and the participants in organisation fulfil the individual objectives along with organisational ones.
(d) All the above.

66. What does organisational objective refer to?

(a) Organisation has a definite goal to achieve.
(b) The goals or objectives, which are service, personal, social and commodity related.
(c) Business objectives.
(d) Profit objectives.

67. "There are eight key areas of organisational needs. These are market-standing, innovation, productivity, physical and financial resources, profitability, manager's performance and development, workers' performance and attitude and public responsibility." Who said this?

(a) William J. Stanton
(b) Jerome McCarthy
(c) Peter Drucker
(d) Louis A. Allen

68. What is the purpose or aim of the organisation?

(a) Direct human efforts in a specific direction.
(b) It helps as a basis for development of organisational objectives
(c) It helps in innovations.
(d) It provides personal benefits.

69. What are the approaches to understand the organisation?

(a) Max Webber's bureaucratic approach and Taylor's scientific management approach.
(b) Mayo's human relation approach and Katz and Khan's open system theory approach.

(c) Public relation approach.
(d) Institutional approach.

70. What is the speciality of Max Webber's bureaucratic model of organisational approach?

(a) This approach is known as Webber's machinistic approach that equates the organisational functioning to a machine type process.
(b) In this, every part of the machine play its own role to perform its expected function. It also stresses on impersonal rationality and a defined procedure, which take care of the members and also proper functioning of the organisation.
(c) Fair and equal treatment to all.
(d) Control and decision making are centralised.

71. What is Taylor's scientific management approach that failed to give importance?

(a) Taylor also produced a machinistic approach in his scientific management to increase productivity
(b) It aimed at the most effective way of integrating men with machines to advancement of maximum production.
(c) In machine like approach, it was noticed that it ignored the human element in organisation.
(d) All the above.

72. What is the main principle of Human Relation approach of Elton Mayo and his colleagues?

(a) Human relation approach emphasises three important elements- perception, motivation and aspiration of members of an organisaton.
(b) The study of Hawthrone shifted the attention of the researchers from the improvement of physical condition of work for increasing production to human relation in the organisation.
(c) In organisation cohesive work groups helping one another to increased productivity.
(d) All the above.

73. On what principles does a formal organisation exist?

(a) Organisation is a cooperative activity of two or more persons with a purpose of common goal.
(b) Proper communication with each other.
(c) Willing to act for a common goal.
(d) Share common objectives.

74. What is the role of informal organisation?

(a) Informal organisations are not formed according to any rules and regulations.
(b) It is of voluntary nature.
(c) The purpose is to fulfil the needs of individuals.
(d) It always has the bearing over the formal organisation.

75. What is meant by basic dimensions of organisational structure?

(a) Job specialisation and departmentation.
(b) Chain of command and span of control.
(c) Formalisation, line and staff and complexity.
(d) All the above.

76. Are organisations static or dynamic?

(a) Organisations are static.
(b) Organisations are dynamic.
(c) Organisations are static as well as dynamic.
(d) They have to adjust constantly with external environment and such adjustments result in change of their structure.

77. "Organisational culture refers to the set of values, beliefs and behavioural pattern from the core identity of

organisation." Who said this?
(a) Denison (b) Simirich
(b) McGregor (d) Peter Drucker

78. What are the components of corporate culture?
(a) Influence of behaviour
(b) Values
(c) Climate
(d) Management style.

79. What is meant by organisational mission?
(a) The purpose to which the organisation exists.
(b) To ensure that organisation shall not encourage conflicting purposes.
(c) It acts as a media for the development of organisational goal.
(d) None of the above.

80. What is the importance of unity of command in an organisation?
(a) It is an important step in an organisation that helps allocation of authority to various levels to achieve the task.
(b) Each person at subordinate level is accountable to his immediate superior.
(c) This method protects the integrity of both, the subordinate and the superior.
(d) This principle clearly states that a subordinate has to comply the orders of one boss at a time.

81. What is the unity of direction in an organisation?
(a) During division of work all connected activities are put together in a particular department.
(b) Each department and section tries to specialise in the activity allotted to it.
(c) If each unit has a single or homogeneous activity/activities, it can bring organisation efficiency.
(d) All the above.

82. What is the concept of an organisational goal?
(a) It is something that an organisation seeks and towards which its all resources and efforts are directed.
(b) The aim of an organisation.
(c) Every level in the organisation has a goal for itself.
(d) Ultimate objective of an organisaton.

83. What are the ingredients of an organisational goal ?
(a) The sum total of its executive plan, which the organisation is striving for.
(b) Combination of objectives, purposes, missions, standards and targets.
(c) Organisations have primary as well as secondary goals.
(d) All the above.

84. What is meant by functions of organisational goal?
(a) The goals of an organisation provide legitimacy to its existence.
(b) Goals provide a starting point to the organisational activities.
(c) Goals act as constraints that organisation must acknowledge.
(d) The goals provide motivational force for organisational activity and the interest of both the individuals and the organisation.

85. What are the types of goals?
(a) Goals are supposed to be followed up by an organisation.
(b) Tangible and intangible goals.
(c) Determinative and constrainable goals.
(d) All the above.

86. What is actually meant by goal?
(a) Goals are targets, that are completed by the organisaton.
(b) Organisations are not achieving goals for which they are created.
(c) Goals are those for which all

organisational resources are spent to reach them.

(d) All the above.

87 What is the internal environment on organisational goals?

(a) In every organisation, there is internal environment and external environment.

(b) Individual or group constitutes the environment of other individual or group.

(c) When interaction takes place between individuals or groups together with organisational norms and values, the atmosphere of mutual trust and adjustment takes place.

(d) None of the above.

88. "Thereare three ways to determine the kind of structure needed in a specifc enterprise, they are (i) activity analysis, (ii) decision analysis, and (iii) relation analysis." Who said this?

(a) Peter Drucker (b) Kast

(c) Selzmick (d) Argyris, C

89. What is meant by organisational theories?

(a) It implies certain generalisations, which have universal applicability.

(b) Ideas formulated by reasoning from facts.

(c) An exposition of the principles on which a subject is based.

(d) All the above.

90. What are organisational theories?

(a) Classical approach

(b) Neoclassical approach

(c) Modern organisational theory.

(d) Contingency approach.

91. What is modern organisational theory?

a) Traditional theory stressing universal principles that were prescriptive.

b) Modern organisation theory derived from general systems theory and has an empirical and analytical base; it views the organisation in a system perspective.

c) Modern theory views organisation as an organic open system.

d) All the above.

92. Why modern organisations are open organic system?

(a) They carry out an exchange relation with environment and are influenced by it.

(b) Organic systems have adaptability and flexibility.

(c) They adapt to environmental situations.

(d) They are probabilistic system and nothing can be said in certainty as the outcome of particular action, that is usually uncertain.

ORGANISATIONAL DEVELOPMENT (OD)

93. What is organisational development?

(a) Organisational development is a complete concept with regard to organisational resources including human resource for organisational effectiveness.

(b) Human resource development is different from an organisational development.

(c) Organisational development provides a planned and systematic change in organisation.

(d) Organisations have their birth, growth, revival, survival and extinction since time immemorial.

94. "Organisational development as a compex educational strategy intended to change the beliefs, attitudes, values and structure of organisations so that they can better adapt to new technologies, market and challenges and the dizzying rate of change itself." Who said this?

(a) Samuel C. Certo and J. Paul Peter
(b) Bennis
(c) Kantz D. and Kahn, R.L.
(d) Clary Carr.

95. What is the process of organisational development?

(a) Organisational development assesses the general health of the organisation.
(b) The process of diagnosis and selection and design intervention.
(c) The process of implementation, evaluation and adjustment and maintenance of system.
(d) OD is a developing and evolving field of activities.

96. What are the major activities involved in organisational development?

(a) Coordination and integration
(b) Managing change and conflict
(c) Team work
(d) Commitment of employees to the work.

97. What are the characteristics of orgnisational development?

(a) Focus on whole organisation and system orientation.
(b) Group process of improvement, development in action research and problem solving.
(c) It is integrated development process of people, structure, technology and social system.
(d) All the above.

98. How will you make the process of organisational development effective?

(a) Determination of the type of OD programme.
(b) Collection of data, reviews and feedback.
(c) Action planning and problem solving, intergroup development and appraisal and follow-up.
(d) All the above.

99. What are the causes responsible for OD's origin?

(a) Requirement of developmental needs.
(b) Reward structure on the job.
(c) Urge for experimental learning process.
(d) Fast and speedy technological and social changes.

100. "OD as a process aimed at enhancing organisational effectiveness through planned change suggested by behavioural science knowledge (about human behaviour). In short, OD involves systematic efforts to enhance organisation's attainment of its major goals." Who said this?

(a) Robbins, Stephen P.
(b) Baron.
(c) Schein, Edgar.
(d) Bennis.

101. What are the training methods used in organisational development?

(a) Use of information technology
(b) Managerial training programme
(c) Conventional training methods.
(d) Laboratory training methods.

102. What is the conventional method of training?

(a) Usual methods of training.
(b) Classroom discussions, presentations, etc.
(c) Audio and Video presentations
(d) All the above.

103. What is laboratory training method?

(a) Methods of learning through experience on the job.
(b) Situations in which trainees experience themselves through their interaction.
(c) This provides greater impact on trainees than conventional training.
(d) All the above.

104. What are the different laboratory training methods of OD?
(a) Case study
(b) Role playing
(c) Gaming knowledge
(d) Sensitivity training.

105. What is role playing?
(a) In this method, two or more persons are assigned different roles to play before other trainees.
(b) Playing the role of particular position by a trainee.
(c) Other trainees observe and comment such roles.
(d) Trainees are given specific problems and they discuss it in their particular roles as per the guidance given to them.

106. What advantage can a trainee get through role playing?
(a) In this, people develop creative ability by observing the roles.
(b) Lot of time is consumed in its conduct and it is expensive too.
(c) One can understand different approaches to a problem in a short time.
(d) He tries to understand others behaviour.

107. What is gaming?
(a) It is an exercise conducted by a group under simulated conditions in sequential decision making.
(b) Under this, two or more trainees are assigned different roles.
(c) A specific realistic problem is given and they discuss the problem in their specific role.
(d Other trainees of the group are observers and they form their opinions

108. What is sensitivity trainng?
(a) Sensitivity training involves no role playing.
(b) It is small group of interaction under stress in an unstructured training group.
(c) It is also known as a T-group.
(d) In order to develop reasonable group activity trainees are encouraged to become sensitive to one other's feelings.

109. Which training method is effective in OD?
(a) Laboratory trainng programmes are the latest and modern.
(b) Conventional training methods are excellent for providing knowledge about behaviour.
(c) Methods like discussions, coaching, lectures, conferences and case studies are being used in organisations with successful results.
(d) All the above.

110. What are the advantages of organisational development?
(a) It deals with organisational change.
(b) It brings overall improvement in the organisation.
(c) It aims at improving the positive factors of development and always reduces negative ones.
(d) All the above.

111. What is organisational conflict?
(a) It is a clash of opposed principles between individuals and groups.
(b) According to March and Simon, conflict in the sense of a breakdown in the standard mechanisms of decision making.

(c) Before taking any step for its elimination one should consider its advantages and disadvantages.

(d) All the above.

112. Is conflict a destructive process?

(a) Conflict is generally not a destructive process, it is structural and inevitable.

(b) Conflict is a powerful process having the capability of both desirable and undesirable consequences.

(c) Before taking any step for its elimination, one should consider its desirable and undesirable consequences.

(d) All the above.

113. What are the positive aspects of conflict?

(a) It gives an individual the opportunity of introspection.

(b) It is essential for the very existence of the organisation because it leads to innovations of various aspects.

(c) Long-standing problems in the organisation continue to irritate the people, as they are seldom represented properly; ultimately they culminate into conflicts.

(d) None of the above.

114. Should conflicts be eliminated?

(a) In general, conflicts bring a dim or gloomy atmosphere in organisation.

(b) The traditionalists in management were of the view that management should enforce strictures so as to help conflicts not to surface.

(c) Neoclassicists stress that management should avoid conflict and provide job satisfaction in the organisation.

(d) Modernists are of the opinion that conflicts are inevitable to appear and management must try to educate personnel to have a better understanding in organisational work ethos rather than eliminate the conflicts as they are bound to appear in organisations.

115. Conflicts can be viewed as a dynamic process consisting of a sequence of episodes. What are they?

(a) Latent conflicts

(b) Perceived conflicts

(c) Felt conflicts

(d) Manifest conflicts

116. What is intraindividual conflict?

(a) An individual having a feeling of conflict in his mind.

(b) Conflict between an individual and/ or a group of people.

(c) An individual is having a problem in decision making, which may be related to the organisation or an individual -Vs- organisational goals.

(d) All the above.

117. What is the meaning of conflict?

(a) An individual will have a clash against opposed principles and loses decision-making capability.

(b) This happens within a person, between members of the group and between groups.

(c) Conflict can occur within organisation or outside organisation also.

(d) All the above.

118. What is interindividual conflict?

(a) When two individuals are in conflict, be the members of the same group or different ones.

(b) Conflict can be between individuals.

(c) It can be between individuals of one group and the other.

(d) All the above.

119. What are the levels of conflicts?

(a) National level

(b) State level

(c) At individual and group level

(d) At organisational level.

120. What are the causes of group level conflict?

(a) Due to disharmony among members of group.
(b) Supervisory staff and group differences.
(c) Need of joint decision making
(d) Differentiation of goals or perception or both.

121 What are the main causes of individual conflict?

(a) Mismatching of individual needs and organisational needs.
(b) Wide spread uncertainty and paucity of right alternatives.
(c) Disparity of aspiration and achievement.
(d) All the above.

122 How does differentiation occur between goal and perception or both?

(a) There are limited resources to be shared.
(b) To determine appropriate area of decision making.
(c) Limitation of authority and functions.
(d) None of the above.

123. What are the causes of conflict at organisational level?

(a) Intra-organisational
(b) inter-organisational
(c) Organisational inefficiency
(d) All the above.

124. What is intra-organisational conflict?

(a) All inter- and intra-individual conflicts.
(b) All inter- and intra-group conflicts.
(c) Conflicts between various groups at various levels of the organisation.
(d) None of the above.

125. What is inter-organisational conflict?

(a) Between an organisation and the government.
(b) Between two organisations.
(c) Conflicts between organisations at State and National levels.
(d) All the above.

126. How can the conflict be resolved?

(a) Making a solution for peaceful co-existence.
(b) Arriving at a compromise.
(c) Solving all existing problems.
(d) Good industrial relations.

127. What are the useful steps taken to resolve the conflict?

(a) Understanding fully various aspects of the conflict.
(b) Proper diagnosis of the present issues.
(c) Use of correct conflict handling method.
(d) All the above.

128. What are the important methods of conflict handling?

(a) Try to avoid eruption of conflict.
(b) Take adequate care not to allow the conflict to surface.
(c) Use tactful 'mediation' method.
(d) Allow the parties to settle their differences through mutual problem solving.

129. How is the conflict diagnosed?

(a) Conflict may arise due to facts, goals, methods and values.
(b) Facts at the disposal of two parties may differ in their goals or methods of performing a particular task. Also, the views about what is right or wrong may differ, but the person who handles the conflict must find out what the conflict is all about.
(c) The correct identification of the problem, as to what caused differences amongst the parties need to be understood by arriving at a right conclusion.
(d) All the above.

130. What is organisational change?

(a) Change is the necessary way of life in most of the organisations.

(b) Change is a part of life but is not always welcome, since it has to be managed. Resistance to change is natural, managing change is to overcome the resistance.

(c) Management must consider the human aspect of change before initiating any action.

(d) All the above.

131. What is the nature of change?

(a) Change creates disequilibrium in the environment of an organisation.

(b) It is the duty of management to introduce adjustments, prior to any major changes.

(c) Resistance to change is psychological factor.

(d) Management must take adequate care not to ignore the fundamental fact of human behaviour.

132. What is known as Hawthrone effect?

(a) Informal groups determine the performance and attitude of workers.

(b) Individual roles and norms differ from those of the formal organisations.

(c) Attitude of the workers is mostly governed by the group interest.

(d) None of the above.

133. What are the reasons of organisational change?

(a) Change in technology, methods and procedures.

(b) Change in business conditions and managerial staff.

(c) Change in formal and informal organisation.

(d) All the above.

134. Why do people resist to change?

(a) Change in the existing stability of the situation.

(b) If the change is detrimental to individual's interest.

(c) Change threatens the security of job.

(d) It also affects emotion, sentiments and social relationship.

135. What are the dimensions of change?

(a) Behavioural dimensions

(b) Psychological dimensions

(c) Logical dimensions

(d) Sociological dimensions.

136. How can a change be successfully introduced?

(a) Proper consultation with employees.

(b) Effective 2-way communication in the organisaton.

(c) Advance planning and introduction of change at the appropriate time.

(d) Always take the trade unions into confidence.

137. Does resistance to change has desirable consequences?

(a) Resistance to change does not always produce undesirable results.

(b) Proposal for an inherent change is not desirable, it requires cost benefit analysis to understand its usefulness in economical aspects.

(c) Rational opposition to change is based on economical aspects; whether the change is more costly than benefits of resistance.

(d) All the above.

138. What steps are taken in the organisational change?

(a) Analysing the existing organisation and initiate clear objectives.

(b) Preparation of a proper plan and experiment it for its usefulness.

(c) Preparation of a phased plan.

(d) Establishment of uniform nomenclature and overcoming the resistance to change.

139. What is meant by group level change?

(a) Group influenced the norms of the individual in change.

(b) Group as a member of change
(c) Group as a target of change
(d) Group as an agent of change.

140. What is the role of a group as the member of change?
(a) Efforts to change individual or subparts of a group, which if successful would have the result of deviation from the norms of the group that will face strong resistance.
(b) Group can attempt to change attitudes, values and behaviour, the more relevant they are to the basis of attraction to the group, the greater will be the influence on members.
(c) The more attractive the group is to its members the greater is the influence that the group can exert on its members.
(d) All the above.

141. What procedure is followed, when a major change is to be effected in the orgnisation?
(a) Analysis of the existing organisation and development of clear objectives.
(b) Preparation of an ideal plan and proper handling of resistance to change.
(c) When an individual accepts the change, he abandons his old learnings.
(d) Change in organisation affects the people in terms of skills, status and social relationship.

142. What are the types of change?
(a) Evolutionary change.
(b) Normal change
(c) Revolutionary change
(d) Extraordinary change.

143. Who developed the technique of total quality management?
(a) Samuel C. Certo and J. Paul Peter
(b) Edward Demming
(c) Gray and Starke
(d) Ewing David, V.

144. What is evolutionary change?
(a) It is gradual, incremental and specially forced on strategy and structure of the organisation.
(b) Slow and systematic change.
(c) A change, which is normal.
(d) Not being resisted by the people.

145. What is revolutionary change?
(a) A change, which is sudden and drastic.
(b) An unexpected change
(c) it is resisted by the people
(d) Change of revolutionary value.

146. How is the TQM change introduced in an organisation?
(a) Through system
(b) Through process
(c) Through management
(d) Through people.

147. What is the significant aspect of change?
(a) Change is inevitable
(b) Change occurs as per the demand of environment and the process of growth
(c) It is pervasive in nature
(d) All the above.

148. What is re-engineering?
(a) Process by which rethinking and redesigning of business process takes place to increase organisational efficiency.
(b) It creates task, role and work to achieve the target.
(c) When failure is faced in business, re-engineering is the best option.
(d) All the above.

149. What are the ingredients of re-engineering?
(a) Business activities and management effectiveness.

(b) Job structure of the organisation, values and beliefs.
(c) Goal orientation
(d) None of the above.

150. What are the external causes of change?
(a) External environmental factors
(b) Globalisation, diversity in employees' culture
(c) Technological change, attitude of the management.
(d) Scarcity of resources, market competition, Government involvement and its policies.

151. What are the internal causes of change?
(a) Indifference in organisational management, lack of efficiency, changing aspiration of employees.
(b) Change in work environment.
(c) Non-cooperation amongst groups.
(d) Unhealthy competitions.

152. What is Lewin's model of change?
(a) Unfreezing (b) Moving
(c) Refreezing (d) All the above.

INTROSPECTION

"Self-actualisation is the transformation of one's own perception into reality."

ANSWERS

1 (a) Deciding the number and type of people required for each job.

2 (d) Work force forecast, man-power assessment and staffing programme.

3 (a), (b) and (c)

(a) Expansion and diversification

(b) Acquisition and merger

(c) Retrenchment

4 (a), (b), (c) and (d)

(a) Ensure optimum utilisation of working personnel.

(b) Assess the requirement of future skills.

(c) Improve the standard of skill, knowledge and ability.

(d) Minimising turn over and filling up turn over vacancies.

5 (d) Leon C. Megginson

6 (d) Mainly line managers furnish the required information on the basis of estimates of operating levels, the staff furnish supplementary data like turn over rates and then final estimates are made.

7 (a), (b) and (c)

(a) Managerial judgement

(b) Ratio trend analysis and work study techniques.

(c) Delfi techniques and others

8 (a), (b) and (c)

(a) Company strategies, human resource planning and formal and informal groups

(b) Job analysis, time horizons and type of information.

(c) Company's production policies and trade unions.

9 (d) (a) Economic forecast

(b) Sales forecast

(c) Expansion programme and employee market forecast.

10 (a), (b), (c) and (d)

(a) Forecasting future needs

(b) Projecting Human Resource supply

(c) Comparison of forecast needs and projection supply

(d) Planning policies and progarammes.

11 (d) Through a scientific selection process.

12 (a) and (b)

(a) Judgement and experience; budgetary planning

(b) Data of work standards and key procedure factors

13 (a) and (b)

(a) Macro level (National)

(b) Micro level (Industry)

14 (a), (b) and (c)

(a) Short period (one year)

(b) Medium period (five years)

(c) Long period (ten-fifteen years)

15 (a) E.B. Geisler

16 (a), (b) and (c)

(a) Forecasting and man-power inventory.

(b) Anticipating man-power problem.

(c) Planning

17 (d) (a) Own competitive position, market opportunities and Government policies.

(b) Import/Export policies/opportunities

(c) Technological change, labour market and audit of existing man-power.

18 (a) Total number of various types of skilled personnel on the strength of the organisation.

19 (c) A prediction of future demands of employees of an organisation.

20 (c) In a labour market, supplies of a particular type of labour and demands for that type of labour seek to obtain a balance.

21 (a) and (c)

(a) The relationship between the buyer and a seller in labour market (except casual labour) is not a temporary one and it lasts for a longer period.

(c) The utilisation of labour markets is for the buyers and sellers, who are in contact with each other for the purchase and sale of workers' services.

22 (c) There is acute shortage of skilled workers for many jobs, such imbalance usually cause hindrance to the development of economy.

23 (b) Unemployment can prevail with unfilled vacancies and rising wages for those who are already working.

24 (d) It is seen that wages do not move flexibly in response to demand and supply of labour.

25 (a), (b) (c) and (d)

(a) Relationship between the employer and employee is long-standing.

(b) Existence of unstable labour force.

(c) Indian labour market is mostly favourable to employer than employee.

(d) Labour market is imperfect therefore, workers do not get proper wages.

26 (d) (a) In the organised labour market, employment generation is the main object of the government both for private and public sectors.

(b) Creation of employment exchange has been a great help for the organised labour market in providing employment opportunities to the local people for certain type of jobs both in private and public sectors.

(c) Organised labour markets are standardised and they operate in a systematic manner.

27 (b) Those, who live below the poverty line, need money to celebrate marriages of their children, hospital expenses etc., and they take loan from their landlords or money lenders, who levy heavy interest on the loan amount. Ultimately the poor man fails to pay back the amount of loan. Such people become bonded labours to the landlords/money lenders.

28 (a) and (b)

(a) This includes small industries, cottage industries, shops and establishments, hotels, mobile business and agriculture, etc.

(b) In this labour market, there is no particular design of job and also no man power planning.

29 (a) and (b)

(a) Employees possess no bargaining power.

(b) No special place of employment.

30 (b) and (d)

(b) Motivation is a function that a manager performs in order to get his subordinates achieve the goal.

(d) Inspiring a person to perform a job by some incentive (monetary or other).

31 (b) Willingness and capacity to work.

32 (b) Peter F. Drucker

33 (d) (a) It is an unending process, by which an individual is motivated.

Explanation : When we motivate an individual, we cannot motivate him partially. Motivation is crried out as a complete process.

(b) A psychological factor; a frustrated individual cannot be motivated.

Explanation : A frustrated person does not have the state of mind to work (i.e., willingness). Therefore, he cannot be easily motivated. The cause of frustration to be understood first, then only he can be motivated to execute the work.

(c) Goals are the motivators.

34 ((d) (a) People are of selfish nature, if that is satisfied, put their best to achieve organisational goal.

(b) Attainable goals give an employee satisfaction.

(c) An executive, who has capabilities to motivate his subordinates, is a successful one.

35 (a), (b) and (c)
(a) Positive motivation
(b) Negative motivation
(c) Extrinsic and intrinsic motivation
<u>*Explanation :*</u> Extrinsic Motivators, (external rewards) which are not directly related to the performance of the job, it occurs after or away from work, such as retirement benefits, health insurance etc. Intrinsic motivators, (internal rewards) are those that occur while performing the work, therefore there is direct motivation to perform the work.

36 (b) Hierarchy of needs

37 (a) E.F.L. Brech

38 (c) It is a psychological concept.

39 (b) It is a key to management actions in its executive form.

40 (c) and (d)
(c) Financial incentives.
(d) Non-financial incentives.

41 (d) Self-actualisation is the transformation of one's perception into reality.

42 (a) Distinction between motivation and maintenance factors in work situation.

43 (c) 'X' and 'Y' theory

44 (c) Achievement oriented people have certain qualities, they prefer a moderate degree of risk, and they feel their efforts and abilities will bring the outcome.

45 (d) Expectancy theory.

46 (b) Motivation is a product of the values one seeks and one's expectation of the probability that a particular action will lead to those values.

47 (d) Skinner

48 (c) Psychological satisfaction of employees on the job largely depends upon the appreciation and recognition of their good work.

49 (a) Employee centered

50 (c) Modification occurs through positive reinforcement (motivation) and negative reinforcement (motivation).

51 (c) ERG means 'Existence', 'Relatedness' and 'Growth'. These three sets of needs are the main force of alternative theory of human needs *(Alderfer's ERG Theory).*

52 (b) and (c)
(b) Equity Theory is a process that does comparison with inequity in organisation.
(c) The main features of Equity Theory are inputs, outputs and comparison.

53 (c) and (d)
(c) Worker is an individual and he is the whole person having both his pleasures and problems.
(d) Management must understand the 'Whole person' and not the 'Part person' for work alone.

54 (a) Mental status or attitude of an individual or a group willing to cooperate.

55 (c) Yoder

56 (a) It can be estimated according to individual's attribute.

57 (a) Using questionnaire and interview technique.

58 (c) Absenteeism, indiscipline problems, employees unrest and increased grievances.

59 (c) Robert M. Guion.

60 (c) Production and productivity are directly affected by high morale.

61 (a) and (b)
(a) Morale refers to total satisfaction of a person from his job, work group and superiors.
(b) Where the morale is high, its output is also high.

62 (a) and (b)
(a) Confidence of an individual member in achievement of the goal of a group.
(b) Confidence of the members in their leader.

63 (d) (a) Proper wage structure based on efficiency.
(b) Security of job and recognition of efforts of people.
(c) Delegation of authority and foolproof grievance system.

64 (d)
(a) Private, profit making organisations.
(b) Public service organisations.
(c) Organisations that are neither private nor public, but they do provide services which are not provided by the business or government.

65 (d)
(a) It is the rational coordination of the activities of a certain number of people.
(b) Its activities are governed by a structure.
(c) In an organisation people involve in interaction and the participants in organisation fulfil the individual objectives along with organisational ones.

66 (a) and (b)
(a) Organisation has a definite goal to achieve.
(b) The goals or objectives, which are service, personal, social and commodity related.

67 (c) Peter Drucker

68 (a) and (b)
(a) Direct human efforts in a specific direction.
(b) It helps as a basis for development of organisational objectives.

69 (a) and (b)
(a) Max Webber's bureaucratic approach and Taylor's scientific management approach.
(b) Mayo's human relation approach and Katz and Khan's open system theory approach.

70 (a) and (b)
(a) This approach is known as Webber's machinistic approach that equates the organisational functioning to a machine type process.
(b) In this, every part of the machine play its own role to perform its expected function. It also stresses on impersonal rationality and a defined procedure, which take care of the members and also proper functioning of the organisation.

71 (c) In machine like approach, it was noticed that it ignored the human element in organisation.

72 (b) The study of Hawthrone shifted the attention of the researchers from the improvement of physical condition of work for increasing production to human relation in the organisation.

73 (a), (b) and (c)
(a) Organisation is a cooperative activity of two or more persons with a purpose of common goal.
(b) Proper communication with each other.
(c) Willing to act for a common goal.

74 (b), (c) and (d)
(b) It is of voluntary nature.
(c) The purpose is to fulfil the needs of individuals.
(d) It always has the bearing over the formal organisation.

75 (d) (a) Job specialisation and departmentation.
(b) Chain of command and span of control.
(c) Formalisation, line and staff and complexity.

76 (c) and (d)
(c) Organisations are static as well as dynamic.
(d) They have to adjust constantly with external environment and such adjustments result in change of their structure.

77 (a) Denison

78 (b), (c) and (d)
(b) Values

(c) Climate
(d) Management style.

79 (a) The purpose to which the organisation exists.

80 (d) This principle clearly states that a subordinate has to comply the orders of one boss at a time.

81 (c) If each unit has a single or homogeneous activity/activities, it can bring organisation efficiency.

82 (a) It is something that an organisation seeks and towards which its all resources and efforts are directed.

83 (b) Combination of objectives, purposes, missions, standards and targets.

84 (a) The goals of an organisation provide legitimacy to its existence.

85 (b) Tangible and intangible goals.

86 (c) Goals are those for which all organisational resources are spent to reach them.

87 (c) When interaction takes place between individuals or groups together with organisational norms and values, the atmosphere of mutual trust and adjustment takes place.

88 (a) Peter Drucker

89 (a) and (c)
(a) It implies certain generalisations, which have universal applicability.
(c) An exposition of the principles on which a subject is based.

90 (a), (b), (c) and (d)
(a) Classical approach
(b) Neoclassical approach
(c) Modern organisational theory.
(d) Contingency approach.

91 (b) Modern organisation theory derived from general systems theory and has an empirical and analytical base, it views the organisation in a system perspective.

92 (a) They carry out an exchange relation with environment and are influenced by it.

93 (c) Organisational development provides a planned and systematic change in organisation.

94 (b) Bennis

95 (c) The process of implementation, evaluation and adjustment and maintenance of system.

96 (a), (b), (c) and (d)
(a) Coordination and integration
(b) Managing change and conflict
(c) Team work
(d) Commitment of employees to the work.

97 (c) It is integrated development process of people, structure, technology and social system.

98 (d) (a) Determination of the type of OD programme.
(b) Collection of data, reviews and feedback.
(c) Action planning and problem solving, intergroup development and appraisal and follow-up.

99 (b), (c) and (d)
(b) Reward structure on the job.
(c) Urge for experimental learning process.
(d) Fast and speedy technological and social changes.

100 (b) Baron

101 (c) and (d)
(c) Conventional training methods.
(d) Laboratory training methods.

102 (b) Classroom discussions, presentations, etc.

103 (a) and (b)
(a) Methods of learning through experience on the job.
(b) Situations in which trainees experience themselves through their interaction.

104 (b), (c) and (d)
(b) Role playing
(c) Gaming knowledge
(d) Sensitivity training.

105 (d) Trainees are given specific problems

and they discuss it in their particular roles as per the guidance given to them.

106 (a) and (c)

(a) In this, people develop creative ability by observing the roles.

(c) One can understand different approaches to a problem in a short time.

107 (a) It is an exercise conducted by a group under simulated conditions in sequential decision making.

108 (b) and (d)

(b) It is small group of interaction under stress in an unstructured training group.

(d) In order to develop reasonable group activity trainees are encouraged to become sensitive to one other's feelings.

109 (a) and (b)

(a) Laboratory trainng programmes are the latest and modern.

(b) Conventional training methods are excellent for providing knowledge about behaviour.

110 (c) It aims at improving the positive factors of development and always reduces negative ones.

111 (b) According to March and Simon, conflict in the sense of a breakdown in the standard mechanisms of decision making.

112 (b) Conflict is a powerful process having the capability of both desirable and undesirable consequences.

113 (b) It is essential for the very existence of the organisation because it leads to innovations of various aspects.

114 (d) Modernists are of the opinion that conflicts are inevitable to appear and management must try to educate personnel to have a better understanding in organisational work ethos rather than eliminate the conflicts as they are bound to appear in organisations

115 (a), (b), (c) and (d)

(a) Latent conflicts

(b) Perceived conflicts

(c) Felt conflicts

(d) Manifest conflicts.

116 (c) An individual is having a problem in decision making, which may be related to the organisation or an individual -Vs- organisational goals.

117 (a) and (b)

(a) An individual will have a clash against opposed principles and loses decision making capability.

(b) This happens within a person, between members of the group and between groups.

118 (a) When two individuals are in conflict, be the members of the same group or different ones.

119 (c) and (d)

(c) At individual and group level

(d) At organisational level.

120 (c) and (d)

(c) Need of joint decision making

(d) Differentiation of goals or perception or both.

121 (d) (a) Mismatching of individual needs and organisational needs.

(b) Wide spread uncertainty and paucity of right alternatives.

(c) Disparity of aspiration and achievement.

122 (a) and (b)

(a) There are limited resources to be shared.

(b) To determine appropriate area of decision making.

123 (a) and (b)

(a) Intra-organisational

(b) inter-organisational.

124 (a) and (b)

(a) All inter- and intra-individual conflicts.

(b) All inter- and intra-group conflicts.

125 (a) and (b)

(a) Between an organisation and the government.

(b) Between two organisations.

126 (a), (b) and (c)

(a) Making a solution for peaceful co-existence.

(b) Arriving at a compromise.

(c) Solving all existing problems.

127 (d) (a) Understanding fully various aspects of the conflict.

(b) Proper diagnosis of the present issues.

(c) Use of correct conflict handling method.

128 (a), (b), (c) and (d)

(a) Try to avoid eruption of conflict.

(b) Take adequate care not to allow the conflict to surface.

(c) Use tactful 'mediation' method.

(d) Allow the parties to settle their differences through mutual problem solving.

129 (c) The correct identification of the problem, as to what caused differences amongst the parties need to be understood by arriving at a right conclusion.

130 (b) Change is a part of life but is not always welcome, since it has to be managed. Resistance to change is natural, managing change is to overcome the resistance.

131 (a) Change creates disequilibrium in the environment of an organisation.

132 (c) Attitude of the workers is mostly governed by the group interest.

133 (d) (a) Change in technology, methods and procedures.

(b) Change in business conditions and managerial staff.

(c) Change in formal and informal organisation.

134 (a), (b), (c) and (d)

(a) Change in the existing stability of the situation.

(b) If the change is detrimental to individual's interest.

(c) Change threatens the security of job.

(d) It also affects emotion, sentiments and social relationship.

135 (b), (c) and (d)

(b) Psychological dimensions

(c) Logical dimensions

(d) Sociological dimensions.

136 (a), (b), (c) and (d)

(a) Proper consultation with employees.

(b) Effective 2-way communication in the organisaton.

(c) Advance planning and introduction of change at the appropriate time.

(d) Always take the trade unions into confidence.

137 (b) and (c)

(b) Proposal for an inherent change is not desirable, it requires cost benefit analysis to understand its usefulness in economical aspects.

(c) Rational opposition to change is based on economical aspects; whether the change is more costly than benefits of resistance.

138 (a), (b), (c) and (d)

(a) Analysing the existing organisation and initiate clear objectives.

(b) Preparation of a proper plan and experiment it for its usefulness.

(c) Preparation of a phased plan.
(d) Establishment of uniform nomenclature and overcoming the resistance to change.

139 (b), (c) and (d)

(b) Group as a member of change.
(c) Group as a target of change.
(d) Group as an agent of change.

140 (b) and ((c)

(b) Group can attempt to change attitudes, values and behaviour, the more relevant they are to the basis of attraction to the group, the greater will be the influence on members.
(c) The more attractive the group is to its members the greater is the influence that the group can exert on its members.

141 (a) and (b)

(a) Analysis of the existing organisation and development of clear objectives.
(b) Preparation of an ideal plan and proper handling of resistance to change.

142 (a) and (c)

(a) Evolutionary change.
(c) Revolutionary change.

143 (b) Edward Demming.

144 (a) It is gradual, incremental and specially forced on strategy and structure of the organisation.

145 (a) A change, which is sudden and drastic.

146 (a), (b), (c) and (d)

(a) Through system
(b) Through process
(c) Through management
(d) through people.

147 (a) Change is inevitable.

148 (a) Process by which rethinking and redesigning of business process takes place to increase organisational efficiency.

149 ((a) Business activities and management effectiveness.

150 (b), (c) and (d)

(b) Globalisation, diversity in employees' culture
(c) Technological change, attitude of the management.
(d) Scarcity of resources, market competition, Government involvement and its policies.

151 (a) and (b)

(a) Indifference in organisational management, lack of efficiency, changing aspiration of employees.
(b) Change in work environment.

152 (a), (b) and (c)

(a) Unfreezing
(b) Moving
(c) Refreezing

Explanation : Unfreezing means making the individual to discard old behaviour. Moving indicates altering the behaviour of an individual and creating new attitudes, values and behaviour. Refreezing denotes reformating new values and behaviour.

◆◆◆◆◆

CHAPTER - 5

- CONCEPT OF LEADERSHIP
- DEVELOPING CREATIVITY
- MANAGERIAL SKILLS
- FUNDAMENTALS OF DECISION MAKING

FEATURES :

- Concept of leadership
- What is leadership?
- Distinction of leader from Boss
- Characteristics
- Effective leader
- Traits (qualities)
- What is empathy
- Leadership style
- Approaches of leadership
- Leadership and motivation
- Management grid
- Leadership theories of Tanneubaum
- What is supervision
- Developing creativity
- Concept
- Nature
- Process of creative abilities
- Creativity techniques
- Brain storming
- Conducting brain storming session
- Creative person
- Proactive organisation
- Role of creativity in managing change
- Management skills
- Concept
- Types of skill
- Development of skills
- Fundamentals of decision making
- Concept
- Process
- Defining problem
- Bounded rationality
- Steps in decision making
- Psychological factors in decision
- Commitment concept
- Quantitative technique
- Quantitative approach
- Prediction of pay off
- Execution and control
- Operation Research (OR)
- PERT
- Decision tree
- Probability theory
- Linear programming
- Managerial statistics in decision making
- Analytical approach to decision making.

KEY NOTE

Concept of leadership

Leadership has been defined differently by different authors. According to Cowley "Leader is one who succeeds in getting others to follow him." It is a complex phenomenon and forms a very important feature of all spheres of human activity. It is seen at work in Industry, administration, sports, politics and on the battlefield. Leadership skill becomes a part of manager's personality. It is not learnt by any training but it is gained by dealing with people under different situations. Leadership is a dynamic man to man relationship between the leader and his subordinates. A leader directly and personally influences the behaviour of those working with him.

Developing creativity

Creativity means the creation of a new thing or an idea. The creative person is one who finds out new spheres and make new observations and novel ideas. Creativity is possessed by every one to some extent. Some may develop it and in others it may be dormant and unnoticed. Creativity in an individual is a natural endowment. It needs encouragement to develop. In organisations where creative talents are not given opportunities for creative expression, they go waste. This quality is very essential for problem solving in critical situations. It is an essential quality for a good leader.

Managerial skills

The job of a manager requires continuous development of skills. A manager can be assessed as a successful one, when he is able to create a team of employees to carry out efficiently the job allotted to such a team under him. This can be possible only if the workers have requisite skills to perform the allotted job. Therefore, a manager need to possess the required professional and supervisory skills and also able to train the staff under him. Broadly speaking a manager must have the ability to transfer experience and knowledge into action. Development of employees' skills is quite vital for the progress of an organisation.

Fundamentals of decision making

Making decision is an integral and continuous process of management. Management is always a decision making process. The decisions may be arrived at after a systematic and detailed analysis. Today any organisational activity for an effective management has to play a vital role in proper decision making. Since the turn of the century old technology is going at a tremendous pace with the rate of growth continuing, a new problem, new variables and also uncertainties that need to be tackled by management. Decision making also has become a complex-phenomenon. Basically, the decision maker faces three major problems, viz., (i) Multiplicity of factors have as bearing upon the decision, (ii) Complexity of relationship existing between these factors, and (iii) The likelihood of the situation being affected more by uncertainties than probabilities.

QUESTIONS

CONCEPTS OF LEADERSHIP

1. **What is leadership?**
   (a) Guiding by persuasion.
   (b) An abstract quality in a human being to induce his followers.
   (c) It helps the entire group to give its maximum for achievement of the goal.
   (d) All the above.

2. **"Subordinates want to be led, and led effectively. They will work just hard enough to get by, if there is a little or no leadership; with effective leadership, they will work with zeal and confidence towards the peak of their capabilities." Who said this?**
   (a) Tosi, H.I., Rizzo, J.R. and Carroll, S.J.
   (b) Pigors and Myers
   (c) Singh, P. and Warrier
   (d) Koontz and O'Donnell.

3. **How will you distinguish a leader from a 'Boss'?**
   (a) He gives orders and instructions to get the job done.
   (b) He knows all the problems thoroughly.
   (c) He inspires enthusiasm into his subordinates for doing better work.
   (d) He will have the answers to solve all problems.

4. **Is leadership quality a born one or acquired by an individual?**
   (a) It is a born quality.
   (b) A quality acquired by an individual.
   (c) It is a quality in-born and acquired too.
   (d) None of the above.

5. **"Leadership is the lifting of man's vision to higher sights, the raising of man's performance to higher standard, the building of man's personality beyond its normal limitations." Whose definition is this?**
   (a) Alfred and Beatty
   (b) Chester I. Barnard
   (c) Peter Drucker
   (d) Koontz and O'Donnell.

6. **What is the main characteristic of leadership?**
   (a) A leader may have many followers.
   (b) The leader coordinates his group and motivates it to work for achieving the goal.
   (c) It is a personal quality of an individual to influence others.
   (d) All the above.

7. **Who can be called as an effective leader?**
   (a) Integration of efforts of his men working under him.
   (b) Authority over subordinates
   (c) Individual, who tackles critical situations effectively.
   (d) The individual, who directs his men effectively to achieve the goal.

8. **Leadership traits (qualities) have been propounded by various thinkers. What are they?**
   (a) Physical and psychological
   (b) Intellectual
   (c) Qualities of character
   (d) All the above.

9. **Who are the famous thinkers of leadership qualities?**
   (a) Viscount Shim
   (b) Ordway Tead

(c) Henry Fayol
(d) Bernard.

10. Are traits common to all leaders?
(a) Certain traits exist in leaders.
(b) All traits are not seen in a particular leader.
(c) Traits can be measured.
(d) None of the above.

11. What is the importance of leadership?
(a) Directing activities of individual and group.
(b) Optimum use of man-power for achievement of goal.
(c) Motivation and human relations.
(d) All the above.

12. What are the attitudes critical to leadership?
(a) Empathy
(b) Self-awareness
(c) Objectivity
(d) Courage

13. What is empathy?
(a) Empathy fosters sympathy.
(b) It is an ability to look at another person's point of view.
(c) A leader should have capacity to identify himself mentally with other person.
(d) This leads to personal identification with other people.

14. What is self-awareness of a leader?
(a) He should understand his role in a leadership situation.
(b) Leader should be aware of his impact on others.
(c) He will understand better, if he knows how he appears to others.
(d) All the above.

15. How objectivity is important to a leader?
(a) Emotional involvement of a leader with subordinates is likely to affect a fair and just appraisal of their performance.
(b) Understanding feelings and problems of subordinates should have an attitude of objectivity to human relations.
(c) Certain psychological distance from the subordinates definitely makes leadership behaviour more objective in nature.
(d) All the above.

16. What is known as environmental structure of leadership?
(a) The factors that influence the leadership.
(b) The organisational hierarchy.
(c) Organisation, job and career.
(d) Supervisors, subordinates and colleagues.

17. What are the attributable factors for the success of a leader?
(a) His success depends upon his relationship with his subordinates.
(b) He should understand the behaviour of his subordinates and also be able to motivate them to achieve the goal.
(c) Mc Gregor's 'X' and 'Y' theory.
(d) Try to reach the organisational performance at its peak.

18. What do you mean by 'goals' in leadership?
(a) Concern for self
(b) Concern for people
(c) Concern for the job
(d) Concern for the organisation.

19. What is leadership style?
(a) Distinctive behaviour of a leader.
(b) Tannebaum and Schimedt depicted various types of leadership style.
(c) Total system of variables like leader, environment, goals and subordinates, that decide the behaviour of the leader and that of his men.
(d) None of the above.

20. Leadership is 'The ability to influence a group towards achievement of goals.' Who said this?

(a) Tannebaum, Weschler, Massarik
(b) Robins
(c) Allen Louis
(d) Koontz and O'Donnel.

21. What does determine the effectiveness of leadership?

(a) Capability of the leader to tackle critical situations.
(b) Personal character of the leader.
(c) Behaviour in the leadership role.
(d) The group of followers and the situation.

22. What are the approaches to leadership study?

(a) Personality approach.
(b) Trait approach
(c) Behavioural approach.
(d) Situational approach.

23. What is meant by leadership phenomenon?

(a) Leader and psychological attriubutes.
(b) The follower with his problems and needs.
(c) Group situation in which the followers and leader interact with one another.
(d) All the above.

24. What is trait approach?

(a) It means distinguishing feature in a character or portrayal of a person.
(b) This approach stresses the in-born qualities or characteristics of an individual.
(c) A leader must have distinguishing character than the followers.
(d) All the above.

25. What are the important characteristics that distinguish a leader?

(a) Physical characters, social background.
(b) Intelligence and personality.
(c) Task related characteristics and socialistic attributes.
(d) Some traits are common to all.

26. What is behavioural approach?

(a) This approach came into being during 1950's and 1960's.
(b) The roots of the approach are how the management viewed workers.
(c) Informal groups and informal leaders laid stress on interpersonal relationship.
(d) The human relation movement in management showed an overriding concern for people.

27. What is a situational approach?

(a) The leader should be able to recognise need of the situation and aspirations of his men.
(b) A good decision taken by a leader always reflects on his intellectual capabilities.
(c) A right decision is always required to tackle a specific situation and is always upheld.
(d) All the above.

28. Are trait and behavioural approach responsible for the leadership style?

(a) The approach of trait is responsible for the adoption of leadership style.
(b) Behavioural pattern of the leader is responsible for leadership style.
(c) Trait and behavioural approach movements give birth to leadership style.
(d) None of the above.

29. What are the leadership styles?

(a) Executive style
(b) Management style
(c) Autocratic style, Free-rein style
(d) Participative or democratic style.

30. What is autocratic style?

(a) In this the leader becomes more powerful as an autocrat .

(b) Subordinates have no power in decision making.

(c) He is not bothered about the feeling of others or subordinates.

(d) This affects the morale and efficiency of the organisation.

31. What is free-rein style?

(a) This is similar to Laissez's fair policy (a policy of non-interference).

(b) Leadership allows the delegation of complete authority of the leader to subordinates.

(c) This type is only possible, where subordinates are highly professional and efficient.

(d) None of the above.

32. What does participative style refer to?

(a) It is democratic or consultative style of leadership.

(b) In this, active participation of subordinates is provided in the process of decision making.

(c) The leader following this style, does not renounce his authority.

(d) This type of leadership is subordinate oriented.

33. What is the main principle behind Douglas McGregor's 'X' and 'Y' theory?

(a) Theory 'X' assumes human being inherently dislikes work; then 'Y' assumes that for human being work is as natural as a game or a play.

(b) Theory 'X' shows that people do not have ambition and dislike responsibility, whereas theory 'Y' assumes that human being has ambition and he willfully shoulders responsibility.

(c) According to McGregor theory 'X' and 'Y' differ in their assumptions.

(d) Under normal circumstances, people like to work and they do not shrink responsibilities.

34 "In the mid 20th century, Ohio University conducted studies on factors of leadership." What is the outcome of categorising the leaders?

(a) People of task accomplishment are 'Task masters.'

(b) People of welfare nature are 'Relation oriented.'

(c) People who understand the 'Human factor' at work.

(d) People follow the middle path, and they balance between task and relation orientation.

35. Who evolved the organisational behaviour modification?

(a) B.F. Skinner

(b) Fred Luthans

(c) Allen Louis

(d) Newsman and Summer

36. What is the relationship between leadership and motivation?

(a) The main object of leadership is to gain faith of the people.

(b) Leadership along with dynamic techniques makes the people faithful and motivate to achieve the goal.

(c) Management is the art of making persons to perform and development of this art depends on the leader.

(d) All the above.

37. What is the contingency theory of leadership?

(a) Human relation approach is towards achieving good impersonal relations and achieving a position of prominence.

(b) Effectiveness of the leadership depends on the ability of the leader to act in terms of situational requirements.

(c) The theory was developed by Fiedler.

(d) Any group performance will be contingent upon the proper matching of leadership and the appropriate group behaviour or leader can elicit in a situation.

38. What is the nature of leadership style?

(a) Positive nature

(b) Negative nature

(c) Positive or negative in nature.

(d) None of the above.

39. What is positive power of the leader?

(a) Power is the ability to influence behaviour of others or impose one's will on others.

(b) A leader may exercise power on his subordinates by virtue of his official position (positive power).

(c) His power may also be of personal nature (personal power), which he derives from his subordinates through human relation.

(d) Use of positive power will force the behaviour of a subordinate to meet the leader's demands. But it is likely that the subordinate may switch on to his old behaviour, when the leader is not present. Effective leadership, to a large extent, depends upon the personal power.

40. What is the negative style of the leader?

(a) Positive style uses assured motivation.

(b) Emphasis is on satisfaction of needs and rewards, etc.

(c) Punishment or creating fear.

(d) A competent leader has to use both positive and negative styles, depending on the environment in which he functions.

41. What should be the guideline for an executive to use his power?

(a) Power to be used to inculcate obedience in subordinates.

(b) Power to be used in extreme conditions to change the behavioural pattern.

(c) Power has its principal effect in its potential use than its actual use.

(d) Fearful anticipation of a punishment is more forceful and deterrent than the actual punishment.

42. What is managerial grid?

(a) This was developed by Robert Blake and James Mouton.

(b) Research studies were conducted for this at Michigan and Ohio universities.

(c) Leadership has task and relation centered behavioural pattern.

(d) None of the above.

43. What are the categories of task/ relation oriented behaviour of leaders?

(a) Impoverished and country club style.

(b) Middle of the road and efficiency

(c) Common stage.

(d) Concern for employees and production.

44. What is impoverished style?

(a) This is a typical irresponsible management developed by certain managers.

(b) It is a poor management that shows a little concern for employees and production.

(c) Employees welfare and development are no concern to the management.

(d) It is only with a principle that the work must carry on somehow.

45. What does country club style refer to?

(a) Country club style means the club is not much serious about its functioning.

(b) It does not follow any principle, since its management is compared to a country club.

(c) Leader exercises extra effors to the welfare of the employees thinking that they will look after the interests of the management.

(d) Leadership ignores the responsibility of target production.

46. What is meant by Middle of the road style?

(a) This kind of leadership is called the balanced leadership style.

(b) Here, the employees are adequately looked after and the leader fixes the target to be achieved.

(c) The leader is equally concerned about the welfare of the employees, as well as the target production.

(d) All the above.

47. What is efficiency style?

(a) In this the leader is only interest about the production, in other words, the task.

(b) He is least bothered about the welfare of the employees.

(c) This style is suited to operation war front and that too for a short period.

(d) In this, production is given top priority leaving aside the welfare of employees.

48. What is common stage or team based style?

(a) In this equal importance is given to the task and welfare.

(b) Maximum care and amiable relations are the watch word of this style. Care is given to the task and the welfare as well.

(c) Importance of assigned task is never lost sight of.

(d) This is the best possible integration style, where task and relation go hand in hand.

49. What is Renis Likert's 4-system leadership?

(a) At Michigan Institute of Social Research, Renis Likert and his associates developed an important concept.

(b) The concept of Likert and his associates is for understanding the leadership behaviour in a continuous structure of 4-system of management.

(c) In this system, Likert has given importance to eight variables.

(d) Exploitative autocrat, benevolent autocrat, participative and democratic leadership.

50. What is the broad spectrum of leadership theories of Tanneubaum and Schmidt?

(a) To enable the managers to choose a particular pattern of leadership behaviour in relation to their subordinates.

(b) Leadership structure (continuum) of manager-non-manager behaviour.

(c) What factors should be considered, while dealing with leadership pattern.

(d) None of the above.

51. What is supervision?

(a) Overseeing the activities of others.

(b) Guiding and controlling the activities of the subordinate staff by a manager.

(c) Ensure the subordinates are working, guide them, and give directions as and when required.

(d) All the above.

52. What are the qualities required for a supervisor?

(a) He must be the leader of his work force, and need to direct and control the activities. He should be impartial and fair to all.

(b) He must have the knowledge of different supervision techniques to function efficiently so as to help achieve the goal with cooperation and team spirit.

(c) He should be tactful with his subordinates.

(d) He must have the managerial skills.

53. What is the role of supervisor?

(a) Supervisor has a unique role to play in the management.

(b) His role is to manage the workers at operating level and get the work executed.

(c) He is the last link in the management group and has direct association with the employees at their work place to achieve the target of production.

(d) All the above.

54. How supervisory conditions are improved?

(a) The jobs should be specified and adequate power provided.

(b) The supervisor should have access to top management in relation to the problems faced by him in execution of jobs.

(c) Due recognisation needs to be given to supervisor along with recommendations, as to his professional status.

(d) All the above.

55. What is the pattern of effective supervision?

(a) The behavioural pattern of a supervisor in a group seeks the overall performance of the group.

(b) Close and general supervisory behaviour.

(c) Employee centered behaviour.

(d) Work centered supervisory behaviour.

56. What does general supervision indicate?

(a) The supervision happens, when supervisor deals with a large quantity of work assignments.

(b) In this, employees are given the freedom, as regards their performance and accomplishment of work.

(c) In general, supervision of employees gets more job satisfaction and they are also satisfied with the supervision and organisation too.

(d) All the above.

57. What is employee centered supervision?

(a) In this, the supervisor considers human factor at the work place.

(b) He makes the people work in a way that the employees feel, they are the part and parcel of the organisation.

(c) He applies the 'Y' theory of McGregor. Hence, they need not be supervised at all times, as they are aware of their duties and responsibilities.

(d) None of the above.

58. What is production centered supervision?

(a) In this, production is the main aspect and nothing is important to the supervisor.

(b) He acts as a task master for the employees.

(c) In this process workers are not motivated to work but are compelled to work to produce the target quantity-the motto being *'Produce or Perish.'*

(d) Such supervisors are not liked by the employees they lose their importance at the work place.

59. Which supervision is the best for an organisation? Employee centered or Production Centered?

(a) Production centered

(b) Employee centered and production centered.

(c) Employee centered

(d) None of the above.

60. What is supportive role of supervision?

(a) The role of supervisor, supporting his subordinates, is needed for effective supervision.

(b) This will usher in feeling of cooperation between the supervisor and his subordinates and also avoid psychological dissonance.

(c) Adequate job training, providing adequate authority to employees, proper scheduling materials and machinery are to be taken care of during supervision, apart from his involvement in the work process.

(d) All the above.

DEVELOPING CREATIVITY

61. What is creativity?

(a) Discovering something new

(b) Imaginative ability of a person.

(c) Capacity or ability of an individual to create something new or novel.

(d) All the above.

62. What is the nature of creativity?

(a) creativity is universal, every individual possesses creative ability to a certain extent.

(b) Creative ability can be developed by training and education.

(c) Creative thinking is a freedom for the varied responses and freedom of actiion.

(d) Highly creative persons are usually found to possess intelligence of quite a high degree; however, there is no hard and fast rule that an intelligent person to be creative.

63. What is meant by creative process?

(a) How the creativity is developed in an individual.

(b) Creative process is an innate ability of a person

(c) Preparation, incubation, inspiration or illumination, and verification process.

(d) All the above.

64. What does preparation refer to?

(a) An earnest work to understand the problem in detail.

(b) It is the initial stage, where facts and materials considered essential are collected and anaysed and then a definite plan of action is set up to start.

(c) Creativity is initiated in the preparation stage and it is then carried on further.

(d) All the above.

65. What is incubation period?

(a) A stage of thinking without any sign of activities externally.

(b) This is characterised by absence of overt activities.

(c) At this stge, one can take rest or engage in understanding other activities.

(d) In the absence of other interference, our conscious mind begins to work in the direction of solving the problem.

66. What does inspiration or illumination indicate?

(a) In this period, the thinker often experiences sudden appearance of the answer to his problem.

(b) This can happen at any time.

(c) At times, while the thinker is sleeping, in dreams.

(d) All the above.

67. What is meant by verification?

(a) During this stage, illumination or inspiration is verified or tried out.

(b) To determine, whether the answer or the solution appeared through insight is correct or not.

(c) In case, it is not found satisfactory, attempts are made afresh to seek solution to the problem

(d) At no stage, a creative thinker feels it

completely perfect. It is open to modification as and when required.

68. What do you understand by creativity abilities?

(a) Abilities to create ideas and also solving problems.

(b) Creativity consists of several distinct abilities.

(c) Certain people having an idea that creativity is a 'God given gift.'

(d) Since creativity consists of many different abilities, it can be developed through training.

69. What are various creative abilities?

(a) Fluency, flexibility and originality.

(b) Problem sensitivity, elaboration and convergent thinking ability.

(c) Principles of attention and principles of consistency.

(d) Productivity and profitability.

70. What is fluency?

(a) Ability to create ideas copiously and very useful to that set of problems, where it is unlikely that a simple proper solution exists.

(b) Fluency is not of much use to mathematical equations, which bring out a single answer.

(c) It is useful to those problems which have many answers to select.

(d) Fluencies is especially useful when resourcefullness is required.

71. What does flexibility refer to?

(a) Flexibility or the ability to shift frames of reference, choose bearing in mind multiple factors and identify various aspects of a situation in dealing with people's problems.

(b) Adaptable to circumstances or situations.

(c) Persons can be trained to have more mental flexibility.

(d) None of the above.

72. What does originality indicate?

(a) Why most people are not original in thinking, for they search for solution in conventional or usual directions.

(b) Originality is an elusive ability and very rare, even though it can be possible to raise.

(c) It is the most essential element of creativity.

(d) Originality producés usual ideas that are not only surprising and novel but also useful, relevant and appropriate.

73. What do you know by problem sensitivity?

(a) People are capable to spot problems, when certain goal is frustrated or uncomfortable symptoms appear themselves.

(b) Ability to guess consequences of situations that others are unable to do so. It requires a mind that is able to identify the crucial features of situations and the relationship.

(c) To create a useful mental model of the situation, the ability to see the situation in an abstract terms seems to be useful.

(d) All the above.

74. What is meant by elaboration?

(a) In creativity, the distance between the initial idea or stimulus and its ultimate outcome need to be considered.

(b) In a process of elaboration in which certain amount of associate thinking is considered, is likely to yield a creative outcome.

(c) In the words of Stephen Splender, 'a gem of an idea gets elaborated into a full-fledged poem' by a poet with his creative talent.

(d) All the above.

75. What is convergent thinking ability?

(a) This ability is called problem solving ability.

(b) An ability capable of making logical inferences to compare and evaluate to select the best alternative in problem solving.

(c) Convergent thinking produces conventional solutions. It is also known as the ability to promote and converge a solution

(d) Convergent abilities do help to understand a problem.

76. "Creative thinking means that the prediction or inferences for the individual are new, original, ingenious, unusual. The creative thinker is the one, who explores new areas and makes new observations, new predictions and new inferences." Who said this?

(a) Kaith Davis.

(b) Elton Mayo.

(c) Skinner.

(d) Wilson Guilford.

77. What is meant by creativity techniques?

(a) This is a technique that usually helps the person in problem solving.

(b) Lateral thinking and forced relationship are used in solving the problem.

(c) These techniques can be used, both, individually or in combination.

(d) All the above.

78. What is lateral thinking?

(a) This leads to new ideas.

(b) It describes a non-rational creative thought process, which is important in finding solutions to problems.

(c) There are two types of thinking, logical (vertical) and lateral in this approach; the logical approach (thinking) is proceeded step by step and standard ways of analysing to arrive at a conclusion.

(d) Lateral thinking creates new concepts and ways of understanding, which ultimately lead to new ideas.

79. What is forced relationship?

(a) Charles Whiking is an eminent authority on this technique.

(b) Creation of a forced relationship between two or more normally unrelated products of ideas used, as the starting point for generation of idea.

(c) The main aspect of the technique that in the process of formulating a relationship between normally incompatible concepts, one has to expand the area of one's mental functioning to think in new directions.\

(d) All the above.

80. What is brain storming?

(a) It is a specific method of generating ideas.

(b) This technique was developed by Alex T. Osborn.

(c) Creative problem solving is a well-known technique.

(d) None of the above.

81. What are the main principles of brain storming?

(a) Solving problems in groups stimulates creative abilities.

(b) If one consciously stops evaluating ideas, it helps in continuous generation of ideas.

(c) Original and creative solutions emerge, when variety of ideas are available.

(d) All the above.

82. What is meant by rule of 'suspended judgement' in brain storming?

(a) Criticism of any idea is not allowed.

(b) Words and phrases that convey negative meaning are to be avoided.

(c) Emphasis to be given on generating and accepting ideas during such a session.

(d) All the above.

83. What is meant by free-wheeling?

(a) Allow a person to think freely.

(b) Allow the mind to ponder over a range of ideas.

(c) Express all ideas, which occur to a person without any restriction.

(d) None of the above.

84. What is cross fertilisation?

(a) Brain storming does not allow criticism and rejection of ideas.

(b) It always modifies and improves upon others' ideas.

(c) Participants are encouraged to combine ideas and develop new alternatives in this process.

(d) Combination of ideas is the main aspect in cross fertilisation.

85. How a brain storming session is conducted and what are its guidelines?

(a) Ideal size of the brain storming group is 10-12 individuals.

(b) Explain the rules of brain storming to the participants.

(c) Pre-session preparations, session procedure and post-session follow up.

(d) When the number of ideas is too large, ask the participants to identify similar ideas and club them together.

86. "The impetus for creativity lies in the desire to improve, the desire to replace the present reality by a better improved one. The ability to recognise that things are wrong or that they can be improved, as the primary factor that underlying creative thinking." Who said this?

(a) Abraham Maslow (b) Guilford

(c) Peter Drucker (d) Robert Owen

87. Who is a creative person?

(a) The conventional culture of the organisation is not suitable for the creative person most of the time.

(b) He is a moderate person by temperament and behaviour, and is more likely to be a generalist rather than a specialist.

(c) He is an anomaly within the organisation, as noted by psychologist, Abraham Maslow.

(d) Creative insight emerges from the synthesis of ideas drawn from unconventional fields.

88. How creative talents are identified?

(a) People get an opportunity to reveal their potential in an organisation through well-implemented suggestion book.

(b) Suggestions of an individual introduce himself to the organisation.

(c) A well-planned suggestion, which gets the approval of the experts is creative resource of an organisation.

(d) The very attempt of making suggestion by an individual reveals the capacity to perceive problems and a desire to improve things and self-motivation to put in efforts to act upon.

89. What is meant by nurturing creative efforts by an organisation?

(a) Creative expression needs certain type of psychological support from the organisational environment.

(b) Normally, pro-creative organisations give adequate support to encourage creative talents.

(c) One of the important organisational criteria for encouraging creativity is the uninhibited flow of ideas and information.

(d) All the above.

90. What is pro-creative organisation?

(a) It is based on sharing of idea, intellectual stimulation, joint ventures, flexible and growth oriented.

(b) Autonomy and opportunity to creative and talented people, recognition and provide speical compensation.

(c) An organisation need to be consultative and participative.

(d) All the above.

91. What is meant by non-creative organisation?

(a) Organisational policies are restrictive and also survival oriented.

(b) Normally they are autocratic or bureaucratic in nature.

(c) Informal group and the relationship are based on conflict, intrigues and baseless gossips.

(d) All the above.

92. What is managing the change with a creative outlook?

(a) A new system or product replaces the old one.

(b) Most of the changes can be avoided by planning and proper vision on the part of the management.

(c) The impact of changes or the consequences cannot be eliminated completely, whereas it can be reduced by appropriate creative actions.

(d) The reason why people do not accept changes, because of its happening abruptly.

93. Who are actually capable to create a support for change?

(a) The feeling of being changed rather than changing voluntarily is another important factor, which leads to resistance.

(b) A creative person alone can put forward an ideal solution like modification, verification and trial, etc., of the change along with the participation of other persons.

(c) It is desirable that a limited interaction should be maintained between the creative persons and members of the work group during the idea generation stage.

(d) All the above.

MANAGEMENT SKILLS

94. What does skill refer to?

(a) An ability to perform something well.

(b) The ability to transfer experience and knowledge into action.

(c) It is wise to know that experience helps to avoid mistakes in the future.

(d) There are two things a manager has to perform — to decide first, what is to be done and who can do it skillfully.

95. What are the different skills required for a manager?

(a) Various skills are required to execute different types of jobs.

(b) Technical skill, human skill,

(c) Conceptual and perceptual skills

(d) General management skill.

96. What is technical skill?

(a) The need for technical skill is more required for the executives at the lower or lower middle level.

(b) Technical skill refers to an understanding and proficiency in handling methods, processing a particular kind of activity.

(c) Mostly of the vocational and on the job training programmes are most concerned with developing the specialised technical skill.

(d) Technical skill is the most popular in the modern era of specialisation.

97. What is human skill?

(a) Man management skill

(b) Human skill is concerned with managing human resource in an organisation
(c) This skill is demonstrated in the way the individual interacts with his superiors, equals and subordinates in an organisastion.
(d) All the above.

98. What is conceptual skill?

(a) The skill that provides awareness or denotes insight, sensitive understanding and provides capability to visualise future actions, etc.
(b) Success of any decision depends upon the conceptual skill of the manager.
(c) Conceptual skill will help a manager to understasnd broader aspect of a situation and how to tackle it.
(d) All the above.

99. What is perceptual skill?

(a) Perceptual skill at times becomes a part of human skill.
(b) Perceive means to be aware through the senses. Perception as a basic cognitive process with many variables affecting the behaviour.
(c) Managerial action emerges from decision making process.
(d) It leads to conception of ideas, judgement and reasoning in managerial activities.

100. How perceptual skill is developed?

(a) There was a time when people through certain qualities like intelligence, creativity, leadership, etc., tried to develop.
(b) Theories of general intelligence and the measurement through IQ tests have been recognised.
(c) Adequate training can develop the scope of intelligence in an individual so as to help improve the perceptual skills.
(d) Through training programme participants get an insight and improve upon their own perceptual skills.

FUNDAMENTALS OF DECISION MAKING

101. What is a decision?

(a) A decision is a behavioural alternative for an executive or any individual.
(b) Management is a decision making process.
(c) A decision is a solution selected after an examination of several alternatives.
(d) Whatever a manager executes, he does it after arriving at a decision.

102. What is the process of decision making?

(a) Defining the problem and analysing the relevant facts.
(b) Preparation of alternative course of action and deciding the best course of action.
(c) Implementation of decision.
(d) All the above.

103. What is meant by defining the problem?

(a) The first step of decision making is knowing the problem, it may be a simple or a complex one.
(b) This requires thorough study of various aspects of the problem so as to understand its nature.
(c) When the nature of the problem is

understood that will lead to critical cause of the problem.

(d) All the above.

104. What is the alternative course of action in decision making?

(a) When a decision is to be taken, alternatives have to be found out.

(b) It is important to find a correct solution.

(c) If alternatives are not properly analysed, there is every possibility of the decision going a wrong way.

(d) Amongst various alternatives the best to be selected.

105. What rationale is involved in decision making?

(a) Decision making is purely a psychological process.

(b) It is not possible to take into consideration all probabilities that can happen in a problem.

(c) There is need to introspect and relate complex factors and variables.

(d) Decision maker must use his experience and ability, while taking a chance in critical stages.

106. What are the principles of bounded rationality?

(a) There are limitations to rationality and some factors are beyond the control of the manager.

(b) Limitation of time does not permit the manager to consider all possible alternatives with their consequences.

(c) The outcome of many decisions is indefinable or probabilistic. The manager cannot evaluate the outcome of a decision prior to taking it.

(d) The rational managerial efforts, therefore go wrong invariably and are spoiled due to inherent confusion of managers in specific situations.

107 "Decision making is a major facilitation of managerial activities. Decision making parameters are each of the management's fundamental functions." Who said this?

(a) George R. Terry,

(b) Franklin G. Moore,

(c) D.E. McForland

(d) Koontz and O'Donnell.

108. What steps are involved in decision making?

(a) Perception, conception and investigation.

(b) Deliberation, selection and promulgation.

(c) Psychological elements of decision.

(d) Tuning of decision and communication.

109. "Whatever a manager does, he does through decision making." Who said this?

(a) John McDonald

(b) Peter F. Drucker.

(c) Koontz and O'Donnell

(d) Earl P. Strong.

110. What do you mean by soundness of a decision?

(a) Information available to the decision maker.

(b) Technique he should follow, while taking the decision.

(c) Sophistication of the decision maker.

(d) Principles of limitations of a decision.

111. What does the decision environment refer to?

(a) Organisational atmosphere, physical as well as psychological has certain effect on the nature of decision taken.

(b) Behaviour of the top management has its effects on the type of decisions and the time frame within which the decisions are taken by the managers.

(c) Decision must be taken in a conducive atmosphere to make it effective in all respects.

(d) All the above.

112. What is the importance of time factor in decision making?

(a) When a strategic decision is taken, the time factor is very important.

(b) A time decision can bring better results, while launching new product in a competitive market.

(c) Communication of the decision must be at appropriate time to achieve results.

(d) All the above.

113. What is the psychological factor in decision making?

(a) Attitudes affect the type of decision that emanates or originates.

(b) Temperament of individuals vary in their approaches.

(c) Certain people may be optimistic, others may be conservative and unwilling to take risk.

(d) Decision may be personal or organisational.

114. What is meant by extent of participation?

(a) How far participation is encouraged by the decision maker is a relevant factor.

(b) The group or the number of people is affected or likely to be affected by the decision.

(c) Some managers encourage the participation, whereas other do not.

(d) All the above.

115. Why the attitude of making decision is important?

(a) The person who possesses willingness to accept the problem in a positive way is far better than the person who wishes only to supervise it.

(b) There are some, who are known as non-decision makers, they normally avoid shouldering responsibility and appoint a committee to look into the problem.

(c) A non-decision maker uses diversionary tactics rather than help solve the problem.

(d) A manager should have the right type of attitude to understand any problem in its entirety and assist to find its solution.

116. Who originated principles of bonded rationality in decision making?

(a) Koontz and O'Donnell

(b) George Terry

(c) Herbert Simon

(d) Peter Drucker

117. What is known as commitment concept in decision?

(a) A decision to be taken with adequate care, supported by relevant facts and should be acknowledged by subsequent events.

(b) A decision taken by higher authorities need to be followed by lower levels of management.

(c) A support to the decision by those affected would increase commitments.

(d) Certain decisions have long-standing effect in administration, such decisions ought to have required degree of stability and desired rationality.

118. What is the importance of decision making?

(a) Decision making is very important for achieving various goals of an organisation.

(b) A good dècision is always selected from various alternatives.

(c) Decision making requires introspection, as it is a psychological process.

(d) Decision making is the function of managerial staff at various levels.

119. What is organisational decision?

(a) A decision taken in organisation.

(b) A manager acts formally in his expected role in an organisation.

(c) The decision taken in the best interest of the organisation.

(d) These decisions are officially taken by a manager in the organisation.

120. What does personal decision refer to?

(a) These decisions are taken by a manager in his personal capacity and not as a part of the organisation.

(b) If an individual wants to change his present job and takes up a new job.

(c) It is difficult to distinguish between personal and organisational decision.

(d) All the above.

121. What is routine or programmed decision?

(a) The decisions are of routine type, which do not require more thinking process. They are often taken by managers for routine matters.

(b) Such decisions have negligible effect on the welfare of the organisation as a whole.

(c) Modern method of dealing with programmed decision is the use of operational research technique.

(d) All the above.

122. What is a group decision?

(a) It is a form of participation by the group in arriving at a decision.

(b) This form of decision will be readily acceptable by subordinates.

(c) This is a modern technique of employees' participation in management decision making.

(d) In decision making the ultimate responsibility lies with the executive. He can collect alternatives and suggestions from the group and arrive at a right conclusion.

123. What is the importance of quantitative techniques in decision making?

(a) Quantitative disciplines include important aspects of management function, *vis-a-vis* modern decision making process.

(b) Quantitative methods are based on scientific methodology, as far as their approach to management problems is concerned.

(c) Application of scientific methods brings objectivity induced decisions.

(d) All the above.

124. What is quantitative approach?

(a) Determining the objective and identifying pertinent variables.

(b) Determination of available strategies and prediction of payoffs

(c) Making a decision and execution of its control.

(d) Quantity approach is concerned with very core of a manager's job of decision making.

125. What does determination of objective refer to?

(a) Determining the objective by a manager to formulate the impact required for a quality and quantity output.

(b) The manager must determine the requirements of resources like men, material and money for this purpose.

(c) The manager should estimate the requirements to fulfil a particular objective.

(d) All the above.

126. What is the identification of pertinent variables?

(a) Collection of related data.

(b) Model building, at this stage, is required for decision making.

(c) To arrive at hypothesis and judge the creativity of an idea for decision making.

(d) All the above.

127. What is determination of available strategies?

(a) The use of mathematics may identify the optimum strategies.

(b) Different strategies may be used according to the situation.

(c) When a number of strategies are available to take a decision, a step by step approach is to be made till the optimum strategy is identified.

(d) None of the above.

128. What is meant by prediction of payoff?

(a) A situation of arriving at a decision may have ample variations, both controllable and uncontrollable.

(b) When products are advertised to attract customers, sales management has to predict the opponents' strategy in addition to their own.

(c) Decision makers have to predict the payoffs which are their objectives under various combinations of controllable and uncontrollable variables.

(d) While predicting payoffs, mathematical and statistical models are employed.

129. How a decision is made with the help of quantitative technlque?

(a) An individual may solve a problem through intuition and common sense and also may use mathematical and operation research method.

(b) The decision maker analyses all the information obtained as result of implementing the mathematical steps and makes a rational strategy.

(c) The choice is made as per the particular criterion and will bring maximum degree of achievement.

(d) The manager will use the mathematical models and optimisation concept in making the decision.

130. What do execution and control refer to?

(a) The ultimate phase of decision making is to find the solution and transform it into proper set of operating procedure.

(b) The operating procedure is to be understood and applied by the concerned persons, who are responsible for its implementation.

(c) The control procedure need to be followed, since the model remains valid representation as along as the input values are retained.

(d) The use of quantitative technique process with proper understanding between the decision maker and the analyst leads to increased use of control method and improve decision making.

131. What is the management science that denotes mathematical technique?

(a) Quantitative or mathematical techniques have been used to solve complicated management problems.

(b) This method was adopted ever since World War II.

(c) This helps the manager to select an optimum alternative course of action in decision making.

(d) This method leads to a number of possible outcomes.

132. What is operation research (OR)?

(a) It includes all quantitative decision making techniques.

(b) It indicates the application of mathematical and optimization concept in decision making.

(c) It develops a mathematical model of a number of complex equations highly worked relationship.

(d) The problems usually having time, cost or profits are to be optimised. This leads to probability and reasonable outcome for a given decision or a number of decisions.

133. What are the different quantitative techniques?

(a) Models, stimulation, resource allocation, waiting line problem and using theory.
(b) Gaming and game theory, PERT/ CPM, decision trees and probability theory.
(c) Derivation of formulae, related formulae and details of inventory control.
(d) Analysis of industrial operations.

134. What are models?
(a) The essence of operation research approach.
(b) A model can be a substitute representation of a reality.
(c) A model of the profit and loss account of a company's operation throughout a particular year in a summary form.
(d) Mathematical conclusions have the advantage of being short and precise. Model is the basis of using OR technique.

135. What does simulation refers to?
(a) Simulation is used in many ways apart from decision making in business.
(b) The use of case study method of teaching management education is an example of simulation.
(c) The application of simulation method provides a systematic approach to solving difficult problems.
(d) All the above.

136. What is resource allocation technique?
(a) While arriving at a decision, many problems relate to optimum use of resources like men and material.
(b) In business the resources have to be used with adequate care to enable maximum profit with minimum cost.
(c) Determination of allocation of resources to be with the motive of profit
(d) Linear programming and inventory models are used for as resource allocation problems.

137. What do the gaming and game theory indicate?
(a) The theory of games and gaming provides adequate insight to trainees, when it is used as a management training method.
(b) This device has been introduced by learned scientists, mathematicians and economists to create real situation.
(c) It is used to find solutions of actual problems involving competitors.
(d) In such games, a rational opponent or opponents are involved, therefore strategic decisions have to be taken.

138. What is meant by PERT (Programme Evaluation and Review technique)?
(a) This technique was designed to shorten the time span project for the Polaris Ballistic Missile Project of the US Navy.
(b) It is a project planning and controlling technique.
(c) The basic device of this system is the network or a pictorial description of the work, activities and events comprising a particular project.
(d) All the above.

139. What is decision tree?
(a) Decision tree is a quantitative technique.
(b) Construction of decision tree is not a mathematical technique.
(c) It is a graphic method used by the decision maker to help him to see the course of action open to him and the possible outcome.
(d) None of the above.

140. What is the probability theory?
(a) In all decisions, there is some element of probability.
(b) Theory of probability provides the basis for rational calculation of obstructions and the possible outcome in complex situations.

(c) The intensity of errors of probability is expressed in mathematical terms.
(d) The outcome of probabilities is compared, distinguished and the decision is made as per the merit of expected values.

141. What does linear programming refer to?

(a) Commonly adopted technique for determining optimum combination of limited reasons to reach the desired objective, such as maximising profits or minimising cost.
(b) This type of problem can be solved by the help of algebraic equations set up to represent the problem and the solving the same mathematically gives the desired result.
(c) The objective is used in linear programming to indicate the relationship between the variables concerned is directly proportional one.
(d) All the above.

142. Why linear programming is used for solving the problem?

(a) Used to achieve objective and maximizing profits for the organisation.
(b) The variables in the problem must be interrelated, e.g., the profit margin per article' A' is Rs. 40 and that of 'B' is Rs. 20, the total profit must reflect the rates of products 'A' to 'B'.
(c) It is useful for mathematical calculations and arriving at correct conclusions.
(d) All the above.

143. What is the role of Managerial Statistics in decision making?

(a) Irrespective of the level or the nature of decision, the most vital input to effective decision making is accurate and timely information.
(b) A number of tools and techniques such as statistical methods, operation research, system analysis, and electronic data processing are helpful to cover the available data.
(c) It is accepted that information when quantified, is precise, less liable to distortion when communicated for decision making.
(d) It is, of course, impossible to quantify all information relevant to a particular decision, but a decision maker cannot afford to ignore such qnantitative information which has a bearing on decision.

144. "It is said, These tools of information processing are not of decision making. As tools of information are the best. The manager may not be able to work these tools personally. But it is essential that he understands them, knows when to call a specialist and knows what to expect of the specialist." Who said this?

(a) Koontz and O'Donnel.
(b) A.R. Palit.
(c) Richard I. Levin.
(d) Peter Drucker.

145. What is meant by decision making environment?

(a) Decision often depends upon a large number of factors which are interrelated and interdependent and the implementation of various alternatives cannot be directly perceived by human mind.
(b) It is not possible to make effective decision instinctively.
(c) Decision maker must make the environmental factors in a rational manner making full use of available information and techniques.
(d) Modern tools and techniques can be of great help for decision maker in analysing data, generating alternatives and computing his implications.

146. What are the analytical approaches to decision making?

(a) Decision under certainty

(b) Decision under risk

(c) Decision under uncertainty

(d) All the above.

147. What is the decision under certainty?

(a) The decision that can be predicted with certainty. A manager can make use of available information according to the degree of certainty or uncertainty expected at a particular time in the future.

(b) The decision maker takes it for granted that there is only one possible future in conjunction with a particular case of action and therefore the decision can be with certainty.

(c) A thorough analysis of the data backed by long experience will provide a manager with the degree of certainty to take a decision.

(d) All the above.

148. What does decision under risk refer to?

(a) While taking a decision for the future, the same can prove to be as risk factor due to two or more possibilities existing along with the main course of action.

(b) Risk means the occurrence of a different state of associated possibilities known or correctly measured to a certain extent.

(c) The probability can be based on the past experience in the outcome of certain events with regard to risk factor.

(d) All the above.

149. How does uncertainty affect the decision?

(a) A particular course of action may face difficult situation in the future, however, probability of each occurrence cannot be estimated correctly.

(b) When decision is not taken with the consideration of all 'pros' and 'cons' the decision will fall under the category of uncertainty.

(c) To avoid uncertainty in decision making, operation research (OR) and managerial statistics have been used in managerial decision process.

(d) All the above.

150. What is the speciality of Operation Research (OR)?

(a) OR is applied to identify the certainty, uncertainty and risk of every decision taken in modern time.

(b) This is to be considered as a broad survey in managerial decision making.

(c) Even though statistical theory has been considered separately, OR discipline too leans heavily on the mathematics of statistics in its application.

(d) None of the above.

INTROSPECTION

"A decision is only the termination of a process and not the result."

ANSWERS

1 (b) An abstract quality in a human being to induce his followers.

2 (d) Koontz and O'Donnell.

3 (c) and (d)

(c) He inspires enthusiasm into his subordinates for doing better work.

(d) He will have the answers to solve all problems.

4 (c) It is a quality in-born and acquired too.

5 (c) Peter Drucker

6 (b) The leader coordinates his group and motivates it to work for achieving the goal.

7 (c) Individual, who tackles critical situations effectively.

8 (d) All the above

(a) Physical and psychological

(b) Intellectual

(c) Qualities of character

9 (a), (b), (c), and (d)

(a) Viscount Shim

(b) Ordway Tead

(c) Henry Fayol

(d) Bernard.

10 (a) and (b)

(a) Certain traits exist in leaders.

(b) All traits are not seen in a particular leader.

11 (d) All the above

(a) Directing activities of individual and group.

(b) Optimum use of man-power for achievement of goal.

(c) Motivation and human relations.

12 (a), (b), (c) and (d)

(a) Empathy

(b) Self-awareness

(c) Objectivity

(d) Courage

13 (c) A leader should have capacity to identify himself mentally with other person.

14 (a) He should understand his role in a leadership situation.

15 (b) Understanding feelings and problems of subordinates should have an attitude of objectivity to human relations.

16 (c) and (d)

(c) Organisation, job and career.

(d) Supervisors, subordinates and colleagues.

17 (b) He should understand the behaviour of his subordinates and also be able to motivate them to achieve the goal.

18 (a), (b) and (c)

(a) Concern for self

(b) Concern for people

(c) Concern for the job

19 (a) Distinctive behaviour of a leader.

20 (b) Robins

21 a Capability of the leader to tackle critical situations.

22 (b), (c) and (d)

(b) Trait approach.

(c) Behavioural approach.

(d) Situational approach.

23 (d) All the above.

(a) Leader and psychological attibutes.

(b) The follower with his problems and needs.

(c) Group situation in which the followers and leader interact with one another.

24 (b) This approach stresses the in-born qualities or characteristics of an individual.

25 (b) and (c)

(b) Intelligence and personality.

(c) Task related characteristics and socialistic attributes.

26 (d) The human relation movement in management showed an overriding concern for people.

27 (c) A right decision is always required to tackle a specific situation and is always upheld

28 (c) Trait and behavioural approach movements give birth to leadership style.

29 (c) and (d)

(c) Autocratic style, Free-rein style

(d) Participative or democratic style.

30 (a) In this the leader becomes more powerful as an autocrat.

31 (b) Leadership allows the delegation of complete authority of the leader to subordinates.

32 (b) In this, active participation of subordinates is provided in the process of decision making.

33 (a) and (b)

(a) Theory 'X' assumes human being inherently dislikes work; then 'Y' assumes that for human being work is as natural as a game or a play.

(b) Theory 'X' shows that people do not have ambition and dislike responsibility, whereas theory 'Y' assumes that human being has ambition and he willfully shoulders responsibility.

34 (a) and (b)

(a) People of task accomplishment are 'Task masters.'

(b) People of welfare nature are 'Relation oriented.'

35 (a) B.F. Skinner

36 (b) Leadership along with dynamic techniques makes the people faithful and motivate to achieve the goal.

37 (d) Any group performance will be contingent upon the proper matching of leadership and the appropriate group behaviour or leader can elicit in a situation.

38 (c) Positive or negative in nature.

39 (b) A leader may exercise power on his subordinates by virtue of his official position (positive power).

40 (c) Punishment or creating fear.

41 (c) Power has its principal effect in its potential use than its actual use.

42 (c) Leadership has task and relation centered behavioural pattern.

43 (a), (b), (c) and (d)

(a) Impoverished and country club style.

(b) Middle of the road and efficiency

(c) Common stage.

(d) Concern for employees and production.

44 (b) It is a poor management that shows a little concern for employees and production.

45 (b) It does not follow any principle, since its management is compared to a country club.

46 (c) The leader is equally concerned about the welfare of the employees, as well as the target production.

47 (d) In this, production is given top priority leaving aside the welfare of employees.

48 (b) Maximum care and amiable relations are the watch word of this style. Care is given to the task and the welfare as well.

49 (b) and (c)

(b) The concept of Likert and his associates is for understanding the leadership behaviour in a continuous structure of 4-system of management.

(c) In this system, Likert has given importance to eight variables.

50 (a) To enable the managers to choose a particular pattern of leadership behaviour in relation to their subordinates

51 (c) Ensure the subordinates are working, guide them, and give directions as and when required.

52 (a) He must be the leader of his work force, and need to direct and control the activities. He should be impartial and fair to all.

53 (c) He is the last link in the management group and has direct association with the employees at their work place to achieve the target of production.

54 (d) All the above

(a) The jobs should be specified and adequate power provided.

(b) The supervisor should have access to top management in relation to the problems faced by him in execution of jobs.

(c) Due recognisation needs to be given to supervisor along with recommendations, as to his professional status.

55 (b), (c) and (d)

(b) Close and general supervisory behaviour

(c) Employee centered behaviour

(d) Work centered supervisory behaviour.

56 (a) The supervision happens, when supervisor deals with a large quantity of work assignments.

57 (b) He makes the people work in a way that the employees feel, they are the part and parcel of the organisation.

58 (b) He acts as a task master for the employees.

59 (c) Employee centered

60 (c) Adequate job training, providing adequate authority to employees, proper scheduling materials and machinery are to be taken care of during supervision, apart from his involvement in the work process.

61 (c) Capacity or ability of an individual to create something new or novel.

62 (b) and (d)

(b) Creative ability can be developed by training and education.

(d) Highly creative persons are usually found to possess intelligence of quite a high degree; however, there is no hard and fast rule that an intelligent person to be creative.

63 (c) Creative process is an innate ability of a person.

64 (b) It is the initial stage, where facts and materials considered essential are collected and anaysed and then a definite plan of action is set up to start.

65 (b) and (d)

(b) This is characterised by absence of overt activities.

(d) In the absence of other interference, our conscious mind begins to work in the direction of solving the problem.

66 (a) In this period, the thinker often experiences sudden appearance of the answer to his problem.

67 (b) To determine, whether the answer or the solution appeared through insight is correct or not.

68 (a) Abilities to create ideas and also solving problems.

69 (a) and (b)

(a) Fluency, flexibility and originality.

(b) Problem sensitivity, elaboration and convergent thinking ability.

70 (a) Ability to create ideas copiously and very useful to that set of problems, where it is unlikely that a simple proper solution exists.

71 (a) Flexibility or the ability to shift frames of reference, choose bearing in mind multiple factors and identify various aspects of a situation in dealing with people's problems.

72 (d) Originality produces usual ideas that are not only surprising and novel but also useful, relevant and appropriate.

73 (b) Ability to guess consequences of situations that others are unable to do so. It requires a mind that is able to identify the crucial features of situations and the relationship.

74 (b) In a process of elaboration in which certain amount of associate thinking is considered, is likely to yield a creative outcome.

75 (d) Convergent abilities do help to understand a problem.

76 (c) Skinner.

77 (b) Lateral thinking and forced relationship are used solving the problem.

78 (d) Lateral thinking creates new concepts and ways of understanding, which ultimately lead to new ideas.

79 (c) The main aspect of the technique that in the process of formulating a relationship between normally incompatible concepts, one has to expand the area of one's mental functioning to think in new directions.

80 (a) It is a specific method of generating ideas.

81 (d) All the above

(a) Solving problems in groups stimulates creative abilities.

(b) If one consciously stops evaluating ideas, it helps in continuous generation of ideas.

(c) Original and creative solutions emerge, when variety of ideas is available.

82 (d) All the above

(a) Criticism of any idea is not allowed.

(b) Words and phrases that convey negative meaning are to be avoided.

(c) Emphasis to be given on generating and accepting ideas during such a session.

83 (b) and (c)

(b) Allow the mind to ponder over a range of ideas.

(c) Express all ideas, which occur to a person without any restriction.

84 (b) and (c)

(b) It always modifies and improves upon others' ideas.

(c) Participants are encouraged to combine ideas and develop new alternatives in this process.

85 (a), (b), (c) and (d)

(a) Ideal size of the brain storming group is 10-12 individuals.

(b) Explain the rules of brain storming to the participants.

(c) Pre-session preparations, session procedure and post-session follow up.

(d) When the number of ideas is too large, ask the participants to identify similar ideas and club them together.

86 (b) Guilford

87 (b) He is a moderate person by temperament and behaviour, and is more likely to be a generalist rather than a specialist.

88 (c) and (d).

(c) A well-planned suggestion, which gets the approval of the experts is a creative resource of an organisation.

(d) The very attempt of making suggestion by an individual reveals the capacity to perceive problems and a desire to improve things and self-motivation to put in efforts to act upon.

89 (c) One of the important organisational criteria for encouraging creativity is the uninhibited flow of ideas and information.

90 (a) and (b)

(a) It is based on sharing of idea, intellectual stimulation, joint ventures, flexible and growth oriented.

(b) Autonomy and opportunity to creative and talented people, recognition and provide special compensation.

91 (a) Organisational policies are restrictive and also survival oriented.

92 (c) The impact of changes or the consequences cannot be eliminated completely, whereas it can be reduced by appropriate creative actions.

93 (b) A creative person alone can put forward an ideal solution like modification, verification and trial, etc., of the change along with the participation of other persons.

94 (b) The ability to transfer experience and knowledge into action.

95 (b) and (c)

(b) Technical skill, human skill.

(c) Conceptual and perceptual skills.

96 (b) Technical skill refers to an understanding and proficiency in handling methods, processing a particular kind of activity.

97 (b) and (c)

(b) Human skill is concerned with managing human resource in an organisation

(c) This skill is demonstrated in the way the individual interacts with his superiors, equals and subordinates in an organisastion.

98 (a) The skill that provides awareness or denotes insight, sensitive understanding and provides capability to visualise future actions, etc.

99 (b) Perceive means to be aware through the senses. Perception as a basic cognitive process with many variables affect the behaviour.

100 (c) Adequate training can develop the scope of intelligence in an individual so as to help improve the perceptual skills.

101 (c) A decision is a solution selected after an examination of several alternatives.

102 (d) All the above

(a) Defining the problem and analysing the relevant facts.

(b) Preparation of alternative course of action and deciding the best course of action.

(c) Implementation of decision.

103 (c) When the nature of the problem is understood that will lead to critical cause of the problem.

104 (d) Amongst various alternatives the best to be selected.

105 (c) There is need to introspect and relate complex factors and variables.

106 (b), (c) and (d)

(b) Limitation of time does not permit the manager to consider all possible alternatives with their consequences.

(c) The outcome of many decisions is indefinable or probabilistic. The manager cannot evaluate the outcome of a decision prior to taking it.

(d) The rational managerial efforts, therefore go wrong invariably and are spoiled due to inherent confusion of managers in specific situations.

107 (a) George R. Terry

108 (a) and (b)

(a) Perception, conception and investigation.

(b) Deliberation, selection and promulgation

109 (b) Peter F. Drucker.

110 (a), (b) and (c)

(a) Information available to the decision maker.

(b) Technique he should follow, while taking the decision.

(c) Sophistication of the decision maker.

111 (b) Behaviour of the top management has its effects on the type of decisions and the time frame within which the decisions are taken by the managers.

112 (a) When a strategic decision is taken, the time factor is very important.

113 (a), (b) and (c)

(a) Attitudes affect the type of decision that emanates or originates.

(b) Temperament of individuals vary in their approaches.

(c) Certain people may be optimistic, others may be conservative and unwilling to take risk.

114 (a) How far participation is encouraged by the decision maker is as relevant factor.

115 (d) A manager should have the right type of attitude to understand any problem in its entirety and assist to find its solution.

116 (c) Herbert Simon

117 (a) A decision to be taken with adequate care, supported by relevant facts and should be acknowledged by subsequent events.

118 (a) and (b)

(a) Decision making is very important for achieving various goals of an organisation.

(b) A good decision is always selected from various alternatives.

119 (c) The decision taken in the best interest of the organisation.

120 (a) These decisions are taken by a manager in his personal capacity and not as a part of the organisation.

121 (a) The decisions are of routine type, which do not require more thinking process. They are often taken by managers for routine matters.

122 (a) and (b)

(a) It is a form of participation by the group in arriving at a decision.

(b) This form of decision will be readily acceptable by subordinates.

123 (b) Quantitative methods are based on scientific methodology, as far as their approach to management problems is concerned.

124 (a), (b) and (c)

(a) Determining the objective and identifying pertinent variables.

(b) Determination of available strategies and prediction of payoffs

(c) Making a decision and execution of its control.

125 (a) Determining the objective by a manager to formulate the impact required for a quality and quantity output.

126 (a) and (b)

(a) Collection of related data.

(b) Model building, at this stage, is required for decision making.

127 (c) When a number of strategies are available to take a decision, a step by step approach is to be made till the optimum strategy is identified.

128 (a), (b) and (c)

(a) A situation of arriving at a decision may have ample variations, both controllable and uncontrollable.

(b) When products are advertised to attract customers, sales management has to predict the opponents' strategy in addition to their own.

(c) Decision makers have to predict the payoffs which are their objectives under various combinations of controllable and uncontrollable variables.

129 (d) The manager will use the mathematical models and optimisation concept in making the decision.

130 (d) The use of quantitative technique process with proper understanding between the decision maker and the analyst leads to increased use of control method and improve decision making.

131 (c) This helps the manager to select an optimum alternative course of action in decision making.

132 (b) and (d)

(b) It indicates the application of mathematical and optimization concept in decision making.

(d) The problems usually having time, cost or profits are to be optimised. This leads to probability and reasonable outcome for a given decision or a number of decisions.

133 (a) and (d)

(a) Models, simulation, resource allocation, waiting line problem and using theory.

(b) Gaming and game theory, PERT/ CPM, decision trees and probability theory.

134 (a) and (c)

(a) The essence of operation research approach.

(c) A model of the profit and loss account of a company's operation throughout a particular year in a summary form.

135 (b) The use of case study method of teaching management education is an example of simulation.

136 (b) In business the resources have to be used with adequate care to enable maximum profit with minimum cost.

137 (c) and (d)

(c) It is used to find solutions of actual problems involving competitors.

(d) In such games, a rational opponent or opponents are involved, therefore strategic decisions have to be taken.

138 (b) and (c)

(b) It is a project planning and controlling technique.

(c) The basic device of this system is the network or a pictorial description of the work, activities and events comprising a particular project.

139 (c) It is a graphic method used by the decision maker to help him to see the course of action open to him and the possible outcome.

140 (b) Theory of probability provides the basis for rational calculation of obstructions and the possible outcome in complex situations.

141 (c) The objective is used in linear programming to indicate the relationship between the variables concerned is directly proportional one.

Explanation : In most of the business activities one has to deal with a number of factors or variables. On such occasions, two characteristics are obvious- (i) There are a number of activities required to be performed and there are a number of alternative ways of doing them, (ii) Resources or facilities for performing each activity is limited to various reasons. The problem, therefore, is to combine activities and resources in such a way as to maximise overall effectiveness. The tools which have been came to be closely associated with these problems are LINEAR PROGRAMMING and other types of mathematical programming. Linear programming has been used extensively based on the fact that constraints subject to which the optimum solution is to be obtained and the most favourable criteria have linear relationship. For example, supply of various urgent medicines to be distributed by Pharmaceutical companies earlier by Air or by Rail, the cost effectiveness can be worked out with the help of linear programming and despatch them according to the urgency of demand.

142 (a) Used to achieve objective and maximizing profits for the organisation.

143 (c) It is accepted that information when quantified, is precise, less liable to distortion when communicated for decision making.

144 (d) Peter Drucker.

145 (c) Decision maker must make the environmental factors in a rational manner making full use of available information and techniques.

146 (d) All the above
(a) Decision under certainty
(b) Decision under risk
(c) Decision under uncertainty.

147 (c) A thorough analysis of the data backed by long experience will provide a manager with the degree of certainty to take a decision.

148 (a) While taking a decision for the future, the same can prove to be as risk factor due to two or more possibilities existing along with the main course of action.

149 (b) When decision is not taken with the consideration of all 'pros' and 'cons' the decision will fall under the category of uncertainty.

150 (a) OR is applied to identify the certainty, uncertainty and risk of every decision taken in modern time.

◆◆◆◆◆

CHAPTER - 6

- ***COMMUNICATION***
- ***TRANSACTIONAL ANALYSIS IN COMMUNICATION***
- ***GROUP DYNAMICS***
- ***INFORMAL ORGANISATION***
- ***COUNSELLING***
- ***JOB SATISFACTION***
- ***HUMAN RELATION***

FEATURES :

- Communication
- Concept
- Importance
- Process
- Source
- Coding
- Verbal and non-verbal communication
- Structure
- Principles
- Methods Informal communication
- Barriers of effective communication
- Effective communication
- Communication gap
- Perception problems in communication
- Transactional analysis in communication
- Meaning of transactional analysis
- Theories of communication
- Strokes
- Ego states in communication
- Group dynamics
- Meaning
- Importance Consequences of group dynamics
- Management communication
- Informal organisations
- Meaning
- Nature
- Advantage
- Disadvantages
- Rumours
- Meaning
- Counselling
- Concept
- Types of counselling
- Who can be a counsellor
- Counselling role of managers
- Job satisfaction
- Meaning
- Job characteristics
- Intrinsic aspect of job
- Productivity and job satisfaction
- Advantage of job satisfaction
- What is frustration
- Human relations
- Meaning
- Philosophy of human relations
- Approaches of human relations
- Objectives
- Meaning of industrial relation (IR)
- How to foster IR?

KEY NOTE

Communication

The word communication has the origin from the Latin word 'Communis' which means common. According to Koontz and O'Donnell communication is the means of organised activity. Communication is an unavoidable part of any management. It is a managerial skill based on human behaviour. It is the process of conveying messages, ideas, attitudes and opinions from one person to another so as to enable them to understand.

Transactional analysis in communication

This is a theory of a communication process that helps predict the future pattern of behaviour. This was introduced by Eric Berne. He after long experimentation through clinical examinations and process; advocated the principle as a rational form of theory for psychic patients. However, the theory was not confined only to people suffering from psychological disorders but also found its use for normal people, who face relation problem in some sphere or the other. This theory has the similarity of Freud's concept of 'Id', 'Ego' and 'Super ego'. According to Berne, personality is the characteristic combination of these ego states in an individual. Parent ego state is similar to that of a parent, the individual with adult ego has an objective approach to reality and the child ego needs for the early period of life. In transactional analysis one can experience transaction (interaction between people). Interaction is there in all forms of communication.

Group dynamics

The word group refers to two or more people, who have certain psychological relation with each other. Dynamics means, the creative force or the capacity to change and adapt new ideas and change with new situations. Therefore, group dynamics refers to the study of the forces existing in group. Groups are formed as a sequel to common interest, whenever any group is formed with a certain interest, it in turn holds its members together. It operates in all types of human interaction in an organisation.

Informal organisation

Activities of such an organisation involve two or more persons having awareness of a given objective. It always operates under the cover of formal relationship in every organisation. Informal organisation is the result of human relations at work place. There are normally many informal groups in an organisation. Each informal group has its social system which activates effectively. Informal organisation is a part of an organisation in its entirety. It is developed through contacts, customs and social interaction between groups. It is a social base formed to cater the personal needs of the members of a group. Informal organisation functions under an informal authority.

Counselling

Counselling is a discussion of emotional problems of an individual or employees with an aim to find a solution. No matter how better human relations at work place is handled, still people may develop emotional problems. Crux of the problem is that each individual differs in behaviour, needs and ideas. Counselling may be required due to work conditions or of personal stress etc., of the individual. Emotional problems can occur by interpersonal and intergroup conflicts. Counselling is needed to judge one's emotional problems and to advise the proper guidance to an individual.

Job satisfaction

According to Kaith Davis, job satisfaction is the favourableness or unfavourableness with which employees view their work. In other words, when the rewards for job performance and one's expectations and execution of the job are in consonance with each other. A worker will be satisfied when he gets what he expected out of the job. Job satisfaction does not mean that a worker is fully satisfied in all respects. He may be satisfied with the work but may be dissatisfied with the work environment. Management cannot establish high job satisfaction once and for all. It needs regular and proper maintenance.

Human relation

It is the integration of people through knowledge and understanding of the activities, attitudes and their interrelationship at the place of work. A good industrial relation can only be possible through good human relation. People need to be respected with dignity, fair dealing and concern for their physical and social needs. An environment where an individual is contented with his job, assured security and bright future are provided with his basic needs in life means an atmosphere of human relation at work.

QUESTIONS

COMMUNICATION

CONCEPTS OF COMMUNICATION

1. What is communication?

(a) It is a Latin word 'Communis' denoting communication.

(b) It is a process through which all forms of information from one person to another are transferred.

(c) Interaction of information between people.

(d) It covers any type of behaviour resulting in an exchange of meaning.

2. What is the nature of communication?

(a) Meaningful interaction amongst people.

(b) The definition of communication does not restrict either written or spoken message.

(c) All means whereby meaning can be conveyed from one individual to another.

(d) Facial expression and gestures often communicate meanings.

3. Communication means- "The transfer of information and understanding from person to person." Who said this?

(a) Elliott Jaques (b) C.I. Barnard

(c) Dale S. Beach (d) Mc Farland

4. What is importance of communication?

(a) Promotional of managerial efficiency, cooperation, thorough understanding.

(b) Basis for leadership action and means of coordination.

(c) Provision of job satisfaction.

(d) All the above.

5. What is the guideline principles of communication?

(a) Clarity, attention and integrity.

(b) Communication must be effective.

(c) There should be two-way communication.

(d) It is a means of modifying behaviour.

6. **What is the process of communication?**
(a) Sender or originator of communication and coding.
(b) Transmitting channel.
(c) Receiving, decoding and destination.
(d) None of the above.

7. **What is meant by 'Source' of communication?**
(a) Process of communication starts with source.
(b) An individual, speaking, writing, gesturing, telecasting, newspaper, organisation, etc.
(c) Communication between individuals.
(d) Information centres.

8. **What is coding?**
(a) Information in the form of idea or concept.
(b) System of words, letters or symbols used to keep secrecy or brevity in communication of messages.
(c) Normally the source first encodes the message as per its requirement.
(d) All the above.

9. **What is verbal communication?**
(a) It takes place usually by means of verbal symbols.
(b) Language or word symbols are most potent tool of communication.
(c) Words derive their meaning from situation in which these are based and the situation to which they refer.
(d) None of the above.

10. **What does non-verbal communication refer to?**
(a) Facial expression and gestures.
(b) Signals other than language are used in a complex-way to indicate feelings and attitudes.
(c) Signals and words are also used precisely to convey the meaning of the message.
(d) All the above.

11. **What is decoding?**
(a) When the recipient receives the message in a code-language, it is made intelligible.
(b) Coded messages are translated into plain language.
(c) When messages are in coded form the same is decoded.
(d) All the above.

12. **What factors influence the process of decoding?**
(a) Recipient's prior knowledge of the situation and beliefs.
(b) Attitude and language.
(c) Cultural background and group affiliations.
(d) None of the above.

13. **What is meant by communication structure?**
(a) Upward communication and downward communication.
(b) Lateral or diagonal communication.
(c) Electronic communication network.
(d) All the above.

14. **What is upward communication?**
(a) Communication of subordinate.
(b) The information flowing from subordinate to superior, may be in written or oral form.
(c) Most employees lack the communication skill.
(d) It can be a report on progress of work to the superior by a subordinate.

15. **What is downward communication?**
(a) Instructions and orders for execution.
(b) Superiors to subordinates in the form of direction, orders, etc., relevant to the work.
(c) The frequency of this communication is more than the upward communication.
(d) All the above.

16. What is horizontal or lateral communication?

(a) Different heads of the departments of an organisation coordinate their work through lateral communication.

(b) It is a good process of effecting coordination in any organisational set up.

(c) In departmentation whereby process, functions or product, different departmental heads have their work completion targets, they need lateral communication network.

(d) All the above.

17. What is a communication network?

(a) The media used for communication.

(b) Computer and internet services.

(c) The route through which a communication flows from sender to the recipient.

(d) None of the above.

18. What are the principles of communication?

(a) Principles of clarity, attention and consistency.

(b) Principles of adequacy, integration and time.

(c) Principles of informality and feedback.

(d) At the time of acceptance of communication recipient must feel that the information received is acceptable.

19. What does the principle of clarity in communication indicate?

(a) Whatever is the message conveyed, should be unambiguous.

(b) The words do not speak themselves, communication must make them meaningful.

(c) Message should be clear, communicated in a simple language and easily understood by the recipient.

(d) Message should be in a concised form and as per the required standard.

20. What is meant by attention in communication?

(a) The communication is always meant for action.

(b) People have emotions and it is the emotion that decides degree of attention.

(c) Recipient's attention to the message communicated is completely drawn to the communication to be effective.

(d) 'Attention' helps the communicator to reduce the time, effect, emotion and mood of the recipient.

21. What does consistency in communication refer to?

(a) Inconsistency in communication creates confusion.

(b) Communication must be consistent with policies and objectives of the organisation.

(c) Consistency in communication needs to be maintained, when interacting with employees.

(d) Consistent communication can bring better coordination in work.

22. What are the principles of adequacy?

(a) Communication should be proper and self-contained.

(b) Communication should not be a piecemeal and inadequate one.

(c) Incomplete message delays action, creates misunderstanding and also strains relations.

(d) Inadequacy affects the efficiency of both the communicator and the recipient.

23. What do principles of integration mean?

(a) It is a means to attain the objectives of an organisation.

(b) Communication brings people together to help accomplish the task satisfactorily.

(c) It should be based on the policy of integration of efforts of people for better cooperation and understanding.

(d) All the above.

24. What is the principle of time?

(a) Information to be communicated at the most appropriate time to have the desired result.

(b) Time has its own value for every action. A message not conveyed on time to the recipient, loses its value and becomes a thing in the past.

(c) A message when it is communicated is the prerogative of the communication, whereas a wrong choice of time may not have the desired result.

(d) None of the above.

25. What do the principles of informality indicate?

(a) An executive should know when to be formal or informal in his actions.

(b) Informality is a quality that brings cordial feelings amongst people.

(c) Politeness and informality bring better results when you communicate in business, while dealing with customers.

(d) All the above.

26. What do principles of feedback refer to?

(a) Communication is a two-way process.

(b) Communication is meant for being communicated.

(c) The recipient should acknowledge the communication/message and transmit the action taken to the communicator.

(d) All the above.

27. What are the methods of communication?

(a) Formal and informal

(b) Oral and written

(c) Downward and Upward

(d) Horizontal

28. What is formal communication?

(a) It is carried out in formal type of organisation.

(b) A formal communication derives its support from the scalar chain system of an organisation.

(c) Formal communication establishes relationship between the two positions.

(d) In this the status or position in the hierarchy of communicator as well as the recipient is important.

29. What does informal communication indicate?

(a) It is based on the informal relationship of people in an organisation.

(b) It is also known as the 'grapevine' system of communication.

(c) This communication is more direct, unofficial, spontaneous and flexible in nature.

(d) All the above.

30. What does oral communication mean?

(a) It is a face to face communication.

(b) It is a communication with spoken words.

(c) It is having a personal touch and more effective.

(d) It brings good relations between management and employees.

31. What is one-way communication?

(a) All types of advertisements are one-way communication.

(b) In this, the sender finishes his responsibility as soon as he transmits his information to other.

(c) The receiver does not have the advantage of clarification after the receipt of the information.

(d) All the above.

32. What do you understand by two-way communication?

(a) This type of communication has the advantage of feedback system.

(b) It can clarify any doubt of the receiver.
(c) Interaction of a teacher and students in classroom establishes proper feedback of communication.
(d) All the above.

33. What are the demands of two-way communication?
(a) Communication, message and recipient.
(b) The connection between sender and receiver.
(c) Sender, transmission, receiver and feedback.
(d) None of the above.

34. What is meant by barriers of effective communication?
(a) Semantic, psychological, organisational barriers.
(b) The transmission barriers between the sender and the receiver.
(c) Personal and mechanical barriers.
(d) All the above.

35. What is semantic barrier of communication?
(a) Poor quality of message and faulty transmission.
(b) Lack of clarity and technical language.
(c) Lack of communication capability of the sender.
(d) This denotes barriers of language and symbols and their interpretation.

36. How does psychological barrier affect the communication?
(a) Premature evaluation and inadequate attention.
(b) Transmission losses and poor retention. Undue stress on written message.
(c) Lack of trust in the sender by the receiver and failure to communicate.
(d) Psychological state of mind of the sender, as well as that of the receiver makes lot of difference.

37. What is the role of organisational barriers in effective communication?
(a) Restriction imposed by the rules of the organisation.
(b) Status, hierarchial position restraining the flow of communication.
(c) complex-structure of the organisation.
(d) All the above.

38. What are the personal barriers of effective communication?
(a) Attitude of superiors and insistence on following proper channel.
(b) Lack of confidence in subordinates and preoccupation of superiors.
(c) Lack of awareness and hesitation to communicate.
(d) It occurs due to constraints at various levels in an organisation.

39. What are mechanical barriers in effective communication?
(a) Inadequate infrastructural arrangements.
(b) Poor office layout and use of wrong medium.
(c) Defective procedures and practices.
(d) None of the above.

40. How can the communication system be improved in the organisation?
(a) Restructuring the organisation.
(b) Promoting upward communication for creative innovations.
(c) Proper follow-up, feedback and by adopting parallel channels.
(d) All the above.

41. How to improve one's ability to communicate?
(a) Be aware of common obstacles for gaining proper understanding.
(b) Understand the process of emphatic listening.
(c) Convey meaning to others.
(d) Get feedback confirmation.

42. What is emphatic listening?

(a) While listening emphatically, a person opens the way for another to talk freely his ideas and feelings without justifying each of his statements.
(b) It is a kind of communication that requires mutual exchange of ideas and feelings between the manager and his subordinate.
(c) In this, the manager must listen and also impart facts and feelings.
(d) All the above.

43. What are the principles of listening?

(a) Attend to the meaning and content of the message.
(b) Listen to idea of the message and identify the main point.
(c) Take notes and use possible recording schemes of the message recording.
(d) Avoid quick judgement, look for areas of interest in the message, and wait till the message is complete.

44. What are the specific requirements of effective listening?

(a) Establish eye to eye contact.
(b) Exhibit affirmative expressions.
(c) Avoid distractive actions during listening.
(d) Paraphrase what is understood by listening.

45. "Communication is the sum of all the things that a person does, when he wants to create understanding in the mind of other. It involves systematic and continuous process of telling, listening and understanding." Who said this?

(a) Newman and Summer,
(b) Louise Allen,
(c) Elliots Jaques,
(d) C.I. Barnard.

46. What are the guidelines for good listening?

(a) Listen patiently what the other person has to say. Try to understand his feelings and what the person is expressing. The factual contents. Repeat the feelings but accurately.
(b) Allow time for discussion to continue without any interruption.
(c) Avoid direct questions, arguments about facts and refrain from comments like- 'That is not correct' etc.
(d) Do not get emotionally involved, try simply to understand first and defer evaluation until later.

47. How to make effective communication?

(a) Make sure that you want to communicate and use proper language.
(b) Use adequate medium and also listen attentively. Communication is a two-way process.
(c) Ensure that your actions do not contradict your communication. Improve your skills in oral and written communication.
(d) All the above.

48. What is grapevine communication?

(a) It is a sort of informal communication.
(b) It is quite fast and spontaneous having a good amount of credibility.
(c) At times, the information transmitted is distorted, when it is passed onto many people in the group.
(d) This channel is used as a supplement to formal channel of communication.

49. What is meant by communication gap?

(a) The gap occurs between the sender and the receiver of the communication.
(b) This is due to simple presumption of mutual understanding.
(c) Merely because the speaker presumes that he has spoken and the one at the other end has heard.
(d) All the above.

50. What is perception problem in communication?

(a) Perception differs with individual's awareness of his environment as well as past experiences.

(b) Usually persons perceive particular learned patterns.

(c) Motives also govern perception as persons tend to select things necessary to their needs and discard those having conflict with their own preconceived ideas.

(d) Perception vary like sensory factors, ability to hear and feel, etc.

TRANSACTIONAL ANALYSIS IN COMMUNICATION

51. What is transactional analysis in communication?

(a) It is concerned with theory and practice of communication.

(b) In this, one can experience interaction between people.

(c) Interactions are always in the form of communication.

(d) In an organisation, a senior directs his junior what he has to do or perform.

52. What is classical communication?

(a) Classical theory stresses on task related communication.

(b) This indicates passing of orders and instructions to subordinates and obedience and coordination are expected in all activities.

(c) In this the direction of communication is 'downward.'

(d) This communication is expected to have full control over subordinates.

53. What is neoclassical view?

(a) In this emphasis on considering the needs of employees is vital.

(b) It is also focused on social interaction of people at the place of work leading to employees' participation in decision making.

(c) In this, employees can have horizontal communication between them and their peers, who are part of the informal work group and have vertical upward communication with the managers.

(d) All the above.

54. What do you understand by 'modernist's' view in communication?

(a) This kind of communication is highly important in organisational activities.

(b) It is felt that proper interaction and communication can create sound and firm relationship between work group and sub-units of the organisation.

(c) For selecting proper and effective pattern of communication, management must study the various aspects of advantages and disadvantages of the pattern to be selected.

(d) The modernists are of the view that proper communication and exchange of information can make the required change in organisational set-up.

55. What is meant by 'Ego' state in transactional analysis?

(a) Personality is a characteristic mix in a person of three ego states.

(b) An ego state is a coherent system of feelings and behaviour pattern.

(c) Transactional analysis is a theory and practice of communication introduced by Eric Berne.

(d) All the above.

56. What ego state does an individual possess?

(a) An ego state which resembles of parental figure (Parental ego).

(b) An ego state which is directed towards an objective appraisal of reality (Adult ego)

(c) An ego state which represents childhood (child ego).

(d) All the above.

57. How can we distinguish the people shifting from one ego state to another?

(a) Ego states are Parent, Adult and Child in transactional analysis.

(b) Words, gestures, facial expressions, tone of voice, feeling expressed and behaviour are clues to ego state in which a person is operating at a given time.

(c) A transaction is an exchange of communication verbal or non-verbal, which takes place between two individuals.

(d) All the above.

58. What is meant by 'strokes' in transactional analysis?

(a) Transactions arise out of person's need for 'stroke'.

(b) A stroke is the sign of recognition which all social beings invariably seek.

(c) Early childhood experience, when an individual completely dependent on others for survival, existed in people is known as 'stroke hunger'.

(d) Stroke hunger is possessed by every individual.

59. What are the types of stroke?

(a) Stroke may be a positive or a negative one.

(b) Those interpersonal experience of early years having approval and acceptance are called positive strokes.

(c) Those of us, whose early experiences are of the nature of disapproval and rejection are called negative strokes.

(d) Strokes may be conditional or unconditional and genuine and not genuine in nature.

60. What happens when two people, each having three egos (Parent, Adult and Child) interact with each other?

(a) Transaction may be simple or complex depending upon the ego stimulus or transactional response originates.

(b) In this the Parent ego and Adult ego may transact .

(c) Child ego of two people may also transact.

(d) None of the above.

61. What are the different types transaction?

(a) Simple transaction is of two kinds- complementary and crossed.

(b) When a transactional stimulus originates in one ego state and the transactional response in the corresponding ego state, the transaction is complementary.

(c) It can be between Adult to Parent and Parent to Child and Child to Adult in a parallel way.

(d) Crossed transaction is when a transactional stimulus originates in one ego state and the transactional response does not come from a corresponding ego state.

GROUP DYNAMICS

62. What is transactional analysis and group dynamics?

(a) Organisation consists of people.

(b) People interact with each other.

(c) Face to face interaction includes transactional analysis and group dynamics (people interact in group).

(d) All the above.

63. What is the importance of group dynamics?

(a) Characteristics of positive attitude may be called as the asset of a group dynamic.

(b) The intention of the supporters of group dynamics is that the work should be done by people in the group.

(c) Individual responsibility and man to man supervision are bad.

(d) Committee meeting, group decision, collective problem solving and group therapy are the indexes of group prosperity.

64. What are the important propositions about groups?

(a) Groups do exist, and they are ubiquitous (omnipresent).

(b) Group mobilises powerful forces.

(c) Group may produce good or bad consequences.

(d) Group dynamics permit desirable consequences.

65. What is meant by the existence of groups?

(a) Groups do exist and they affect the human behaviour to a great extent.

(b) A child is born in a family (group) that may be good or bad for the family.

(c) Any new addition to a group may bring change the very structure of the group. It may also affect the attitude, feeling and behaviour of other members of the group (good or bad).

(d) A man lives in a group (family) and continues to stay till his last.

66. Why groups are inevitable and ubiquitous?

(a) Man cannot live without groups.

(b) Biological nature, language, capacity and environment are different factors which make a man to live in group.

(c) The gregarious nature of man force him to stay in group.

(d) All the above.

67. Is it a fact that groups mobilise powerful forces?

(a) They mobilise powerful forces that produce effects, which are important to individuals.

(b) Evidences show that members of high cohesive groups have less problems than the less cohesive ones.

(c) There are two main reasons of relationship between cohesiveness of groups and the individual anxiety.

(d) Cohesive groups provide support to their members and group membership provides satisfaction to the individual which result in reducing the anxiety.

68. What are the consequences of group dynamics?

(a) The knowledge of group dynamics suggests necessary adjustment in human behaviour.

(b) Consequence may be positive as well as negative.

(c) Results may be advantageous to some and disadvantageous to others.

(d) In order to remove the lacunae in consequences one must emphasise alike both the positive and negative aspects.

69. What do you understand by transactional analysis in organisational meetings?

(a) This exists when people come together and discuss ideas and views.

(b) Organisational meetings refer to committees, conferences, and other groups where face to face discussions on various workers'

problems concerning the group in the organisation take place.
(c) To decide the course of action in performance of the specific act by the group.
(d) To initiate creative thinking.

70. What are the advantages of meetings?
(a) Participation improves group performance.
(b) It provides encouragement and support to arrive at decisions.
(c) Helps to promote creative thinking.
(d) All the above.

71. Why some meetings are unproductive?
(a) When required persons do not attend the meeting it become unproductive.
(b) Members attend the meeting, however, at times they do not get what is expected of it.
(c) Some people developed the attitude that meetings are quite unproductive and they do not attend them.
(d) All the above.

72. What is the disadvantage of meetings?
(a) Meetings are not productive enough to cater the requirements of all the people.
(b) They are slow and expensive too.
(c) They loose creative thinking in people.
(d) All the above.

73. What is meant by a team?
(a) When people perform tasks together is called a team.
(b) People seek to develop a corporate state is teamwork.
(c) A small group of people interacting regularly.
(d) None of the above.

74. "Coordination by a small cooperative group in regular conduct, wherein members contribute responsibility enthusiastically to task achievement is operation team." Who said this?
(a) Kaith Davis,
(b) Koontz and O'Donnell
(c) Berne, E.
(d) Skimmer, B.F.

75. What are different types of a team according to its work?
(a) Process team
(b) Goal team
(c) Sequential team
(d) None of the above.

76. What is process team?
(a) This team has a number of skill and unskill levels.
(b) This team works together very cohesively and with loyalty.
(c) Members are having the cooperation in such a way that they interact effectively. Among them is a formal leader, whereas their relations are informal.
(d) This is most effective and challenging team.

77. What is meant by goal team?
(a) This type of team usually have a minimum quota of work goals.
(b) The tasks are allotted to the team according to its capabilities.
(c) All members of the team will be allotted their work according to their capacities so as to achieve the team goal in a specific time-frame.
(d) Good teams are normally used in sales of products by various companies.

78. What does sequential team refer to?
(a) In this, members are dependent on each other.
(b) The work of a group is distributed to the members of its team, according to the sequence of work.
(c) In this the work piles up slowly with the person.

(d) Normally, the employees agree with the pace of the slowest employee in the team so as to avoid making the slow employee ineffective.

79. What is management communication?

(a) There are various aspects of communication in the organisation.

(b) Communication, when referred to organisation is for employees at lower level.

(c) Communication within the management group is called management communication or intramanagement communication.

(d) In every organisation certain important subjects, which are discussed only by top management, such secrets are to be safeguarded.

80. What is the importance of management communication?

(a) It is the prerequisite to employee communication.

(b) Necessary for good decisions and with greater scope of managerial influence.

(c) Links in communication chain are within the management group and self-communication of management group for better knowledge about the policies of organisation.

(d) All the above.

81 How can the management communication be improved?

(a) Committees and conferences

(b) Written communication like-newsletters, bulletins and special booklets, etc.

(c) Organising conferences on various matters, projects and policies of organisation and subjects connected to development and progress.

(d) All the above.

INFORMAL ORGANISATIONS

82. What is informal organisation.

(a) There are two types of relationship viz., formal and informal between persons.

(b) Underformal organisations exist with more complex system of social relationship consisting of informal organisations.

(c) Informal organisations cannot be identified through organisation charts. They have their own system of interaction and communication network to protect the interest of their members.

(d) Authority and leadership in an informal organisation are earned from a number of groups. Informal organisation has a powerful influence over productivity and job satisfaction.

83. What do you know about the 'aims' of the informal organisation?

(a) It is a product of human interaction at work place.

(b) It satisfies the human needs of working in a group.

(c) It shares common ides and values communicating in familiar language and protecting group interest.

(d) All the above.

84. What are the characteristics of informal organisation?

(a) Informal organisation is a part of total organisation.

(b) It develops from habits, contacts, and customs of social group.

(c) It usually try to remain small not prominent and unstable.

(d) None of the above.

85. What is the nature of informal organisation?

(a) Informal organisation arises from social interaction.
(b) Informal leadership.
(c) Role of informal leader.
(d) All the above.

86. What are the advantages of informal organisation?

(a) Stability to work group, influence on the productivity and job satisfaction.
(b) It is social structure to meet personal needs of its members.
(c) It is a useful channel of communication.
(d) Informal organisation may fill-in the gaps of a manager's ability.

87. What are the disadvantages of informal organisation?

(a) There is possibility of a clash between objectives of formal and informal organisations.
(b) It may act , at times, on mob psychology and as such it can create difficulties for formal organisation.
(c) It is difficult to integrate the formal and informal organisations on various aspects.
(d) None of the above.

88. What are the main functions of informal organisation?

(a) Perpetuation of cultural values and satisfaction of individual needs.
(b) Source of informal communication.
(c) Regulatory device of social control.
(d) All the above.

89. What are the difficult potential areas for the management due to informal organisation?

(a) Resistance to change
(b) Role conflict
(c) Spreading of rumours.
(d) None of the above.

90. What is grapevine?

(a) Whenever people gather, they interact, talk about their work, colleagues, associates, friends, families, etc., any communication received on such occasions is spread very rapidly.
(b) Grapevine information may be oral or written or by observation.
(c) Information received through this medium may be 100% correct or entirely false.
(d) The communication that could not be communicated efficiently may be sent to this channel for wide circulation.

91. Kalth Davis has suggested three situations for becoming an active communicator, which are they?

(a) It is fickle, dynamic and varied as people are.
(b) When there is excitement and insecurity about job.
(c) When our friends and associates are involved in the situation.
(d) If it is not a news or a stale information, research shows that the greatest spread of information takes place immediately after it becomes known.

92. What are the factors of grapevine?

(a) It has tremendous capacity to carry information.
(b) It moves speedily.
(c) It has unusual ability to penetrate even the top most company security cordons.
(d) Whenever a message is to be passed very quickly.

93. What is the importance of grapevine?

(a) Grapevine provides the manager required feedback. He can seek support of the employees through grapevine.

(b) It is a good way to know the reaction of people and also groups and persons may be persuaded.

(c) It is useful for trade unions.

(d) It is a very good medium for passing information very quickly.

94. What is the disadvantage of grapevine?

(a) It is an important channel of communication for the management as well as workers.

(b) Due to its fast speed, at times, information is unheard or misinterpreted, while spreading it.

(c) Leakage of any important and confidential information with regard to organisation may prove disastrous.

(d) All the above.

95. What do you understand by rumours?

(a) Rumour is the most undesirable feature of grapevine.

(b) Grapevine serves as a source of information, but all information passed through it is not always wrong and not correct either.

(c) Rumour is the product of over enthusiasm and ambiguity of situation.

(d) All the above.

96. How the organisation can control rumours?

(a) Make all possible efforts to prevent spreading of rumours.

(b) Rumour should be listened carefully to find out if there is any fact in that.

(c) Any serious rumours to be stopped immediately and the measures undertaken for corrective actions.

(d) If the employees' union does have a strong informal leadership, necessary cooperation can be sought.

COUNSELLING

97. What is counselling?

(a) It is the discussion of an emotional problem.

(b) Despite better relations at work places, employees still develop emotional problems.

(c) Counselling needs discussion.

(d) Main purpose of counselling is to understand or decrease an employees emotional disorder.

98. What are the main functions of counselling?

(a) proper advice and reassurance.

(b) Release of emotional tension and communication.

(c) Clarified thinking and reorientation.

(d) All the above.

99. What is meant by reassurance in counselling?

(a) It is the method of giving courage to the employee to face a problem.

(b) A supervisor can reassure his subordinate in critical situations

(c) This is to encourage a person to have confidence.

(d) Reassurance to be given to the affected person at the right time.

100. How to release the emotional tension?

(a) It is one of the primary functions of counselling.

(b) A good counsellor, who is sympathetic to the counselee's problem, can easily relax his tension.

(c) The release of tension does not always solve the problem, but it does remove the mental blockade and give courage to the counselee to face the problem boldly.

(d) All the above.

101. What does clarified thinking refer to?

(a) Clarified thinking is a result of emotional release.

(b) A skilled and able counsellor brings about clear thinking more quickly.

(c) In clarified thinking, counsellor does not advise what is right but he encourages the individual to accept the reality for emotional problem and to be more rational in solving the problem.

(d) All the above.

102. What is reorientation?

(a) It brings a change in the employee's psychological aspects through a change in basic goals and values.

(b) In this a revision of the workers' level of aspiration and keep on par with actual attainment.

(c) Management recognises those, who are in need of reorientation and does the needful.

(d) All the above.

103. "Successful counselling depends on communication skills, primarily oral by which other person's emotions can be shared with another." Who said this?

(a) Kaith Davis

(b) EFL Brech

(c) Koontz and O'Donnell

(d) Hersey and Blanchard.

104. What are the causes of counselling?

(a) Frustration

(b) Conflicts

(c) Stress

(d) All the above

105. What are the types of counselling?

(a) Directive counselling.

(b) Indirect counselling.

(c) Cooperative counselling

(d) Non-directive counselling.

106. What is directive counselling?

(a) The counsellor patiently listens the emotional problem of the employee.

(b) The counsellor decides with the employee what to do and further motivates the employee to do so.

(c) The counsellor takes an active part in discussing every aspect of the problem and helps to arrive at a conclusion.

(d) All the above.

107. What is non-directive counselling?

(a) A client centered counselling.

(b) It is a type of counselling in which the counselee is important and not the counsellor.

(c) In this the role of counsellor is to listen to the person and try to understand the feelings and follow improved course of action.

(d) The counsellor throughout the interview should attempt to ask discerning questions.

108. What is the limitation of non-directive counselling?

(a) It is much time consuming.

(b) It is not economical to implement.

(c) It is client oriented.

(d) All the above.

109. What are the distinctive features of directive and non-directive counselling?

(a) Methods followed in counselling

(b) Responsibility of solving the problem.

(c) Status (to be maintained).

(d) Role (to be carried out).

110. What is cooperative counselling?

(a) It is an integration of both type of counselling.

(b) Directive and non-directive counselling are two extremes of counselling problems.

(c) The counsellor incites discussion and deals in a broader perspective before the employee for comparison.

(d) It is a mutual discussion of employees' problems.

111. "Cooperative counselling means-a mutual discussion of an employees' emotional problem and a cooperative effort to set-up conditions that will remedy it." Who said this?

(a) Peter Drucker (b) Chris Argyris
(c) Keith Davis (d) William H. Whyte

112. Who can be a counsellor?

(a) Who can do the counselling.
(b) Supervisors in a formal organisation.
(c) Specialists.
(d) Professional counsellors.

113. What is the role of supervisors as counsellors in a formal organisation?

(a) Supervisors have direct contact with the employees and therefore they are in a better position to manage all minor emotional problems.

(b) Supervisors will be able to manage the mental health of the employees working directly under them.

(c) Supervisors will be able to tackle appropriately mental situations as they are the immediate superiors of the employees.

(d) Supervisors can also understand the seriousness of problems that require professional counselling and refer the same accordingly.

114. Who is specialist counsellor?

(a) One, who is technically qualified and expert in the field.

(b) Experts in the fields of HRM, Social Welfare, Legal and doctors.

(c) Emotional problems normally involve some technical aspects in individual's job.

(d) All the above.

115. Who can be called a professional counsellor?

(a) One, who is trained in psychology (Psychologist) and deals with emotional upsets and behavioural pattern of the individual.

(b) A psychiatrist, who can treat mental disorders of people ON and OFF the job.

(c) Who has taken the counselling as his profession.

(d) Who can advise the management to look after the proper mental health of its employees.

116. What do you understand by the counselling role of a manager?

(a) Manager of a formal organisation normally interact with his subordinates in day to day work and he will be able to understand the emotional problems.

(b) Manager is the person, who tries to resolve the problem, as soon as it comes to his notice.

(c) All problems have objective facts and emotional contents to a certain extent.

(d) A manager can carry out all functions of counselling except reorientation for which he may refer to a professional counsellor.

JOB SATISFACTION

117. What is meant by job satisfaction?

(a) This refers to an individual's feeling of satisfaction on the job, which induces to do the work.

(b) It is not synonymous with organisational morale.

(c) It is a behavioural pattern of an individual or a group.
(d) All the above.

118. "Job satisfaction is the favourableness or unfavourableness with which employees view that work." Who said this?
(a) Keith Davis.
(b) Calvin Coolidge,
(c) Hersey Blanchard,
(d) None of the above.

119. Is there a correlation between job satisfaction and one's life satisfaction?
(a) This relationship can either be positive or negative.
(b) If a person is satisfied at home and in his social life, he is normally satisfied with his job also.
(c) Any management cannot continue job satisfaction at all times, it requires regular review and maintenance.
(d) At times, it may be seen that all employees may be dissatisfied with their family and social lives leading to an average job satisfaction level.

120. What are the major factors governing job satisfaction?
(a) Characteristics of the individual.
(b) Characteristics of the work.
(c) Attitude of the management.
(d) Environmental factors.

121. What is performance standars?
(a) Whatt activities are to be perfomed.
(b) It makes explicit quality and quantity of performance.
(c) They are logical expression of job description.
(d) All the above.

122. What is meant by job characteristics?
(a) Higher the level of job, greater is the job satisfaction.
(b) If job contents are having variation, the job satisfaction will also change.
(c) Social interaction and working conditions.
(d) Compensation and promotional avenues.

123. How does social interaction affect job satisfaction?
(a) An employee's interaction with skilled workers in performing a job may improve his performance and lead to job satisfaction.
(b) If the supervision is of poor standard, it may affect the performance of an ordinary employee.
(c) For achieving organisational goal, an employee need to cooperate with other employees. His involvement in job and with coworkers is vital.
(d) None of the above.

124. What is the intrinsic aspect of job?
(a) It is the intrinsic value of job.
(b) Intrinsic value of job differs from individual to individual.
(c) Intrinsic value differs the same way as that of job satisfaction.
(d) An expert skilled worker may have dissatisfaction if there is low job requirement.

125. How does job satisfaction depend on the nature and the situation?
(a) There are a number of factors viz., economical, social and environmental, etc., that contribute to job satisfaction.
(b) Wage may be important to one person, whereas others may prefer job security.
(c) Working conditions in an organisation need to be conducive.
(d) All the above.

126. What role does job satisfaction play to improve morale of workers?
(a) Job satisfaction is one of the important factors that help improve morale standard.

(b) Job satisfaction involves many factors like wage, supervision, working conditions, job security, promotion, working hours so on and so forth.

(c) Apart from job related factors, individual's group relationship outside the work environment is of vital importance that contributes to job satisfaction.

(d) All the above.

127. What job satisfaction does an employee seek?

(a) Recognition as an individual.

(b) An opportunity for advancement and job security.

(c) Proper compensation and satisfactory working conditions.

(d) Efficient leadership, proper work ethos and organisational environment.

128. What is the relationship between productivity and job satisfaction?

(a) Job satisfaction and productivity depend upon management techniques.

(b) A satisfied employee may be a high or low producer.

(c) In many cases, job satisfaction and productivity are interrelated.

(b) Both influence each other

129. What advantage does one get by study of job satisfaction?

(a) It gives an indication of general job satisfaction level of an organisation.

(b) Workers' attitude towards management.

(c) It improves communication level in the organisation.

(d) Survey can also indicate the need for training programmes.

130. What kind of job satisfaction surveys are conducted in an organisation?

(a) Objective surveys.

(b) Subjective surveys.

(c) Descriptive surveys

(d) Projective surveys.

131. What is meant by an objective survey?

(a) Objective type of questionnaire is prepared with multiple choice answers.

(b) The respondents have to select the answer, which is nearest to the feeling as correct.

(c) They have to tick mark the right answer.

(d) Multiple answers are normally prepared by the management.

132. What does the descriptive survey indicate?

(a) In this, management prepares the questions.

(b) Employees are given opportunity to give answers in a descriptive way.

(c) Questions are of 'Direct' and 'Indirect' type.

(d) All the above.

133. What is projective survey?

(a) It is meant for interpreting job satisfaction.

(b) The tests are prepared for personality probe.

(c) These tests are developed by Psychiatrist to find out the mental health of an individual.

(d) All the above.

134. How are the data of job satisfaction survey used by the organisation?

(a) Apprising the concerned personnel.

(b) Interpretation of data for further necessary action by the management.

(c) Results of such data are to be made available to all concerned personnel for their appropriate action.

(d) All the above.

135. What is frustration?

(a) It is opposite to job satisfaction.

(b) A state of effectiveness to achieve the goal.

(c) An outcome of a motive drive being blocked and unable to reach the desired goal by an individual.

(d) All the above.

HUMAN RELATIONS

136. What is human relation

(a) It is the integration of people in work situations.

(b) Human relation is the medium through which the employees and organisation mutually cooperate to achieve more productivity.

(c) Human relation seeks to emphasise employees' aspects of work rather than technical or economic aspects.

(d) Human relations try to make employment and working conditions less impersonal.

137. Human relations is the integration of people into work situation, in that it motivates them to work together productively, cooperatively and with economic psychological and social satisfaction." Who said this?

(a) Mc Ferland, B.E. (b) Kaith Davis

(c) Robert R. Blake (d) Peter Drucker

138. What is the principle or philosophy of human relations?

(a) Employers should ,as far as possible, provide economic security to their employees to a maximum extent.

(b) Cooperation of employees to be won in productive process without any duress.

(c) Proper personnel policies and practices must be followed to safeguard the rights, interests and welfare of the employees, stockholders, consumers and members of the society.

(d) All the above.

139. What are the different approaches to human relation?

(a) Fear and punishment or hard approach.

(b) Reward and soft or weak approach.

(c) Carrot and stick approach.

(d) Path goal approach.

140. What is meant by fear and punishment approach?

(a) In this use of coercion and threat, close supervision and strict control of personnel is involved.

(b) People work for the sake of money.

(c) People work only to the required standard so as not to lose the job.

(d) None of the above.

141. What is reward, soft or weak approach?

(a) People work expecting some reward.

(b) For getting better work, motivation and good relations with the employees are required.

(c) It is assumed that people are motivated to work to the extent they are rewarded.

(d) In case of excessive motivation, it leads to disadvantageous situation.

142. What does carrot and stick approach refer to?

(a) This is a motivation technique used to reward the people, if they show improvement in work and if the work is not of the required standard, the rewards are withheld.

(b) This approach is successful as long as the employee struggles for subsistence.

(c) It is ineffective, when an individual is satisfied with his primary needs.
(d) All the above.

143. What is meant by path goal approach?
(a) This approach is the one in which employees' needs are sufficiently high and the goal is prominent to achieve.
(b) According to this, people work hard to attain the desired goal.
(c) An individual, in such an approach, must be free from all barriers to follow the desired path.
(d) All the above.

144. What is the objective of human relations in an industry?
(a) Human relation is an area of management that is concerned with integration of people in work situation.
(b) It is a study of methods through which both the individuals and organisational goals can be achieved.
(c) All principles of human relations are based on the primacy of the individual himself.
(d) Human relation stands in the forefront of management thinking.

145. What is meant by industrial relations?
(a) Industrial relations can only be based on human relations.
(b) A fair dealing and concern for human beings, their physical and social needs.
(c) It is also concerned with determination of wages and conditions of employment.
(d) Industrial and human relations are distinctly two indispensable factors in industry.

146. What is the basic requirement of a good industrial relation?
(a) In any organisation good relations between the management and the workers depend upon mutual confidence.
(b) Development of good industrial relations is a good labour policy.
(c) The aim of industrial policy should be to secure the best possible cooperation of employees.
(d) All the above.

147. What are the basic needs of an industrial worker?
(a) The needs of an industrial worker are freedom of fear, security of employment and freedom of wants.
(b) Adequate food, better health, clothing and housing are human requirements.
(c) An environment in which the labourer is contended with his job.
(d) All the above.

148. What are the objectives of Industrial relations?
(a) Good industrial relation means presence of industrial peace and to secure industrial cooperation.
(b) Prejudices, provincialism etc., have no place where good industrial relations prevail.
(c) To have industrial peace, the employees must be provided with fair wages, good working conditions, reasonable working hours, holidays and required minimum amenities of life.
(d) None of the above.

149. How to foster industrial relations (IR)?
(a) The employer, Human resource manager, the individual employee, Trade unions and Government play a significant role in fostering and maintaining good industrial relations.
(b) Various labour laws prescribe the minimum requirements of protection, safety, health and security of the workers, made statutory obligations on the part of employers.
(c) It is the duty of management to safeguard an individual's work

satisfactorily and satisfying part of his life.

(d) A good employer is always ahead of law.

150. What is the role of an Industrial manager?

(a) Work is an important part of development for human efficiency.

(b) An individual being social, finds his main aspects of satisfaction of life in association with others at his work place.

(c) Progressive form of industrial management is based on democratic methods.

(d) Through cooperation of workers maintenance of good industrial relations is the basic aim.

INTROSPECTION

"The bright prospects of approach to human relation is related to infinite potential of human mind."

ANSWERS

1 (b) and (d)
(b) It is a process through which all forms of information from one person to another are transferred.
(d) It covers any type of behaviour resulting in an exchange of meaning.

2 (c) All means whereby meaning can be conveyed from one individual to another.

3 (c) Dale S. Beach

4 (d) All the above
(a) Promotional of managerial efficiency, cooperation, thorough understanding.
(b) Basis for leadership action and means of coordination.
(c) Provision of job satisfaction.

5 (a) Clarity, attention and integrity.

6 (a), (b) and (c)
(a) Sender or originator of communication and coding.
(b) Transmitting channel.
(c) Receiving, decoding and destination.

7 (b) An individual, speaking, writing, gesturing, telecasting, newspaper, organisation, etc.

8 (b) and (c)
(b) System of words, letters or symbols used to keep secrecy or brevity in communication of messages.
(c) Normally the source first encodes the message as per its requirement.

9 (b) Language or word symbols are most potent tool of communication.

10 (a) and (b)
(a) Facial expression and gestures.
(b) Signals other than language are used in a complex-way to indicate feelings and attitudes.

11 (a) When the recipient receives the message in a code-language, it is made intelligible.

12 (a), (b) and (c)
(a) Recipient's prior knowledge of the situation and beliefs.
(b) Attitude and language.
(c) Cultural background and group affiliations.

13 (a) and (b)
(a) Upward communication and downward communication.
(b) Lateral or diagonal communication.

14 (b) The information flowing from subordinate to superior, may be in written or oral form.

15 (b) Superiors to subordinates in the form of direction, orders, etc., relevant to the work.

16 (a) and (b)
(a) Different heads of the departments of an organisation coordinate their work through lateral communication.
(b) It is a good process of effecting coordination in any organisational set up.

17 (c) The route through which a communication flows from sender to the recipient.

18 (a), (b) and (c)
(a) Principles of clarity, attention and consistency.
(b) Principles of adequacy, integration and time.
(c) Principles of informality and feedback.

19 (c) Message should be clear, communicated in a simple language and easily understood by the recipient.

20 (c) Recipient's attention to the message communicated is completely drawn to the communication to be effective.

21 (b) Communication must be consistent with policies and objectives of the organisation.

22 (a) Communication should be proper and self-contained.

23 (c) It should be based on the policy of integration of efforts of people for better cooperation and understanding.

24 (a) Information to be communicated at the most appropriate time to have the desired result.

25 (c) Politeness and informality bring better results when you communicate in business, while dealing with customers.

26 (c) The recipient should acknowledge the communication/message and transmit the action taken to the communicator.

27 (a), (b), (c) and (d)

(a) Formal and informal

(b) Oral and written

(c) Downward and Upward

(d) Horizontal.

28 (b) A formal communication derives its support from the scalar chain system of an organisation.

29 (c) This communication is more direct, unofficial, spontaneous and flexible in nature.

30 (b) It is a communication with spoken words.

31 (a) and (b)

(a) All types of advertisements are one-way communication.

(b) In this, the sender finishes his responsibility as soon as he transmits his information to other.

32 (d) All the above.

(a) This type of communication has the advantage of feedback system.

(b) It can clarify any doubt of the receiver.

(c) Interaction of a teacher and students in classroom establishes proper feedback of communication.

33 (c) Sender, transmission, receiver and feedback.

34 (a) and (c)

(a) Semantic, psychological, organisational barriers.

(c) personal and mechanical barriers.

35 (d) This denotes barriers of language and symbols and their interpretation.

36 (a), (b), (c) and (d)

(a) Premature evaluation and inadequate attention.

(b) Transmission losses and poor retention. Undue stress on written message.

(c) Lack of trust in the sender by the receiver and failure to communicate.

(d) Psychological state of mind of the sender, as well as that of the receiver makes lot of difference.

37 (d) All the above

(a) Restriction imposed by the rules of the organisation.

(b) Status, hierarchial position restraining the flow of communication.

(c) complex-structure of the organisation.

38 (a), (b) and (c)

(a) Attitude of superiors and insistence on following proper channel.

(b) Lack of confidence in subordinates and preoccupation of superiors.

(c) Lack of awareness and hesitation to communicate.

39 (a), (b) and (c)

(a) Inadequate infrastructural arrangements.

(b) Poor office layout and use of wrong medium.

(c) Defective procedures and practices.

40 (d) All the above

(a) Restructuring the organisation.

(b) Promoting upward communication for creative innovations.

(c) Proper follow-up, feedback and by adopting parallel channels.

41 (a), (b), (c) and (d)

(a) Be aware of common obstacles for gaining proper understanding.

(b) Understand the process of emphatic listening.

(c) Convey meaning to others.

(d) Get feedback confirmation.

42 (a) While listening emphatically, a person opens the way for another to talk freely his ideas and feelings without justifying each of his statements.

43 (a), (b), (c) and (d)

(a) Attend to the meaning and content of the message.
(b) Listen to idea of the message and identify the main point.
(c) Take notes and use possible recording schemes of the message recording.
(d) Avoid quick judgement, look for areas of interest in the message, and wait till the message is complete.

44 (a). (b). (c) and (d)
(a) Establish eye to eye contact.
(b) Exhibit affirmative expressions.
(c) Avoid distractive actions during listening.
(d) Paraphrase what is understood by listening.

45 (b) Louise Allen.

46 (a), (b), (c) and (d)
(a) Listen patiently what the other person has to say. Try to understand his feelings and what the person is expressing. The factual contents. Repeat the feelings but accurately.
(b) Allow time for discussion to continue without any interruption.
(c) Avoid direct questions, arguments about facts and refrain from comments like- 'That is not correct etc'.
(d) Do not get emotionally involved, try simply to understand first and defer evaluation until later.

47 (d) All the above
(a) Make sure that you want to communicate and use proper language.
(b) Use adequate medium and also listen attentively. Communication is a two-way process.
(c) Ensure that your actions do not contradict your communication. Improve your skills in oral and written communication.

48 (a), (b), (c) and (d)
(a) It is a sort of informal communication.
(b) It is quite fast and spontaneous having a good amount of credibility.
(c) At times, the information transmitted is distorted, when it is passed onto many people in the group.
(d) This channel is used as a supplement to formal channel of communication.

49 (d) All the above.
(a) The gap occurs between the sender and the receiver of the communication.
(b) This is due to simple presumption of mutual understanding.
(c) Merely because the speaker presumes that he has spoken and the one at the other end has heard.

50 (a) Perception differs with individual's awareness of his environment as well as past experiences.

51 (a) and (b)
(a) It is concerned with theory and practice of communication.
(b) In this, one can experience interaction between people.

52 (b) This indicates passing of orders and instructions to subordinates and obedience and coordination are expected in all activities.

53 (c) In this, employees can have horizontal communication between them and their peers, who are part of the informal work group and have vertical upward communication with the managers.

54 (b) It is felt that proper interaction and communication can create sound and firm relationship between work group and sub-units of the organisation.

55 (b) An ego state is a coherent system of feelings and behaviour pattern.

56 (d) All the above
(a) An ego state which resembles of parental figure (Parental ego).
(b) An ego state which is directed towards an objective appraisal of reality (Adult ego)
(c) An ego state which represents childhood (child ego).

57 (b) Words, gestures, facial expressions, tone of voice, feeling expressed and behaviour are clues to ego state in which

a person is operating at a given time.

58 (b) A stroke is the sign of recognition which all social beings invariably seek.

59 (a) Stroke may be a positive or a negative one.

60 (a) Transaction may be simple or complex depending upon the ego state from which the transactional stimulus or transactional response originates.

61 (a), (b), (c) and (d)

(a) Simple transaction is of two kinds- complementary and crossed.

(b) When a transactional stimulus originates in one ego state and the transactional response in the corresponding ego state, the transaction is complementary.

(c) It can be between Adult to Parent and Parent to Child and Child to Adult in a parallel way.

(d) Crossed transaction is when a transactional stimulus originates in one ego state and the transactional response does not come from a corresponding ego state.

62 (c) Face to face interaction includes transactional analysis and group dynamics (people interact in group).

63 (a) and (d)

(a) Characteristics of positive attitude may be called as the asset of a group dynamic.

(d) Committee meeting, group decision, collective problem solving and group therapy are the indexes of group prosperity.

64 (a), (b), (c) and (d)

(a) Groups do exist, and they are ubiquitous (omnipresent).

(b) Group mobilises powerful forces.

(c) Group may produce good or bad consequences.

(d) Group dynamics permit desirable consequences.

65 (c)

(c) Any new addition to a group may bring change the very structure of the group. It may also affect the attitude, feeling and behaviour of other members of the group (good or bad).

66 (b) Biological nature, language, capacity and environment are different factors which make a man to live in group.

67 (b) and (d)

(b) Evidences show that members of high cohesive groups have less problems than the less cohesive ones.

(d) Cohesive groups provide support to their members and group membership provides satisfaction to the individual which result in reducing the anxiety.

68 (d) In order to remove the lacunae in consequences one must emphasise alike both the positive and negative aspects.

69 (b) Organisational meetings refer to committees, conferences, and other groups where face to face discussions on various workers' problems concerning the group in the organisation take place.

70 (a) and (b)

(a) Participation improves group performance.

(c) Helps to promote creative thinking.

71 (b) Members attend the meeting, however, at times they do not get what is expected of it.

72 (a) Meetings are not productive enough to cater the requirements of all the people.

73 (c) A small group of people interacting regularly.

74 (a) Kaith Davis.

75 (a), (b) and (c).

(a) Process team

(b) Goal team

(c) Sequential team

76 (c) Members are having the cooperation in

such a way that they interact effectively. Among them is a formal leader, whereas their relations are informal.

77 (c) All members of the team will be allotted their work according to their capacities so as to achieve the team goal in a specific time-frame.

78 (b) The work of a group is distributed amongst the members of its team, according to the sequence of work.

79 (c) Communication within the management group is called management communication or intramanagement communication.

80 (d) All the above

(a) It is the prerequisite to employee communication.

(b) Necessary for good decisions and with greater scope of managerial influence.

(c) Links in communication chain are within the management group and self-communication of management group for better knowledge about the policies of organisation.

81 (d) All the above.

(a) Committees and conferences

(b) Written communication like-newsletters, bulletins and special booklets, etc.

(c) Organising conferences on various matters, projects and policies of organisation and subjects connected to development and progress.

82 (c) and (d)

(c) Informal organisations cannot be identified through organisation charts. They have their own system of interaction and communication network to protect the interest of their members.

(d) Authority and leadership in an informal organisation are earned from a number of groups. Informal organisation has a powerful influence over productivity and job satisfaction.

83 (d) All the above.

(a) It is a product of human interaction at work place.

(b) it satisfies the human needs of working in a group.

(c) It shares common ides and values communicating in familiar language and protecting group interest.

84 (a), (b) and (c)

(a) Informal organisation is a part of total organisation.

(b) It develops from habits, contacts, and customs of social group.

(c) It usually try to remain small not prominent and unstable.

85 (d) All the above.

(a) Informal organisation arises from social interaction.

(b) Informal leadership.

(c) Role of informal leader.

86 (a), (b) and (c)

(a) Stability to work group, influence on the productivity and job satisfaction.

(b) It is social structure to meet personal needs of its members.

(c) It is a useful channel of communication.

87 (a) and (b)

(a) There is possibility of a clash between objectives of formal and informal organisations.

(b) It may act , at times, on mob psychology and as such it can create difficulties for formal organisation.

88 (a) and (b)

(a) Perpetuation of cultural values and satisfaction of individual needs.

(b) Source of informal communication.

89 (a), (b) and (c)

(a) Resistance to change

(b) Role conflict

(c) Spreading of rumours.

90 (b), (c) and (d)

(b) Grapevine information may be oral or written or by observation.

(c) Information received through this medium may be 100% correct or entirely false.

(d) The communication that could not be communicated efficiently may be sent to this channel for wide circulation.

91 (b), (c) and (d)

(b) When there is excitement and insecurity about job.

(c) When our friends and associates are involved in the situation.

(d) If it is not a news or a stale information, research shows that the greatest spread of information takes place immediately after it becomes known.

92 (a), (b) and (c)

(a) It has tremendous capacity to carry information.

(b) It moves speedily.

(c) It has unusual ability to penetrate even the top most company security cordons.

93 (a), (b) and (c)

(a) Grapevine provides the manager required feedback. He can seek support of the employees through grapevine.

(b) It is a good way to know the reaction of people and also groups and persons may be persuaded.

(c) It is useful for trade unions.

94 (b) and (c)

(b) Due to its fast speed, at times, information is unheard or misinterpreted, while spreading it.

(c) Leakage of any important and confidential information with regard to organisation may prove disastrous.

95 (a) and (c)

(a) Rumour is the most undesirable feature of grapevine.

(c) Rumour is the product of over enthusiasm and ambiguity of situation.

96 (a), (c) and (d)

(a) Make all possible efforts to prevent spreading of rumours.

(c) Any serious rumours to be stopped immediately and the measures undertaken for corrective actions.

(d) If the employees' union does have a strong informal leadership, necessary cooperation can be sought.

97 (d) Main purpose of counselling is to understand or decrease an employees emotional disorder.

98 (d) All the above.

(a) proper advice and reassurance.

(b) Release of emotional tension and communication.

(c) Clarified thinking and reorientation.

99 (a) It is the method of giving courage to the employee to face a problem.

100 (b) A good counsellor, who is sympathetic to the counselee's problem, can easily relax his tension.

101 (c) In clarified thinking, counsellor does not advise what is right but he encourages the individual to accept the reality for emotional problem and to be more rational in solving the problem.

102 (a) It brings a change in the employee's psychological aspects through a change in basic goals and values.

103 (a) Kaith Davis

104 (a) All the above

(a) Frustration

(b) Conflicts

(c) Stress

105 (a), (c) and (d)

(a) Directive counselling.

(c) Cooperative counselling

(d) Non-directive counselling.

106 (d) All the above.

(a) The counsellor patiently listens the emotional problem of the employee.

(b) The counsellor decides with the employee what to do and further motivates the employee to do so.

(c) The counsellor takes an active part in discussing every aspect of the problem and helps to arrive at a conclusion.

107 (b) It is a type of counselling in which the counselee is important and not the counsellor.

108 (d) All the above
(a) It is much time consuming.
(b) It is not economical to implement.
(c) It is client oriented.

109 (a), (b), (c) and (d)
(a) Methods followed in counselling
(b) Responsibility of solving the problem.
(c) Status (to be maintained).
(d) Role (to be carried out).

110 (a) It is an integration of both type of counselling.

111 (c) Keith Davis

112 (b), (c) and (d)
(b) Supervisors in a formal organisation.
(c) Specialists.
(d) Professional counsellors.

113 (a) and (d)
(a) Supervisors have direct contact with the employees and therefore they are in a better position to manage all minor emotional problems.
(d) Supervisors can also understand the seriousness of problems that require professional counselling and refer the same accordingly.

114 (a) One, who is technically qualified and expert in the field.

115 (a) One, who is trained in psychology (Psychologist) and deals with emotional upsets and behavioural pattern of the individual.

116 (a) and (d)
(a) Manager of a formal organisation normally interact with his subordinates in day to day work and he will be able to understand the emotional problems.
(d) A manager can carry out all functions of counselling except reorientation for which he may refer to a professional counsellor.

117 (a) This refers to an individual's feeling of satisfaction on the job, which induces to do the work.

118 (a) Keith Davis.

119 (b) If a person is satisfied at home and in his social life, he is normally satisfied with his job also.

120 (a) and (c)
(a) Characteristics of the individual.
(c) Attitude of management.

121 (c) They are logical expression of job description.

122 (a), and (b)
(a) Higher the level of job, greater is the job satisfaction.
(b) If job contents are having variation, the job satisfaction will also change.

123 a) An employee's interaction with skilled workers in performing a job may improve his performance and lead to job satisfaction.

124 a) It is the intrinsic value of job.

125 a) There are a number of factors viz., economical, social and environmental, etc., that contribute to job satisfaction.

126 b) Job satisfaction involves many factors like wage, supervision, working conditions, job security, promotion, working hours so on and so forth.

127 a), b), c) and d)
(a) Recognition as an individual.
(b) An opportunity for advancement and job security.
(c) Proper compensation and satisfactory working conditions.
(d) Efficient leadership, proper work ethos and organisational environment.
Explanation (d) : As for leladership, it has a paramount role to play in an organisastion. One would definitely love to work under a dynamic and effficient leader-as the adage goes. *"It is alwlays better to be in the group of sheep led by a lion rather than be in the group of lions led by a sheep."* Other aspects have their own priorities.

128 (a) Job satisfaction and productivity depend upon management techniques.

129 (a) It gives an indication of general job satisfaction level of an organisation.

130 (a), (c) and (d)
(a) Objective surveys.
(c) Descriptive surveys
(d) Projective surveys.

131 (a) and (b)
(a) Objective type of questionnaire is prepared with multiple choice answers.
(b) The respondents have to select the answer, which is nearest to the feeling as correct.

132 (d) All the above.
(a) In this, management prepares the questions.
(b) Employees are given opportunity to give answers in a descriptive way.
(c) Questions are of 'Direct' and 'Indirect' type.

133 (d) All the above.
(a) It is meant for interpreting job satisfaction.
(b) The tests are prepared for personality probe.
(c) These tests are developed by Psychiatrist to find out the mental health of an individual.

134 (a) Apprising the concerned personnel.

135 (c) An outcome of a motive drive being blocked and unable to reach the desired goal by an individual.

136 (c) Human relation seeks to emphasise employees' aspects of work rather than technical or economic aspects.

137 (b) Kaith Davis.

138 (a) and (c)
(a) Employers should ,as far as possible, provide economic security to their employees to a maximum extent.
(c) Proper personnel policies and practices must be followed to safeguard the rights, interests and welfare of the employees, stockholders, consumers and members of the society.

139 (a), (b), (c) and (d)
(a) Fear and punishment or hard approach.
(b) Reward and soft or weak approach.
(c) Carrot and stick approach.
(d) Path goal approach.

140 (a) In this use of coercion and threat, close supervision and strict control of personnel is involved.

141 (b) and (d)
(b) For getting better work, motivation and good relations with the employees are required.
(d) In case of excessive motivation, it leads to disadvantageous situation.

142 (a) This is a motivation technique used to reward the people, if they show improvement in work and if the work is not of the required standard, the rewards are withheld.

143 (b) and (c)
(b) According to this, people work hard to attain the desired goal.
(c) An individual, in such an approach, must be free from all barriers to follow the desired path.

144 (a) Human relation is an area of management that is concerned with integration of people in work situation.

145 (b) A fair dealing and concern for human beings, their physical and social needs.

146 (a) In any organisation good relations between the management and the workers depend upon mutual confidence.

147 (a) The needs of an industrial worker are freedom of fear, security of employment and freedom of wants.

148 (a) Good industrial relation means presence of industrial peace and to secure industrial cooperation.

149 (c) It is the duty of management to safeguard an individual's work satisfactorily and satisfying part of his life.

150 (d) Through cooperation of workers maintenance of good industrial relations is the basic aim.

◆◆◆◆◆

CHAPTER - 7

- ***INFLUENCE AND POWER IN ORGANISATIONS***
- ***ORGANISATIONAL CULTURE***
- ***INDUSTRIAL PLANNING***
- ***CONCEPTS OF ORGANISATIONAL BEHAVIOUR (OB)***
- ***STRESS MANAGEMENT***
- ***CONCEPTS OF HUMAN RESOURCE ACCOUNTING SYSTEM***

FEATURES :

- Influence and power in organisations
- Concept
- Basis of influence
- Legitimacy of influence and power in an organisation
- Coercive power
- Expert power
- Charismatic power
- Right to privacy
- Consistent policy
- Organisational culture
- Concept
- Characteristics
- Pattern of culture
- Role of custom in organisation
- Cultural dimensions
- Action learning
- Cultural change
- Role of technology
- Industrial planning concept
- Characteristics
- Nature
- Industrial policy
- Concepts of organisational behaviour (OB)
- Characteristics of OB
- Historical background
- OB research methods
- Tackling of management problems
- Social system in organisations
- Challenges of work force
- Global perspective
- Multiple regression technique
- Theories of OB
- Kelley's theory
- Corporate behaviour
- Role measurement
- Behavioural self-management
- Multinational corporations
- Globalisation
- Stress management
- Concept and forms of stress
- Stages of stress
- Causes Role pressure in stress
- Concepts of human resource accounting system
- Control of cost on man-power

KEY NOTE

Influence and power in organisation

Influence is a process that a person tries to take advantage of compliance with his intention from other individuals. It is necessary for having an effective influence that two parties must be in continuous and dependable relationship between each other.

Power, in other words, is an ability to influence others behaviour. Power occurs, when an individual induces force on other person to mould his behaviour according to his desire.

Organisational culture

It can be viewed as a cognitive set up having values, attitudes, behavioural aspects and aspirations shared by members in an organisation. When these norms and values are established once, they are bound to be stable and exert influence on organisation and its members.

Industrial planning

Industrial planning is an organised and planned effort in the field of industry. Planning is the persistent effort to maximise the available resources to meet the need of growing population. Thus, industrial planning is the maximum and organised use of human resource and material available in an industry.

Concepts of organisational behaviour

Organisational behaviour is the systematic analysis of people, group and organisations. It aims at production and enhances their performance and that of the organisation in which they work. How people behave in formal organisation is the subject matter of organisational behaviour. There are four elements viz., (i) people, (ii) technology, (iii) structure and (iv) social system.

Stress management

Stress at work is unavoidable, because thought process is required for job performance. Stress is nonspecifically induced, which means that it develops from many different environmental factors and spreads effect of each, which is difficult to isolate. According to Prof. Robbins, stress is a condition in which an individual is confronted with an opportunity, constraint or demand, related to what he or she desires and for which the outcome is perceived to be both uncertain and important. When one is exposed to stress, several psychological changes like a' tremendous alarm' reaction followed by a stage of resistance do occur and finally if stress persists, exhaustion and the individual fails to cope with the stress due to lack of physical ability to withstand the stress -condition.

Human resource accounting system

This is the system, which evaluates and accounts for the value of human resource. It is a computerised data processing system used by the modern organisations. It provides adequate data to enable the management to control and monitor utilisation of human resource. This system can easily store and retrieve the information like various categories of personnel, skilled and unskilled workers and where they are deployed, cost of procurement of man-power, training and development, career planning and also wastage of productive man-hours, etc. This system can help the management to save man-power and optimum utilisation in various departments. Also, it can give proper account of absenteeism and turnover. If properly installed, this system can adequately update and utilise the data available for optimum resource planning at a future date.

QUESTIONS

INFLUENCE AND POWER IN ORGANISATIONS

1. **What is influence?**
   (a) A process of inducement
   (b) To respond in an intended way
   (c) When two persons react with each other for settlement
   (d) A process by which an individual extracts the compliance with his intentions from others.

2. **What is meant by the bases of influence in an organisation?**
   (a) Psychological contact
   (b) Legitimate authority
   (c) Use of power
   (d) None of the above.

3. **What is meant by legitimacy of organisational influence?**
   (a) Conformity to organisational norms by the members of the organisation in action or by thought.
   (b) Legitimacy to organisation by workers in avoiding conflicts.
   (c) Organisation must confirm through its policies and systems to maintain unified action towards objectives.
   (d) In an organisation legitimacy is confirmed by managers, unions and the work force.

4. **What do you understand by legitimate authority?**
   (a) Legitimate authority is embedeed in the psychological contract and a supervisor can expect subordinates to comply accordingly
   (b) It refers to whether or not, the person, who is the subject of influence.
   (c) It is normally reflected in the structure of an organisation.
   (d) All the above.

5. **What is power in an organisation?**
   (a It is a force that can be used to extract compliance.
   (b) Power can be used to achieve sanctioned processes of the organisation.
   (c) People often comply power, when it is exercised by legitimate authority.
   (d) None of the above.

6. **What is coercive power?**
   (a) Coercive power is used to extract information from a person.
   (b) Normally, it is used, when the norms of the organisation are not adhered to.
   (c) Coercive means to force obedience by power.
   (d) When one person has control over reward deserved by another.

7. **What is expert power?**
   (a) Expert power is the very task and the person oriented.
   (b) Experts normally have the power of decision making in their specification.
   (c) Expert power usually takes time to develop in an individual.
   (d) We rely on the recommendations of experts.

8. **What is charismatic power?**
   (a) Power has the capacity to inspire enthusiasm and devotion.
   (b) When individuals are susceptible to influence by other person.
   (c) It is based on the feeling of oneness that a person has with another.
   (d Charismatic power cannot be

transformed from one person to another.

9. What does legitimacy of an individual in an organisation indicate?

(a) Workers' behaviour towards work and organisation.

(b) High legitimacy is mainly non-job related like family relationship, place of residence and religion and political affiliation.

(c) High legitimacy always correlates with the organisational management and about union activities.

(d) All the above.

10. Why do people need organisation?

(a) Organisation provides many opportunities and resources to an individual.

(b) It fulfils socio-economic goals of individuals.

(c) Organisation needs people, without whom the very existence is suspicious.

(d) The goals of an individual and organisation differ from each other, but they are not necessarily describable.

11. "An analysis of basic properties of relatively mature human beings and formal organisation lead to the conclusion that there is an inherent incongruence between the self-actualisation of the two. The basic congruency create a situation of conflict, frustration, failure and loss of self-esteem" Who said this?

(a) Maslow

(b) Argyris

(c) Calvin Coolidg

(d) Urwick

12. What is the right to privacy in the organisation?

(a) Private opinions, views, and motives of an individual.

(b) This refers to the employees' privacy, psyche and non-organisational activities.

(c) It is said, it is part of an individual's own inner-self and is not subject to analysis for getting or losing the job.

(d) All the above.

13. What is infringement on privacy?

(a) Privacy is the right of every individual and encroachment on it is considered as undesirable.

(b) Secret observation such as unknown surveillance.

(c) Infringement on privacy may be justified by the authorities on compelling reasons.

(d) None of the above.

14. What is the role of management in maintaining the discipline?

(a) Management should frame the rules and regulations and also penalties for their violation.

(b) Employees' consent to the rules and regulations to be obtained through their unions.

(c) Rules should be positive in nature and management fairly consistent and flexible in maintaining discipline.

(d) All the above.

15. What is meant by consistent policy of organisation?

(a) Policy is based on consistent action for similar offence.

(b) It cannot be deviated according to situations.

(c) It must secure a better labour management relation.

(d) All the above.

16. What is known as flexible policy of an organisation?

(a) Policy which can be adaptable to different circumstances.

(b) Flexible policy does not mean inconsistency with basic standards of discipline.

(c) A flexible interpretation should be allowed to establish standards of conduct for compromise.

(d) All the above.

17. What can be the comparison of consistent and flexible policy?

(a) Consistent and flexible policies are two extremes of the problem.

(b) One is strict rules and the other is special consideration.

(c) In compromise between the rules should be defined accordingly.

(d) Flexibility should be adopted within the framework of the organisation.

ORGANISATIONAL CULTURE

18. What is culture?

(a) Culture consists of manifestation of human behaviour.

(b) Culture is man made.

(c) All the ways of doing and thinking of as group.

(d) Behaviour of man is not constant, as it changes with the change of place and time.

19. "Culture is the totality of group ways of thoughts and action duly accepted and followed by a group of people." Who said this?

(a) Gillin and Gillin (b) A.F. Walter Paul, (c) Mac Iver (d) Petaer Drucker

20. What are the characteristics of culture?

(a) Culture is a learned behaviour as opposed to natural one.

(b) Culture is social heritage.

(c) It is normally linked with the past.

(d) It is embodiment of refinement.

21. What is the pattern of culture?

(a) It develops trait by trait or to say itemwise.

(b) Interrelation and interaction of complexes of traits in a given society determines its pattern.

(c) The pattern of culture is traceable to the very beginning of human society.

(d) All the above.

22. What is the functional role of culture in business?

(a) It emphasises the role of a vision that gives organisation a momentum leading to organisational success.

(b) Culture is the combination of behavioural pattern that creates the norms of interpersonal behaviour pattern.

(c) Culture in reality encompasses the total behavioural pattern of a group of people with regard to cultural changes, or evolving new dimensions in a changing environment.

(d) None of the above.

23. "Culture as a set of fundamental assumptions and beliefs about reality that are shared by as group of individuals that are working towards common purpose." Who said this?

(a) Schein (b) Tries and Beyer (c) J.L. Massie (d) D.R.Hampton

24. How can an organisation develop culture within?

(a) Managers should distinguish between how they want the people to behave and the organisational objectives, policies to adhere.

(b) Actual values and the behavioural pattern the employees should adopt to help bring the desired change.

(c) Organisational strategy and the

policies cannot remain for ever in a changing technical, social and cultural scenario.

(d) In an internal organisational change, people within have to alter both their social structure and personal views.

25. What is the role of customs in the organisation?

(a) One has to observe the customs and rules for understanding the culture.

(b) People heavily depend on customs and habits to understand the behaviour.

(c) Organisations have standard customs for absorbing new employees through their beneficial programmes; work customs are expected roles of each employee.

(d) All the above.

26. What is organisational culture and managing change?

(a) When people interact, their behavioural regularities, language, customs, differences and demeanor need to be observed.

(b) Cultural norms are learned and taught through various formal and informal ways in the organisation.

(c) Important values of the organisation are product quality and price, etc.

(d) All the above.

27. What are the cultural dimensions that affect in managing change?

(a) Personal values, attitudes and beliefs

(b) Rewards and punishments.

(c) The way decisions are made and informal information are passed onto others.

(d) None of the above.

28. What are the factors that require attention to design a well-integrated management structure in an organisation?

(a) Well-integrated planned structural approach.

(b) Organisational relationship amongst people.

(c) Proper attention with regard to human needs of the organisation.

(d) Flexibility of the management in making adjustments on required basis.

29. What are the major psychological factors involved in a structural change?

(a) Learning

(b) Confidence

(c) Misapprehensions and confusions.

(d) All the above.

30. Why does the mass or group learning required for successful change programme?

(a) To improve interpersonal skills.

(b) Susceptibility of employees to behavioural change.

(c) Changing the management process.

(d) Altering the behviour of people in the organisation.

31. What is meant by organisational change analysis?

(a) Changed programmes are undertaken with specific action research.

(b) Survey feedback is an action research.

(c) Action research provides initial motivation and progress to change for improvement.

(d) All the above.

32. What is organisational change methods?

(a) Team building

(b) Positive reinforcement programme.

(c) Management by objectives and high involvement organisational strategies.

(d) None of the above.

33. What are the main characteristics of organisational culture?

(a) Assumptions and values, sharing of perception, risk taking and management attitude.

(b) Employees' inclination, team building and competitiveness.

(c) Stability and structure.

(d) All the above.

34. What is meant by types of culture?

(a) Organisations have different forms of cultural levels with distinctive features.

(b) Functional

(c) Descriptive

(d) Perceptual

35. What is detrimental to progress of culture?

(a) All types of cultural barriers are detrimental to the progress.

(b) If the organisational culture is not changed according to the environment, it will adversely affect the organisational growth and progress.

(c) Dynamic culture improves the effectiveness of organisation.

(d) The cave culture inhibits acceptance of changes.

36. How is the culture learned?

(a) Through instructions

(b) Written records and relevant stories

(c) Rituals, language and material symbols.

(d) None of the above.

37. "Culture is the realm of final valuations and human beings must interpret the whole world, including their own devices, techniques and power in the light of their valuations." Who said this?

(a) Mc Clelland

(b) Mc Iver and Page

(c) M. Bond

(d) Hofstede, G.

38. What are the objectives of group learning that need to be understood?

(a) Understanding inadequacies of interpersonal skills.

(b) Acquire effective interpersonnel strategies.

(c) Provisioning of job learning process and reinforcement of already learned methods.

(d) All the above.

39. What is known as action learning?

(a) Any type of learning becomes easier when the theory and practical are carried out simultaneously.

(b) Action learning has higher acceptance amongst the management trainees, because it involves learning by doing.

(c) This approach in training programme is not easy to implement.

(d) None of the above.

40. How to implement culture in new organisation?

(a) In the new organisation, managers try to implement self-sufficient culture to support high performance.

(b) It has the advantage of cost that may be lower due to less direct supervision.

(c) Workers' morale and satisfaction to be made higher and also absenteeism and turnover to be reduced.

(d) All the above.

41. Why are some organisations distinguished with their cultural values?

(a) Understanding the needs of customers and employees.

(b) Freedom to innovate ideas.

(c) Free to communicate and willingness to take risks.

(d) None of the above.

42. Why and how does the organisational culture change?

(a) The world in which organisations operate often change.

(b) External forces like market conditions, new technology, and Government policies change over a period of time.

(c) Change is essential for development.

(d) All the above.

43. What is the main role of technology in an organisation?

(a) It being the physical as well as mental process creates input into usable output.

(b) All automated equipment used in industrial and other places are examples of technological device.

(c) Technology creates the behaviour of people in effective functioning of the organisation.

(d) Technology makes an important external face in the modern organisation.

44. What is the impact of automation?

(a) It makes workers efficient in their performance.

(b) Reduces the work force to perform routine jobs.

(c) It is cost effective.

(d) All the above.

45. What are the consequences of organisational culture?

(a) Organisational culture is associated with successful performance of an organisation.

(b) Voluntary turnover of individuals is related to organisational culture.

(c) Organisational culture is like to change due to factors like-change in composition of work force, planned change, merger and acquisition, etc.

(d) None of the above.

INDUSTRIAL PLANNING

46. What is industrial planning?

(a) In this modern era, there is persistent effort to maximise the utilisation of available resources to meet the needs of on-growing population.

(b) Attempts are also made to check and control the population.

(c) National phenomenon is governed by natural laws but in the sphere of human activity control and planning is very essential.

(d) None of the above.

47. "Economical planning is a system under which the enlightened experts after planning make a prior survey of resources, make the critical decisions as to what should be produced and where. Moreover, they decide as to how and among whom should it be distributed." Who said this?

(a) B. Wooton

(b) H.D.Dickson

(c) Peter Drucker

(d) Robins Stephen, P.

48. What are the characteristics of industrial planning?

(a) It is a continuous process and coordination of human aspect.

(b) Maximum use of economic means.

(c) It has to be carried out by specialised professionals.

(d) All the above.

49. What is the nature of industrial planning?

(a) It has two aspects, the theoretical and practical with direct and indirect goals.
(b) It makes use of scientific methods.
(c) Jobs are either eliminated or changed into new jobs.
(d) All the above.

50. What is the industrial policy of India?
(a) This visualises a mixed economy with an overall responsibility of Government for planned development of industries in the national interest.
(b) This policy was announced in 1948 after independence of India.
(c) Under this policy, two categories of industries have been made through Schedule-'A' and Schedule-'B'.
(d) All the above.

CONCEPTS OF ORGANISATIONAL BEHAVIOUR (O(B)

51. What is organisational behaviour?
(a) Applying the scientific methods to practical management problems.
(b) It mainly deals with analysis of individual, groups and organisation.
(c) How people do behave in formal organisation.
(d) It coordinates the work and people.

52. What is significant characteristics of OB?
(a) It enhances the betterment of human resources.
(b) OB controls the problems of work force diversity.
(c) It has global perspective.
(d) It attempts to improve people-organisation relation.

53. "From the administrative point of view, organisation behaviour seeks to improve the people-organisation relationship in such a way that people are motivated to develop teamwork that effectively fulfils their needs and achieve organisational needs." Who said this?
(a) Leonardo da Vinci (b) Keith Davis
(b) E.F.L. Breck (d) B.F. Skinner

54. How will you identify a modern organisation?
(a) It involves huge investment, complicated technology and sophisticated machinery.
(b) System of working and mutually agreed purpose.
(c) Systematic division of labour and assignment of authority.
(d) Adaptation and mutual interaction.

55. What do you mean by organisationai behaviour- system?
(a) Constitution of internal social system by people. It is the study of human action in an organisation.
(b) Structure created by relationship of the people in the organisation.
(c) Tecchnology imparts physical and economic conditions within which the people work.
(d) Social system provides environment in which the organisation operates.

56. What are the important concepts of OB?
(a) OB is based on certain fundamental concepts.
(b) Human dignity and individual differences.
(c) The concept of whole person and motivation.
(d) All the above.

57. What is the historical background of OB?
(a) Scientific management.
(b) Human relation movement.
(c) Classical organisation theory
(d) None of the above.

58. What are the methods followed for the study and research on OB?
(a) Theory
(b) Survey research
(c) Experimental research
(d) Quantitative researach.

59. What are the main characteristics of OB?
(a) Understand the dynamic nature of an organisation.
(b) Face the challenges of work force diversity.
(c) Visualise the well-being of human resources.
(d) All the above.

60. What is organisational behaviour management?
(a) Adapting positive reinforcement in the organisation to elicit desirable organisational behaviour.
(b) To enforce discipline at work place.
(c) Manage the human resource to attain the desired behaviour pattern.
(d) Encourage positive and negative reinforcement programmes.

61. What are the different points to be considered by the management for organisational behaviour modification programme?
(a) Exactly pin-point the required programme to be followed.
(b) Undertake a survey as to how people respond to behaviour they wish to change.
(c) Adopt a time-bound programme
(d) All the above.

62. Is it possible to discourage undesirable behaviour through disciplinary action?
(a) Punishment is resorted to eliminate undesirable organisational behaviour.
(b) Systematic way, if punishments are awarded to undesirable behaviour it may lead to positive results.
(c) A system of progressive discipline is ideal in organisation to discourage undesirable behaviour.
(d) None of the above.

63. What is the criterion followed to award punishment?
(a) Award the punishment to delinquent at the earliest after occurrence of undesirable response.
(b) Administer moderate punishment in a progressive manner.
(c) Award of punishment should always be dispassionate.
(d) All the above.

64. How the managerial problems are tackled by OB?
(a) The knowledge of OB depends on behavioural sciences.
(b) OB develops the knowledge base through empirical and research oriented programme.
(c) Scientific orientation is the standard adopted by OB.
(d) All the above.

65. Why is it significant to study behaviour in organisational settings?
(a) Social scientists always study human behaviour in organisational settings.
(b) Knowledge acquired from scientific studies can bring better results in practical applications.
(c) Organisational function and quality of life is improved by OB.
(d) OB can be used in scientific methods to arrive at general behaviour pattern in an organisation.

66. What are the levels of analysis used in OB?

(a) Individual
(b) Groups
(c) Organisations
(d) Environment

67. What is social system in an organisation?

(a) Informal groups are formed in an organisation.
(b) Social system influences jobs in many ways.
(c) It can be taken as a set of values and relations that interacts.
(d) All the above.

68. How will you define the organisation, as an open system?

(a) It operates in a self-sustaining manner.
(b) It transforms inputs into output in a continuous manner.
(c) These outputs get transformed back to inputs in a cyclical manner.
(d) All the above.

69. What is future of organisations?

(a) In the early twentieth century, there was a change from agriculture economy to manufacturing economy.
(b) Now (in the 21st century), we have electronic devices that can store and transmit information quite fast to distant locations.
(c) These machines have created more job opportunities and one can work with more creative jobs.
(d) Future organisations will be more in technical nature and small sized.

70. What are the challenges confronted by work force in diversity?

(a) Changes in work force and behavioural pattern at work place in an organisation.
(b) Community life and characteristics of work force have been changing in the past and such change have been the study process of OB continuously.
(c) Goal achievement behaviouar that emerges from work force leads to better performance.
(d) All the above.

71. What is meant by global perspective of organisation?

(a) Comparative nature in economy determines global perspective of organisation.
(b) Assuming unicultural nataure of organisations, it seems to be difficult.
(c) The challenges in the field of economy that our nation faces are different from other nations.
(d) OB has its own applicability all over the globe.

72. What is the main source of OB?

(a) Economic stability of an organisation.
(b) Scientific management study.
(c) Rapid industrialisation and technological change.
(d) All the above.

73. Who did identify the inefficient working practices of employees in the industrial set-up?

(a) Peter Drucker
(b) Bakke, E.W.
(c) F.W. Taylor
(d) Keithi Davis

74. Who is the author of the book, Scientific Management?

(a) Taylor, F.W.
(b) Maslow
(c) Mintzberg, H.
(d) Weber, J.

75. Peter Drucker described, "The first man who did not work for granted, but looked at it and studied it." Who is this?

(a) Robbins P. Stephen
(b) F. W. Taylor

(c) Koontz and O'Donnell
(d) Mintzberg

76. Who made 'the time and motion study approach in scientific mangement?'
(a) F. W. Taylor
(b) Lisa A. Mainiero
(c) Victor H. Varoom
(d) Frank and Lillian Gilberth

77. What are the methods adopted for understanding the behaviour in an organisation?
(a) It is a fact that a large number of researches confirm things already believed to be correct.
(b) If we cannot trust our own beliefs, then the scientific methods take over to analyse the facts of belief.
(c) OB is strongly based on research carefully conducted to establish the facts.
(d) All the above.

78. Is 'theory' an essential ingredient of OB research?
(a) OB is a part of an applied science.
(b) Theory describe the relationship between concepts.
(c) When theory has been made, its prediction is tested through direct research.
(d) When theory does not conform to research, it is either modified, related or rejected completely.

79. What is correlation coefficient method in research?
(a) It contains relation of variables.
(b) Measurement of variables.
(c) Association of variables can be either positive or negative.
(d) Researchers depend upon estimation of relationship, a statistics known as correlation.

80. What is multiple regression technique?
(a) Researchers may be able to tell the possibility to each of different variables subscribed in predicting the particular behaviour.
(b) The complex nataure of human behaviour at work site.
(c) Researchers usually use the OB, multiple regression technique in their respective fields.
(d) None of the above.

81. What are the main elements of organisational behaviour system?
(a) Philosophy and goals and system controls.
(b) Formal and informal organisations.
(c) Social environment, attitudes and situation.
(d) Human relation factors.

82. How the organisational climate is measured?
(a) There are a number of instruments that have been developed for this purpose
(b) Litwin and Stringer's approach
(c) Lickert's scale.
(d) All the above.

83. What are the main ingredients of organisational climate?
(a) System concept
(b) Supportive approach
(c) Its relation with situational variables
(d) Interaction.

84. Why is the organisational climate considered an important factor in management?
(a) For its impact on motivation, productivity and job satisfaction.
(b) It has an unforeseen relationship with organisation.
(c) It projects the overall social system of work group.
(d) It directs the behavioural pattern.

85. What are the theories of organisational behaviour?

(a) Autocratic theory of model
(b) Custodial theory
(c) Supportive theory
(d) Collegial theory.

86. What is autocratic model?

(a) Those who are in power, use dictatorship for ruling.
(b) Employees are to obey the orders of their superiors, otherwise they will be punished.
(c) The theory assumes that management only knows what is right and what is wrong.
(d) All the above.

87. What is meant by custodial model?

(a) Custodial model makes the employees dependable in the organisation.
(b) The model follows the programme of economic reward to employees.
(c) Security of job and organisational dependence are also the specialities of this model.
(d) It provides maintenance factors of motivation.

88. What is collegial model?

(a) This model is based on the principles of mutual contribution of employer and employees.
(b) Each employee should feel that he is a part and parcel of the organisation.
(c) Management supports the employees' job performance.
(d) Employees feel responsible to the organisation and the society at large.

89. What is supportive model?

(a) This model mainly motivates the employees to work.
(b) Management supports the job performance and not the employee.
(c) It emulates a feeling of participation and involvement in organisational work
(d) This model is very effective in organisation, where complex and modern technologies are used.

90. How to evaluate the different models of OB?

(a) The assumptions could be of specific goals; what is expected of people is motivation for hardwork and people's performance at high level.
(b) None of the models is the best for all time, as needs do change.
(c) Models are related to hierarchy of human needs.
(d) All the above.

91. What popular research method is used in OB?

(a) Scientific research method.
(b) Qualitative research method
(c) Experimental research method
(d) All the above.

92. What is experimental method of OB?

(a) This method is popularly used in OB.
(b) This is based on 'Cause and effect' method.
(c) Understanding the casual connections between variables that lead to knowing the causes and effects of behaviour.
(d) None of the above.

93. What is meant by naturalistic observation?

(a) An observation naturally made by an investigator.
(b) It is a qualitative research technique used for observation of events.
(c) A researcher with the help of qualitative technique observes events occurring and making an effort not to affect them, even if they are present in the process of investigation.
(d) All the above.

94. What is known as dependent variables?

(a) An independent variable is systematically analysed by the investigator to find out its dependable nature.

(b) A dependent variable is the behaviour of interest exhibited that is being measured by the investigator.

(c) A behaviour that is an independent variable.

(d) None of the above.

95. What is the 'time and motion' study?

(a) A study carried out with regard to performance of individuals.

(b) A type of applied research, famous in the early twentieth century, was to classify the individuals movement to carry out the job.

(c) The time and motion study was used by the followers of scientific management.

(d) Gilberths have modified the principles of scientific management.

96. What is Kelley's theory of casual attribution?

(a) A process, through which people try to establish the causes of others' behaviour.

(b) It is a process involving the judgement of people's behaviour.

(c) Casual attribution has three ingredients-consensus, consistency and distributiveness.

(d) All the above.

97. What is behavioural response to managerial controls?

(a) Understanding the significance of employees' acceptance

(b) Setting attainable standards of performance at all levels.

(c) Knowing the feedback within the behavioural control system.

(d) All the above.

98. How to decentralise control without loss, while delegating?

(a) Each time, when a manager delegates work to his subordinate, creates a problem of knowing whether the work is performed satisfactorily.

(b) Delegation invariably raises the question of proper control.

(c) In decentralisation, the manager usually depends on how far he can deacentralise without losing the control.

(d) When a manager delegates a large measure of planning, he need not lose control, if he is ready to change his existing system of direct control.

99. What is social loafing phenomenon?

(a) Any combined operation by people.

(b) Work performed by more than one individual.

(c) More individuals who are contributing to a big task, the less each individual's contribution to be to the work task or additive task.

(d) All the above.

100. "From the administrative point of view, OB seeks to improve the people-organisation relationship in such a way that people are motivated to develop team work that effectively fulfil their needs and achieve organisational objectives." Who said this?

(a) Kaith Davis (b) Cohen, R.

(c) Mc Clelland (d) Adler, N.J.

101. What are the essential features of effectively managing an organisation?

(a) Knowledge about organisation.

(b) People as personality perception.

(c) Groups, their relations and development.

(d) Management process.

102. What is meant by corporate behaviour?

(a) Behaviour is governed by individual, group and structure..

(b) Corporate behaviour includes

perception, learning, personality and motivation at individual level.

(c) It is the behaviour of personnel in a corporate environment.

(d) This creates better performance and more job satisfaction to employees.

103. What is the significance of individual behaviour in corporate environment?

(a) Individual behaviour is socially and psychologically conditioned for creating the employees capable of better performance.

(b) All individuals are properly oriented to have a common behaviour in the organisation.

(c) Job behaviour is very essential for individual performance in an organisation.

(d) Individual behaviour is modified after analysing the problems related to achievement of goal.

104. What is structural behaviour?

(a) It is mainly influenced by the different type of structures, line and functional organisations.

(b) The design of structures has different impact on behaviour.

(c) Social responsibility and accountability have attributed to behavioural dimensions.

(d) All the above.

105. Why is the stress on corporate behavioural modification given in modern management?

(a) The role of environment is accountable in corporate behaviour.

(b) Corporate behavioural modification is an essential factor in human resource development.

(c) Perception, learning and personality development make the basic for behavioural modification.

(d) The following factors like identification, measurement, analysis, evaluation and intervention techniques are useful methods for behavioural modification.

106. What is the important identification in behavioural modification?

(a) In behavioural modification the initial action is identification of various problems.

(b) Immediate supervisor of an employee who knows the job can correctly identify the critical behaviour.

(c) The immediate supervisor can execute the modification process efficiently.

(d) All the above.

107. What role does the measurement play in behavioural modification?

(a) Certain standards are used to find out the critical behaviour.

(b) Measurement standard is an indicator for subjective evaluation.

(c) Comparison in frequencies of measured data that reveals the critical behaviour of each employee.

(d) All the above.

108. What is the purpose of analysis in the behavioural modification?

(a) Functional analysis is usually carried out after a primary observation, counting, checking of personal records and various attributes.

(b) Critical behaviour affecting performance is always analysed.

(c) Causes and consequences of behaviour are analysed to infer proper behaviour for getting the desired results.

(d) Critical behaviour is a function of consequences.

109. What is the need of intervention in behavioural modification?

(a) It prevents people from undesirable behaviour.

(b) Desirable alternative behaviour is positively reinforced for replace undesirable behaviour.

(c) It is applied to strengthen and accelerate the desirable behaviour.
(d) There are mainly two types of intervention--positive and negative reinforcement.

110. How evaluation is carried out in behavioural modification?

(a) Accountability, effectiveness, and productivity, etc., are applied to measure performance behaviour.
(b) Corporate behaviour modification is evaluated at frequent intervals to make it effective.
(c) Behavioural modification is evaluated through reaction, learning, behavioural change and performance improvement methods.
(d) All the above.

111. What is self-management of behaviour?

(a) It involves one's introspection and self-modification.
(b) It creates positive thinking, development of will power and self-motivation.
(c) Success of self-management depends on one's ability to manage the antecedents (Stimuli).
(d) All the above.

112. What is the important strategy of self-management?

(a) It controls emotions.
(b) Directs mental process to arrive at correct conclusion.
(c) Stimuli strategies, attention to strategies, recognition and consequences are enhanced.
(d) All the above.

113. What is the role of cognitive process in the consequence of behavioural process?

(a) The mental process translates the stimuli into behaviour.
(b) Stimuli, attention and recognition.
(c) Translation, forming the behaviour.
(d) All the above.

114. What is the culture difference affecting managing practice?

(a) Performance of work procedures in one country may be a failure in some other country.
(b) The differences are the customs and practices and the religious diversity and beliefs.
(c) Individualistic beliefs are always seen in all cultures, especially business 'pay off' are routine in all transactions.
(d) In the above.

115. What is multinational corporation?

(a) They perform in a larger perspective globally; produce and sell the products in various countries.
(b) Multinational corporations acquire the markets with latest products and services.
(c) They have the competitive spirit with other firms globally.
(d) All the above.

116. What are the well-known dimensions of Hofestede with regard to culture and work place?

(a) It must influence thinking and behaviour.
(b) It should influence managing institutes.
(c) Power distance and uncertainty avoidance.
(d) Individualism and masculinity.

117. What is globalisation?

(a) International business activity.
(b) Future economic success of business enterprises depends upon how effectively they meet demands of foreign companies.
(c) Disappearance of political boundaries of a country in the financial and industrial activity.
(d) All the above.

118. "On political map the boundaries between countries are as clear as ever. But on the competitive map, a map showing the real flows of financial and industrial activity, those boundaries have largely disappeared. Today, however, the pressure of globalisation is driven not so much by diversification or competition as by the needs of customers. Their needs have globalised and the fixed costs of meeting them have soared. That is why we must globalise." Who said this?

(a) Walter, R.E.
(b) Ghani, A.H.
(c) Kenicki Ohamae
(d) Vip, G.S.

119. How can a company achieve international competitiveness?

(a) Nature of competitive advantage differs amongst industries at international level.
(b) A marketing plan which can make international appeal.
(c) Employees' knowledge on global focal point of companies.
(d) Selection of right partners and avoidance of mistakes committed by others.

120. What is the reason for globalisation?

(a) Desire to exploit new markets.
(b) Companies took bold steps to cross natural boundaries.
(c) Some business firms, due to quest of lower factor of costs like wage, raw materials and emerging better opportunitaies.
(d) None of the above.

121. Do ethical values differ across the country?

(a) Ethical differences are significant.
(b) Ethical beliefs lack theoretical or conceptual understanding.
(c) Cross cultural studies related to cross cultural issues show definite variation across the natural boundaries.
(d) one of the above.

122. What is the functional role of culture?

(a) Culture is a topic influenced by both in business and management studies apart from psychology and cultural anthropology.
(b) It is a set of fundamental values by a group of people and are reflected in their behaviour.
(c) It is a set of fundamental assumptions and belief.
(d) Culture makes it possible for a group to improve and put together the responses to inputs from the environment that becomes a threat to its survival.

123. How is organisational culture created?

(a) The founders of any organisation possess certain values and visions that may lead to creation of culture.
(b) Organisational culture develops from the experience and external environment.
(c) Organisational culture may develop through contact between groups and individuals within the organisation.
(d) All the above.

STRESS MANAGEMENT

124. What is stress?

(a) Stress is condition in which a person is faced with constraint and strains.

(b) A discomfort of an individual.
(c) Stress does not have a negative impact at all times.
(d) Stress becomes a troublesome affair for an employee.

125 "Stress is a condition in which an individual is confronted with an opportunity, constraint or demand related to what he or she desires and for which the outcome is perceived to be both uncertain." Who said this?
(a) Robbins,
(b) R.L.Khan,
(c) Oliver L. Niehouse and Karen B Massoni
(d) None of the above.

126. What are the different forms of stress?
(a) Constructive stress.
(b) Destructive stress,
(c) Role ambiguity
(d) Transition related stress.

127. What is constructive stress?
(a) It is positive manner action for the benefit of the individual and organisation.
(b) Low and moderate form of stress can act in a constructive manner.
(c) Moderate type of stress can increase stimulative creativity, care and effort in one's work.
(d) All the above.

128. What is distractive stress?
(a) It is not suitable for the individual and organisation
(b) These are effects that are beyond the tolerance of individuals.
(c) These type of stress can lead to breakdown of mental and physical strength of an individual.
(d) It creates dissatisfaction and leads to shortfall in performance.

129. What are the prominent signs and symptoms of stress?
(a) Prolonged worry and nervous tension.
(b) Problems of rise in blood pressure.
(c) Emotional imbalance, mental and physical disorders.
(d) All the above.

130. What are the stages of stress?
(a) Alarming stage of body system.
(b) Development of resistance that leads to other complications in the body system.
(c) Individual develops frustration, uneasiness and conflictive feeling.
(d) Natural resistance of the body fails (natural immunity) and the individual feels exhausted and fatigued.

131. What are the causes of stress?
(a) Organisational factors.
(b) Environmental factors.
(c) Individual and group factors.
(d) None of the above.

132. What are the effects of stress?
(a) A low level stress is not very harmful to an individual but it may improve performance.
(b) Psychological
(c) Physical
(d) Behavioural.

133. What are symptoms of stress?
(a) Physical (b) Social
(c) Psychological (d) Behvioural

134. What are the organisational factors that contribute to the source of stress?
(a) Some jobs are stressful than others.
(b) Role conflict
(c) Interpersonal relationship, lack of proper communication.
(d) Responsibility, change in job.

135. What are the personal factors that contribute to stress?
(a) Traumatic experience of life.

(b) Death of near and dear ones and problems in the family.

(c) Change in responsibilities of job.

(d) Fired by the superior.

136. What is the behavioural impact of stress?

(a) Stress always changes the normal behavioural pattern of an individual.

(b) People under stress may not be able to control their physical and mental balance.

(c) People under stress need to avoid tension; for this they take alcohol, drugs and keep themselves aloof from others.

(d) They become moody, lazy and irritative also.

137. How to overcome stress?

(a) Physical exercise, self-control.

(b) Practising relaxation and meditation to reduce tension on body and mind.

(c) Change life style through modification; practise Yoga regularly and proper physical exercise.

(d) All the above.

138. What does the organisation provide to reduce the tension on employees?

(a) Job designing, goal setting.

(b) Develop career plans by reducing conflicts.

(c) Provide healthy organisational climate.

(d) Counselling employees and recreational facilities.

139. "Burn out is a state of fatigue or frustration brought out by devotion to a cause, way of life or relationship that failed to produce expected reward." Who said this?

(a) H.J. Frendenberger,

(b) R.L. Khan,

(c) Oliver L. Niehouse

(d) Hans Selye

140. What is occupational factor of stress?

(a) Certain jobs are more stressful than others.

(b) Blue collar workers are more likely to have job related stress.

(c) Those who work on routine jobs have high level of stress problems like tension, anxiety, depression, irritation than others.

(d) All the above.

141. What is the role of pressure in stress?

(a) It happens in an organisation to the extent of role conflict and role ambiguity.

(b) This occurs where pressures persist to comply with different and inconsistent demands.

(c) If one complies with a demand, it is difficult to comply with other demands.

(d) None of the above.

142. What is the role of ambiguity in stress?

(a) It is a type of role problem.

(b) An uncertainty about work requirements.

(c) Responsibility is not clear because of vague job description.

(d) Lack of professional experience.

143. What connection does self-esteem have with stress?

(a) Self-esteem is the way an individual look upon and evaluates himself.

(b) One's own concepts can have effect on one's performance and also one responds to stress factors.

(c) Self-esteemed people possess confidence.

(d) They know their capabilities and act accordingly in any situation.

144. How does a person with high-ability is susceptible to stress?

(a) It is less likely that a person will experience with role overload.

(b) Persons with high ability are aware of their upper limit.
(c) They are normally able to assess their possibility of success in stress situations.
(d) All the above.

CONCEPTS OF HUMAN RESOURCE ACCOUNTING SYSTEM

145. What is human resource accounting system?
(a) Human resource is the most important asset of an organisation.
(b) Expenses incurred in recruitment, training and development of employees are charged against the income of the organisation for a specified accounting period yearly.
(c) It is an audit system of human.
(d) None of the above.

146. Why does an organisation require human resource accounting system?
(a) It enables the organisation to have information with regard to human resource activities and the cost involved for the same.
(b) Monitor whether human resources are having the added values or depreciation over a period of time.
(c) It enables the management to conduct various management activities in accordance with its financial capacity.
(d) All the above.

147. How to control the cost of man-power in an organisation?
(a) By application of MBO system.
(b) Reduction of cost in human resource recruitment, training etc.
(c) Control cost of turnover.
(d) Keeping the priority in maintaining optimum level of man-power in all organisational activities.

148. What is human resource information system?
(a) It is a method adopted by the organisation to collect information on the analysis of people and their jobs.
(b) Data based system provides information about employees.
(c) A comprehensive data based system is unavoidable for better functioning of an organisation.
(d) All the above

149. What is the purpose of human resource information system in an organisation?
(a) To provide continuous information of people and their jobs with properly safeguarding the confidentiality.
(b) It is a cost effective data bank.
(c) To provide personal privacy of information
(d) Security of the information with regard to business activities.

150. Why Human Resource Information System (HRIS) is essential for an organisation?
(a) To avoid loss of man-power, which is time consuming and costly.
(b) While transfer of data from one record to another, it may lead to errors and confusions and also maintenance of records.
(c) To centralise the information at one place in an organisation for ready reference.
(d) A computerised information system is convenient for ready reference at all times.

INTROSPECTION

"While understanding Organisational Behaviour (OB), one has to consider the process of changes happening within people, groups and in organisations."

ANSWERS

1(d) A process by which an individual extracts the compliance with his intentions from others.

2 (a), (b) and (c)
(a) Psychological contact
(b) Legitimate authority
(c) Use of power

3(a) Conformity to organisational norms by the members of the organisation in action or by thought.

4 (a) and (c)
(a) Legitimate authority is embedeed in the psychological contract and a supervisor can expect subordinates to comply accordingly
(c) It is normally reflected in the structure of an organisation.

5 (c) People often comply power, when it is exercised by legitimate authority.

6 (a) Coercive power is used to extract information from a person.

7 (a), (b) and (c)
(a) Expert power is the very task and the person oriented.
(b) Experts normally have the power of decision making in their specification.
(c) Expert power usually takes time to develop in an individual.

8 (a) Power has the capacity to inspire enthusiasm and devotion.

9 (b) High legitimacy is mainly non-job related like family relationship, place of residence and religion and political affiliation.

10 (b) It fulfils socio-economic goals of individuals.

11 (b) Argyris

12 (b) This refers to the employees' privacy, psyche and non-organisational activities.

13 (a) Privacy is the right of every individual and encroachment on it is considered as undesirable.

14 (d) All the above
(a) Management should frame the rules and regulations and also penalties for their violation.
(b) Employees' consent to the rules and regulations to be obtained through their unions.
(c) Rules should be positive in nature and management fairly consistent and flexible in maintaining discipline.

15 (d) All the above
(a) Policy is based on consistent action for similar offence.
(b) It cannot be deviated according to situations.
(c) It must secure a better labour management relation.

16 (a) Policy which can be adaptable to different circumstances.

17 (d) Flexibility should be adopted within the framework of the organisation.

18 (a) Culture consists of manifestation of human behaviour.

19 (b) A.F. Walter Paul

20 (a) Culture is a learned behaviour as opposed to natural one.

21 (b) Interrelation and interaction of complexes of traits in a given society determines its pattern.

22 (c) Culture in reality encompasses the total behavioural pattern of a group of people with regard to cultural changes, or evolving new dimensions in a changing environment.

23 (a) Schein

24 (a) and (b)

(a) Managers should distinguish between how they want the people to behave and the organisational objectives, policies to adhere.
(b) Actual values and the behavioural pattern the employees should adopt to help bring the desired change.

25 (d) All the above
(a) One has to observe the customs and rules for understanding the culture.
(b) People heavily depend on customs and habits to understand the behaviour.
(c) Organisations have standard customs for absorbing new employees through their beneficial programmes; work customs are expected roles of each employee.

26 (d) All the above
(a) When people interact, their behavioural regularities, language, customs, differences and demeanor need to be observed.
(b) Cultural norms are learned and taught through various formal and informal ways in the organisation.
(c) Important values of the organisation are product quality and price, etc.

27 (a), (b) and (c)
(a) Personal values, attitudes and beliefs
(b) Rewards and punishments.
(c) The way decisions are made and informal information are passed onto others.

28 (b), (c) and (d)
(b) Organisational relationship amongst people.
(c) Proper attention with regard to human needs of the organisation.
(d) Flexibility of the management in making adjustments on required basis.

29 (d) All the above
(a) Learning
(b) Confidence
(c) Misapprehensions and confusions.

30 (a), (b) and (d)
(a) To improve interpersonal skills.
(b) Susceptibility of employees to behavioural change.
(d) Altering the behviour of people in the organisation.

31 (c) Action research provides initial motivation and progress to change for improvement.

32 (a), (b) and (c)
(a) Team building
(b) Positive reinforcement programme.
(c) Management by objectives and high involvement organisational strategies.

33 (a) Assumptions and values, sharing of perception, risk taking and management attitude.

34 (b), (c) and (d)
(b) Functional
(c) Descriptive
(d) Perceptual

35 (a) All types of cultural barriers are detrimental to the progress.

36 (a), (b) and ((c)
(a) Through instructions
(b) Written records and relevant stories
(c) Rituals, language and material symbols

37 (b) Mc Iver and Page

38 (d) All the above
(a) Understanding inadequacies of interpersonal skills.
(b) Acquire effective interpersonnel strategies.
(c) Provisioning of job learning process and reinforcement of already learned methods.

39 (b) Action learning has higher acceptance amongst the management trainees, because it involves learning by doing.

40 (c) Workers' morale and satisfaction to be made higher and also absenteeism and turnover to be reduced.

41 (a), (b) and (c)

(a) Understanding the needs of customers and employees.
(b) Freedom to innovate ideas.
(c) Free to communicate and willingness to take risks.

42 (b) External forces like market conditions, new technology, and Government policies change over a period of time.

43 (c) Technology creates the behaviour of people in effective functioning of the organisation.

44 (a) and (b)
(a) It makes workers efficient in their performance.
(b) Reduces the work force to perform routine jobs.

45 (a) and (c)
(a) Organisational culture is associated with successful performance of an organisation.
(c) Organisational culture is like to change due to factors like-change in composition of work force, planned change, merger and acquisition, etc.

46 (a) In this modern era, there is persistent effort to maximise the utilisation of available resources to meet the needs of on-growing population.

47 (b) H.D. Dickson

48 (a) and (b)
(a) It is a continuous process and coordination of human aspect.
(b) Maximum use of economic means.

49 (d) All the above
(a) It has two aspects, the theoretical and practical with direct and indirect goals.
(b) It makes use of scientific methods.
(c) Jobs are either eliminated or changed into new jobs.

50 (a) This visualises a mixed economy with an overall responsibility of Government for planned development of industries in the national interest.

51 (a) and ((c)
(a) Applying the scientific methods to practical management problems.
(c) How people do behave in formal organisation.

52 (a) and (b)
(a) It enhances the betterment of human resources.
(b) OB controls the problems of work force diversity.

53 (a) Leonardo da Vinci

54 (a), (b) and (c)
(a) It involves huge investment, complicated technology and sophisticated machinery.
(b) System of working and mutually agreed purpose.
(c) Systematic division of labour and assignment of authority.

55 (a) (a) Constitution of internal social system by people. It is the study of human action in an organisation.

56 (b) and (c)
(b) Human dignity and individual differences.
(c) The concept whole person and motivation.

57 (a) Scientific management.

58 (a), (b), (c) and (d).
(a) Theory
(b) Survey research
(c) Experimental research
(d) Quantitative researach.

59 (d) All the above
(a) Understand the dynamic nature of an organisation.
(b) Face the challenges of work force diversity.
(c) Visualise the well-being of human resources.

60 (a) Adapting positive reinforcement in the organisation to elicit desirable organisational behaviour.

61 (b) Undertake a survey as to how people respond to behaviour they wish to change.

62 (c) A system of progressive discipline is ideal in organisation to discourage undesirable behaviour.

63 (d) All the above
(a) Award the punishment to delinquent at the earliest after occurrence o undesirable response.
(b) Administer moderate punishment in a progressive manner.
(c) Award of punishment should always be dispassionate.

64 (b) and (c)
(b) OB develops the knowledge base through empirical and research oriented programme.
(c) Scientific orientation is the standard adopted by OB.

65 (c) Organisational function and quality of life is improved by OB.

66 (a), (b) and (c)
(a) Individual
(b) Groups
(c) Organisations

67 (c) It can be taken as a set of values and relations that interacts.

68 (a) It operates in a self-sustaining manner.

69 (d) Future organisations will be more in technical nature and small sized.

70 (b) Community life and characteristics of work force have been changing in the past and such change have been the study process of OB continuously.

71 (a) Comparative nature in economy determines global perspective of organisation.

72 (b) Scientific management study.

73 (c) F.W. Taylor

74 (a) F.W. Taylor

75 (b) F. W. Taylor

76 (d) Frank and Lillian Gilberth

77 (c) OB is strongly based on research carefully conducted to establish the facts.

78 (c) and (d)
(c) When theory has been made, its prediction is tested through direct research.
(d) When theory does not conform to research, it is either modified, related or rejected completely.

79 (d) Researchers depend upon estimation of relationship, a statistics known as correlation.

80 (a) Researchers may be able to tell the possibility to each of different variables subscribed in predicting the particular behaviour.

81 (a), (b) and (c)
(a) Philosophy and goals and system controls.
(b) Formal and informal organisations.
(c) Social environment, attitudes and situation.

82 (b) and (c)
(b) Litwin and Stringer's approach
(c) Lickert's scale.

83 (a), (b) and (c)
(a) System concept
(b) Supportive approach
(c) Its relation with situational variables.

84 (a) For its impact on motivation, productivity and job satisfaction.

85 (a), (b), (c) and (d)
(a) Autocratic theory of model
(b) Custodial theory
(c) Supportive theory
(d) Collegial theory.

86 (a) Those who are in power, use dictatorship for ruling.

87 (a) Custodial model makes the employees dependable in the organisation.

88 (a) This model is based on the principles of mutual contribution of employer and employees.

89 (a) This model mainly motivates the employees to work.

90 (a) The assumptions could be of specific goals; what is expected of people is motivation for hardwork and people's performance at high level.

91 (c) Experimental research method.

92 (b) This is based on 'Cause and effect' method.

93 (c) A researcher with the help of qualitative technique observes events occurring and making an effort not to affect them, even if they are present in the process of investigation.

94 (b) A dependent variable is the behaviour of interest exhibited that is being measured by the investigator.

95 (b) A type of applied research, famous in the early twentieth century, was to classify the individuals movement to carry out the job.

96 (c) Casual attribution has three ingredients- consensus, consistency and distributiveness.

97 (d) All the above
(a) Understanding the significance of employees' acceptance
(b) Setting attainable standards of performance at all levels.
(c) Knowing the feedback within the behavioural control system.

98 (d) When a manager delegates a large measure of planning, he need not lose control, if he is ready to change his existing system of direct control.

99 (c) More individuals who are contributing to a big task, the less each individual's contribution to be to the work task or additive task.

100 (a) Kaith Davis

101 (a), (b) and (c)
(a) Knowledge about organisation.
(b) People as personality perception.
(c) Groups, their relations and development.

102 (b) Corporate behaviour includes perception, learning, personality and motivation at individual level.

103 (a) Individual behaviour is socially and psychologically conditioned for creating the employees capable of better performance.

104 (b) The design of structures has different impact on behaviour.

105 (b) Corporate behavioural modification is an essential factor in human resource development.

106 (d) All the above.
(a) In behavioural modification the initial action is identification of various problems.
(b) Immediate supervisor of an employee who knows the job can correctly identify the critical behaviour.
(c) The immediate supervisor can execute the modification process efficiently.

107 (b) and (c)
(b) Measurement standard is an indicator for subjective evaluation.
(c) Comparison in frequencies of measured data that reveals the critical behaviour of each employee.

108 (c) Causes and consequences of behaviour are analysed to infer proper behaviour for getting the desired results.

109 (c) It is applied to strengthen and accelerate the desirable behaviour.

110 (c) Behavioural modification is evaluated through reaction, learning, behavioural change and performance improvement methods.

111 (d) All the above
(a) It involves one's introspection and self-modification.
(b) It creates positive thinking, development of will power and self-motivation.
(c) Success of self-management depends on one's ability to manage the antecedents (Stimuli).

112 (c) Stimuli strategies, attention to strategies, recognition and consequences are enhanced.

113 (b) and (c)
(b) Stimuli, attention and recognition.
(c) Translation, forming the behaviour.

114 (b) The differences are the customs and practices and the religious diversity and beliefs.

115 (d) All the above
(a) They perform in a larger perspective globally; produce and sell the products in various countries.
(b) Multinational corporations acquire the markets with latest products and services.
(c) They have the competitive spirit with other firms globally.

116 (c) and ((d)
(c) Power distance and uncertainty avoidance
(d) Individualism and masculinity.

117 (c) Disappearance of political boundaries of a country in the financial and industrial activity.

118 (c) Kenicki Ohamae

119 (d) Selection of right partners and avoidance of mistakes committed by others.

120 (a) Desire to exploit new markets.

121 (a) Ethical differences are significant.

122 (d) Culture makes it possible for a group to improve and put together the responses to inputs from the environment that becomes a threat to its survival.

123 (a) The founders of any organisation possess certain values and visions that may lead to creation of culture.

124 (a) Stress is condition in which a person is faced with constraint and strains.

125 (a) Robbins,

126 (a) and (b)
(a) Constructive stress.
(b) Destructive stress,

127(a) It is positive manner action for the benefit of the individual and organisation.

128 (a) and (b)
(a) It is not suitable for the individual and organisation
(b) These are effects that are beyond the tolerance of individuals.

129 (d) All the above
(a) Prolonged worry and nervous tension.
(b) Problems of rise in blood pressure.
(c) Emotional imbalance, mental and physical disorders.

130 (b), (c) and (d)
(b) Development of resistance that leads to other complications in the body system.
(c) Individual develops frustration, uneasiness and conflictive feeling.
(d) Natural resistance of the body fails (natural immunity) and the individual feels exhausted and fatigued.

131(a), (b) and (c)
(a) Organisational factors.
(b) Environmental factors.
(c) Individual and group factors.

132 (b), (c) and (d)
(b) Psychological
(c) Physical
(d) Behavioural.

133 (a), (c) and (d)

(a) Physical
(c) Psychological
(d) Behavioural.

134 (b), (c) and (d)
(b) Role conflict
(c) Interpersonal relationship, lack of proper communication.
(d) Responsibility, change in job.

135 (a), (b) and (d)
(a) Traumatic experience of life.
(b) Death of near and dear ones and problems in family.
(d) Fired by the superior.

136 (b), (c) and (d)
(b) People under stress may not be able to control their physical and mental balance.
(c) People under stress need to avoid tension; for this they take alcohol, drugs and keep themselves aloof from others.
(d) They become moody, lazy and irritative also.

137 (b) and (c)
(b) Practising relaxation and meditation to reduce tension on body and mind.
(c) Change life style through modification; practise Yoga regularly and proper physical exercise.

138 (a) to (d)
(a) Job designing, goal setting.
(b) Develop career plans by reducing conflicts.
(c) Provide healthy organisational climate.
(d) Counselling employees and recreational facilities.

139 (a) H.J. Frendenberger,

140 (b) and (c)
(b) Blue collar workers are more likely to have job related stress.
(c) Those who work on routine jobs have high level of stress problems like tension, anxiety, depression, irritation than others.

141(b) This occurs where pressures persist to comply with different and inconsistent demands.

142 (c) Responsibility is not clear because of vague job description.

143 (b) One's own concepts can have effect on one's performance and also one responds to stress factors.

144 (a) It is less likely that a person will experience with role overload.

145 (a) Expenses incurred in recruitment, training and development of employees are charged against the income of the organisation for a specified accounting period yearly.

146 (a) It enables the organisation to have information with regard to human resource activities and the cost involved for the same.

147 (d) Keeping the priority in maintaining optimum level of man-power in all organisational activities.

148 (a) It is a method adopted by the organisation to collect information on the analysis of people and their jobs.

149 (a) To provide continuous information of people and their jobs with properly safeguarding the confidentiality.

150 (c) To centralise the information at one place in an organisation for ready reference.

◆◆◆◆◆

CHAPTER - 8

- *INTERNATIONAL HUMAN RESOURCE MANAGEMENT (IHRM) : AN OVERVIEW*
- *CAREER PLANNING*
- *PERSONALITY*
- *ATTITUDE*

FEATURES :

- International HRM
- Concept
- Difference between HRM and IHRM
- Main issues of IHRM
- Strategic role of IHRM
- Importance of IHRM
- Empowerment of work force
- Multinational operations
- Ideology of IHRM
- Global competitiveness
- Business needs at global arena
- Customer based vision
- Cultural and organisational effectiveness
- Strong and stable culture
- Procurement of staff for international assignment
- HRD dimensions of IHRM
- International performance management
- Intrinsic compensation for employees
- Total concept of remunerative package
- Industrial relation
- International negotiation
- International project management
- Responsibilities of Project Manager IHRM
- Training personnel for foreign assignment
- Career planning
- Concept
- Career planning process
- Organisational career development
- Effective career planning
- Personality
- Attitude

KEY NOTE

International Human Resource Management (IHRM)

Rapidly advancing technology is likely to bring change at every pace. We are now in the world in which electronic gadgets are controlling the activities of an organisation along with skilled human resource. In the twenty-first century what is ahead for the organisational performance, to be more skilled work force and electro-mechanical machines based operations, so as to enable them execute more and more work of routine nature. Thus, the surplus ones are fully utilised for more innovative jobs.

International Human Resource Management (IHRM) has a vital role in understanding the changing demographic characteristics of the work force in the present scenario. This task includes resource strategy, allocation of optimum level of man-power, human relation and human behaviour within the organisation, human resource development and performance evaluation, and so on.

Nowadays, the HR Manager is not simply to perform personal and administrative functions, but he must possess adequate knowledge of business strategy, relation of culture and work place and negotiations, etc. Therefore, when we look upon the global executives, we candidly feel that they are required to have self management skills, skills for independently managing the business of their establishments in a foreign country, capability of integration, social and international skills like political, legal and adaptability to social and environmental conditions abroad, etc.

Career planning

Career planning is a personnel function. This programme is normally carried out in well-established organisations. Nowadays, workers have high expectations about their jobs and career prospects. This has a great bearing on the quality of life among the working class. The driving force behind career planning is the need of modern organisations to make the best use of available human resource.

The most significant factors of career planning are— to acquire the right person for the right job, to keep the morale of the employees high at all times, open new avenues for employees to higher placement levels and promotions. A good career planning provides much needed development process of human resource.

Personality

In common parlance personality refers to the impression, which an individual forms on others through his personal attributes making an attractive or unattractive view. However, the psychological factors of an individual are rarely known to others. Personality is not a superficial fact or occurrence that can easily be understood on an individual's personal appearance. In fact, personality is the whole aspect of an individual from the general point of view. It includes a person's physical psychological and emotional aspects. Personality which makes an individual to stand apart. In short, it is the impression of characteristic attributes of an individual.

Attitude

It is an indication of mind to certain actions. According to G.W. Allport, "Attitude is mental and neural state of readiness organised through experience exerting a dynamic influence upon the individual's response to all situations and objects with which it is related." In other words, it is a process that affects the behavioiur of an individual. This is associated with physical and psychological aspects of a person. It is a comprehensive reflection of various mental activities. This is also known as expression relating to objects, people and events; e.g., How does an individual feel about something if someone says, "He likes his friend." this expression has attitude towards his friend.There are many more qualities of an executive at an international level. The above are only illustrative and not exhaustive ones.

QUESTIONS

INTERNATIONAL HUMAN RESOURCE MANAGEMENT (IHRM)

1. **What is international human resource management?**
   (a) Managing of human resource from the host country and from parent country.
   (b) Managing human resource from a third country.
   (c) Procurement, allocation and utilisation of man-power from international sphere.
   (d) Managing human resources at International organisations.

2. **What modification has been suggested by Poole in the Harward Model of IHRM?**
   (a) The global development of business.
   (b) Power of different stake holders.
   (c) The more specific link between corporate and human resource strategies.
   (d) None of the above.

3. **What is the difference between HRM and International IHRM?**
   (a) There is no much difference between HRM and IHRM.
   (b) International HRM deals with many functions, which are not within the scope of domestic HRM.
   (c) Responsible for functions like selection, training and management of international assignees.
   (d) IHRM has to comply with foreign cultures and laws and enhance multinational image and dealing with human rights, etc.

4. **What are the main issues of IHRM?**
   (a) International assignments, selection of proper employees.
   (b) Adjustment of employee and his family in host country.
   (c) Language and communication problems.
   (d) All the above.

5. **What is the strategic role of IHRM?**
   (a) Staffing to the optimum level and its policy.
   (b) Management training and development
   (c) Performance rating or appraisal.
   (d) Regulation of compensation policy.

6. **What are the barriers of effective IHRM?**
   (a) Variations in social, political and economic barriers.

(b) Perceived value of HR activities differ according to places.
(c) HR Management is merely viewed as an administrative function.
(d) Cultural differences and resistance to change.

7. What are the reasons for development of IHRM?
(a) Domestic industrialisation
(b) Economic development.
(c) Technological development
(d) Relationship between strategy and organisational structure.

8. What is the importance of IHRM?
(a) It deals with the practices of managing people at international level.
(b) IHRM requires quality of performance and skills.
(c) In a global work force, a need to be studied to face the challenges in international competition of business to succeed in diverse culture.
(d) All the above.

9. What is known as empowerment of workforce?
(a) Quality circles, job enrichment, union of employees.
(b) Codetermination, work council
(c) Self-management
(d) Comparative analysis of workforce.

10. What is the use of IHRM?
(a) It helps in the success of any multinational organisation.
(b) Involvement in the employees' personal or informal lives to understand their needs and aspirations.
(c) Deals with host country, parent country and third country according to the existing polices of the organisation to keep up their morale.
(d) Provide adequate guidance to personnel on taxation and compensation aspects.

11. What are the phases of growth of globalisation to be managed by IHRM?
(a) Corporations in the global market have to meet the challenges on the face of growth.
(b) Domestic operations.
(c) International operations.
(d) Multinational operations.

12. What are domestic operations?
(a) In this, there is not much exposure to international arena.
(b) There can be short trips to foreign agents, and also small assignments of projects in foreign countries.
(c) Manager has to be exceptionally qualified in a particular field.
(d) Having more focus on domestic markets.

13. What do you mean by international operations?
(a) In IHRM operations, managers are assigned to foreign countries, who have requisite expertise in general, technical and financial management.
(b) In international operations, different markets require approaches as per the product, and business methods according to local conditions.
(c) Personnel deputed must have language skill, cross cultural adaptability and flexibility to various circumstances. For this purpose, managerial staff and sales personnel are usually selected from the host countries on various occasions.
(d) None of the above.

14. What are multinational operations?
(a) It is very important to explore the cost effectiveness of the organisation for multinational operations.
(b) Management executives are selected for multinational operations on their merits.
(c) The basic aim for the corporation at

multinational level is the goal integration.

(d) All the above.

15. What is the difference between IHRM and (domestic) HRM?

(a) IHRM comprises different workforce categories of various nations.

(b) Management has to focus on broader perspective.

(c) Considerable involvement is there in employees' personal problems and their solutions.

(d) In domestic setting involvement of HR Department in personal problems of employees and their families is limited.

16. What are the specific needs for international HRM?

(a) In global business new challenges have to be faced.

(b) Corporations have to develop global attitudes of knowing markets and the people.

(c) Human Resource management at international level to identify skills needed for success and avoid failure.

(d) All the above.

17. What is the ideology of International HRM?

(a) Commitment

(b) Competence

(c) Cost effectiveness and congruence

(d) Good orientation.

18. What are the strategic advantages of IHRM?

(a) Commitment to management for human resource development.

(b) Skilled personnel of expertise in the organisation

(c) Better motivated personnel and their morale

(d) Well-developed organisational structure and system procedures.

19. Is planning of strategy an essential part of IHRM?

(a) Corporate development requires right person at the right place in the organisational structure.

(b) Technological advancement and innovative process for the strategy planning is devised by the management before overseas operations.

(c) Staffing policy need to be drawn well in advance for international business.

(d) Alternative arrangements for suitable managers to be provided at international locations to help run the business smoothly.

20. What is the aim of IHRM?

(a) High job commitment

(b) Quality control

(c) Flexible working relations

(d) All the above.

21. What is the source of organisational competitiveness?

(a) Quality of workforce

(b) Capital available with the organisation.

(c) Technology innovations

(d) Accessibility to markets.

22. What are the business needs at global arena?

(a) Acquiring perfect business performance.

(b) Development of human resource and effective use.

(c) Relation with the customers in a competitive scenario of international business sphere.

(d) None of the above.

23. What is meant by customer oriented approach?

(a) An important characteristic of business organisation is the customer at its centre of quality strategy.

(b) Business firms must look at the

interest of internal and external customers.

(c) Customer based vision must be the strategy of an organisation.

(d) All the above.

24. "Work is primarily structured around a small number of business processes or workflows, which link the activities of employees, to the needs and capabilities of suppliers and customers in a way that improves the performance of all the three." Who said this?

(a) Pralhad Ck. and Gary Hamel

(b) Ostroff and Smith

(c) Vogel, F.F.

(d) Whitely, R

25. What is competitiveness in business?

(a) A standard to which a country can under market conditions produce goods and services which can compete in the international market.

(b) Competition of business at international level

(c) A firm has got the advantage over its competitors in any market.

(d) All the above.

26. What are the main implications of globalisation?

(a) Government relations.

(b) Finance, competition and international conditions.

(c) Organisational challenges.

(d) All the above.

27. What is the criterion to be followed to create workforce?

(a) Proper identification of business needs.

(b) Specify the needed skills.

(c) Structure the development process.

(d) Establish the process and improve the same as and when needed.

28. What is the set of skills required for an IHRM executive?

(a) Technical, professional and self-management

(b) Organisational management

(c) Skills for integration and competitive skills

(d) Political, social and legal skills to tackle situations at international level to manage the organisation.

29. What is the role of corporate human resource function?

(a) Centralised human resource function of companies

(b) Decentralised human resource function of companies

(c) Transition human resource function of companies

(d) All the above.

30. Who is the author of the book "Cultures and Organisation-Software of mind?"

(a) Greert Hofstede

(b) Kluckhokn-Strodthbeck

(c) Andre Lauzent

(d) Tohbanainen

31. What are the findings of 'Hofstede' research on culture and workforce?

(a) Work related values are not universal.

(b) Always underlying values persist, when multinational company tries to impose the same norms on all its foreign interests.

(c) Local values are determined according to headquarters regulations are interpreted

(d) Though a multinational company tries, out of way, to insist on uniformity that may endanger the morale and efficiency of the workforce.

32. What are the organisational dimensions that Hofstede made as the landmark study of cross culture?

(a) Power distance, uncertainty avoidance

(b) Individualism and masculinity
(c) Groupism
(d) Collectivism.

33. What is the evaluation of Hofestede' study?
(a) It had certain inherent weaknesses and strengths.
(b) Hofstede's respondents worked within a single multinational industry.
(c) Unskilled manual labourers were not considered for the study.
(d) All the above.

34. What are the main advantages or strengths of Hofstede's research?
(a) Four dimensions of his study went deep into cultural values and made very important comparisons between national cultures.
(b) The connotations of each dimension are considered highly relevant to issues of importance to international managers.
(c) No other study had compared such a volume of national culture in detail.
(d) All the above.

35. What is the Hall's theory of cultural context?
(a) Hall distinguished between high and low context cultures.
(b) High context cultures are Arabic, Chinese and Japanese and have indirect style of communication and ability to understand the same.
(c) Low context culture is seen in USA, Sweden and UK. In this the environment is not important and non-verbal behaviour is usually ignored. Communication is distinct and clear.
(d) People pay more attention towards them to gesture in low context culture.

36. What is meant by strength of organisational culture?
(a) Agreement about the importance of specific values amongst the members of organisation.
(b) If a consensus, on the important values of culture is cohesive and stable, exists amongst a large number of people.
(c) If the consensus happens to be apparently less in number, the culture is not considered strong and stable.
(d) None of the above.

37. What are the characteristics of business organisations lead to performance?
(a) Organisations have a definite philosophy regarding the conduct of business.
(b) Management is committed to adopt the values in conformity economic and the environment of business organisations.
(c) The cultural values are known and shared by one and all business firms to adhere to business practices.
(d) This is an important task of IHRM.

38. What is meant by strong and stable culture of an organisation?
(a) Unifying corporate philosophy and goal.
(b) Access to top management and open communication with a sense of accomplishment.
(c) Employees become part and parcel of the company.
(d) High ethical standards and satisfaction with performance and reward system.

39. How the effectiveness of an organisation identified?
(a) Through contingency theory approach
(b) The goal attainment approach
(c) Through competitive value approach
(d) Task oriented approach.

40. What is autonomy and entrepreneurship?
(a) It is a process of breaking up

corporations in small companies and motivating them to work independently and competitively.

(b) This creates entrepreneurial responsibility, as autonomy is given to the bottom line.

(c) Personnel are provided with substantial reward system.

(d) All the above.

41. What does the productivity through people mean?

(a) Employees' awareness that their whole-hearted efforts are required for the success of company.

(b) Treat the workers with respect and dignity and make them feel that they are part and parcel of the organisation.

(c) Workers be allowed to have freedom at their job and take necessary decision to improve their jobs.

(d) None of the above.

42. How are ethical values of culture in an organisation determined?

(a) Ethical conduct is within each employee and the organisation too.

(b) Rules, policies, reward system and code of ethics are seen in the structure of organisational system.

(c) Behaviour of each individual is responsible for maintenance of ethical standards of the organisation.

(d) All the above.

43. How diversions and challenges are managed in global business?

(a) The challenges for international business and managing the diversions amongst employees and differences in the social, economic, technlogical and political factors are to be tackled skilfully.

(b) IHRM has to develop adaptability to local conditions to the maximum advantage of the organisation.

(c) Those corporations, which achieve parity of their important values and business goals of the country where they are functioning is likely to over come their competitors and also cut across the barriers.

(d) All the above.

44. What are cross-cultural hurdles in international business?

(a) International business may face cross cultural barriers in different countries.

(b) Different languages, nationality feelings and prejudices.

(c) Different socio-political framework, economic policy, tariffs and laws prevailing in foreign countries.

(d) If the actions of management offend the feelings of the people of that country, it will culminate into failure of the business.

45. What are the cross-cultural factors that put hurdles in business interactions?

(a) Individual behaviour

(b) Language

(c) Social customs

(d) Business practices and etiquettes.

46. What are the factors influencing the image of national culture?

(a) Truth or reality influence favorably in advance and also interpersonal dynamics.

(b) Role of value of product in managing the play of indisposition.

(c) Investor's view point.

(d) Predisposition as determinant of price has multiple effect on changing pre-indisposition.

47. What are the attributes of cultural maturity?

(a) Acceptance and tolerance

(b) Adaptability and resilience

(c) Ability to induce reciprocal adoption

(d) Flexibility.

48. What are the assumptions of people in different cultures about human nature?

(a) No assumptions regarding this
(b) Good
(c) Evil / bad
(d) Mixed opinions.

49. According to common personal values, mangers around the world have been categorised having the values, they possess like highly pragmatic, highly individualistic, high moral, etc. Identify managers of which nation possess 'High pragmatic values?'

(a) Japanese managers
(b) US managers
(c) Australian managers
(d) Indian ones.

50. "Since organisational values can powerfully influence what people actually do, we think that values ought to be a matter of great concern to managers. In fact, shaping and enhancing values can become the most important job a manager can do." Who said this?

(a) Murdock, George, P.
(b) Kluckholm, F and Strodtbeck
(c) Greet Hofstede
(d) Deal and Kennedy

51. What are the main types of interpersonal communications in a cross-culture?

(a) Verbal communication
(b) Para-verbal communication
(c) Non-verbal communication
(d) None of the above.

52. What are the different processes of selection and recruitment in human resource cycle in an organisation?

(a) Selection and recruitment
(b) Performance, appraisal and reward
(c) Development of personnel
(d) Transfer.

53. What are the sources of multinational companies to make up the requirement of human resource?

(a) Parent country nationals
(b) Host country nationals
(c) Third country national
(d) Any where the man-power is available

54. Why parent country nationals are mostly preferred by the management to fill-up the managing positions by multinational companies?

(a) Non-availability of proper managerial talent in the host country.
(b) Multi-racial population of the host country, entails that selecting a manager of a particular race would result in social and political problems.
(c) Need to maintain organisational coordination and control.
(d) All the above.

55. Why has Tung preferred to induct personnel from the host country in the foreign companies?

(a) Individuals are familiar with the customs and culture.
(b) They know the language
(c) They are economical and are aware of the routine job, and local market, hence, hiring them would bring good public relations.
(d) All the above.

56. Why do US companies usually prefer third country-nationals for their enterprises?

(a) They possess requisite expertise.
(b) They were judged to be the best ones for the job.
(c) They are economical
(d) All the above.

57. What is meant by expatriate national?

(a) Who has been deputed to foreign country.

(b) The person, who belongs to the host country.
(c) Remove oneself from one's native country
(d) None of the above.

58. What is the advantage of employing personnel from the parent country?
(a) Providing a chance to able managers for international exposure.
(b) It can facilitate better organisational control and coordination.
(c) Helps in keeping the morale of the personnel high.
(d) All the above.

59. What are the main disadvantages of employing parent country personnel?
(a) Emoluments of parent country nationals and those of host country nationals may differ.
(b) Parent country personnel may take more time to adopt themselves to new environment.
(c) The attitudes and approaches of parent country personnel may sometimes affect adversely.
(d) All the above.

60. What is the advantage of employing personnel from host country?
(a) The language problem is eliminated.
(b) Economy of hiring workers and also avoiding work permits.
(c) Continuity in management improves and also morale of host country personnel improves, as they are career oriented.
(d) None of the above.

61. What are the disadvantages in employing host country personnel?
(a) This may create problems of control and coordination for the Headquarters of the Company.
(b) Employing host country personnel limits opportunities for parent country nationals to gain foreign experience.
(c) Hiring of host country personnel could discourage the functioning of global units efficiently .
(d) All the above.

62. What criterion is followed in the selection of personnel for foreign assignments?
(a) Required experience and skill for the job.
(b) Adaptability to cultural norms of host country.
(c) Special knowledge of languages of foreign countries.
(d) All the above.

63. What is meant by an individual's technical suitability for expatriate selection in multinational companies?
(a) Skills required to perform the job.
(b) Ability to communicate.
(c) Technical and managerial skills.
(d) Interpersonal skill.

64. What type of traits are required in cross-cultural business environment?
(a) Maturity, emotional control and positive attitude.,
(b) Knowledge of language/languages.
(c) Diplomacy and adaptability
(d) Tolerance.

65. What is the requirement of multinational companies other than the expatriate standard?
(a) Technical and managerial skills.
(b) Ability, capacity and suitability for the particular job assigned to the individual.
(c) Evaluation of past performance record of the individual.
(d) Suitable tests can be conducted before selection.

66. What factors do contribute to better performance of the expatriate?
(a) Individuals must have willingness to serve in a foreign country, they need

to be sufficiently motivated for the job and their families must be of supportive nature.

(b) Technical capability to perform the assigned job.

(c) They must be adaptable to situations and also flexible in their attitude.

(d) Persons must possess good interpersonal skill and communication ability.

67. What are the special managerial skills needed in the new global business perspective?

(a) Managers must be leaders in all respects. They must be able to develop others in the shortest period to shoulder independent responsibility.

(b) They must have broad outlook, need to have international attitude, and also be able to negotiate workforce anywhere, as and when needed.

(c) Managers need to have generalistic skills to visualise the global business perspective from all angles like-technical, financial, organisational, business related and human resource of the organisation.

(d) All the above.

68. How to make the best use of human resource management?

(a) It involves continuous innovation within the company by utilising the knowledge and abilities of individuals.

(b) IHRM strategy to be customer-oriented.

(c) Creative talents to be procured, while making selections of people and also those who are already in service to be encouraged for creative ideas.

(d) Empowerment to people can only make innovations through free thinking and expression.

69. What are the HRD dimensions of international human resource management?

(a) The need of empowerment, self-discretion and self-motivation.

(b) Re-engineering organisational control system.

(c) Self-monitoring and self-evaluation

(d) Re-orientation.

70. What is global corporate restructuring?

(a) Usually corporate restructures itself once in every ten years.

(b) Traditional Indian family business structure of Indian corporate is an hindrance to the progress of global business trend.

(c) Corporate restructuring takes place once in 20 years.

(d) All the above.

71. Is compensation system in Indian corporates adequate for the global operations in the new global business perspective?

(a) A well-developed incentives and wage structure is very essential.

(b) International corporates cannot sustain the *ad hoc* wage system as followed still in Indian corporates.

(c) Compensation plans for Indian human resource should be made by a National Commission and must continuously update on market requirement and fluctuation of human resource and a balance to be worked out by inter-industry wage structure.

(d) All the above.

72. What is the objective of international compensation?

(a) Encourage performance to achieve the organisational goals.

(b) Enable the organisation to have the capable personnel of various categories.

(c) Create the company to optimise its complete wage-system.

(d) Motivate the employees to take up assignments at international arena.

73. What is intrinsic compensation for the employees?

(a) Job content
(b) Career prospects
(c) Personal development (scope)
(d) Recreational facilities.

74. How financial compensations are classified?

(a) Direct
(b) Indirect
(c) Through contract payments
(d) All the above.

75. What are the indirect financial compensations?

(a) Pension (b) Insurance
(c) Benefits (d) Bonus

76. What is meant by economic reward?

(a) Basic pay
(b) Performance incentive, profit sharing
(c) Special reward for extended service
(d) All the above.

77. What are the causes of compensation differences?

(a) Due to income and expenditure power of the company.
(b) Institutional set-up and the wage bargaining are at variance in many countries.
(c) Impact of cultural difference between countries.
(d) Possible differences between organisations and industries due to labour policy differences in productivity and labour capital ratio, etc.

78. How to interpret the concept of remuneration package?

(a) Employee's cost involved.
(b) Gross benefit of the employee.
(c) Net benefit and interpretation.
(d) All the above.

79. What are the common elements in a standard compensation package? Although compensation packages differ from country to country due to legal mandate.

(a) Basic pay (or salary)
(b) Benefits
(c) Allowances, incentives and taxes.
(d) Standard deductions.

80. What are the main ingredients of an expatriate's compensation package?

(a) Basic salary
(b) Benefits and allowances
(c) Incentives
(d) Perks

81. What are the major issues of managing international compensation?

(a) Many of the multinational companies find it difficult to establish a consistent compensation plan between countries that create credibility at domestic and overseas levels.
(b) Creation of standard of living for an individual would have had at the home establishment which is known as a balance sheet approach.
(c) Some of the US companies have long-term incentive programme for overseas managerial staff. This seems to be not feasible for all other countries.
(d) All the above.

82. What does repatriation indicate?

(a) After expatriation, repatriation takes place.
(b) On completion of international assignment of an employee is transferred to his parent country.
(c) Expataraiation includes repatriation and also re-entry again.
(d) All the above.

83. What is the repatriation process known as?

(a) Preparation
(b) Relocation

(c) Transition and readjustment
(d) All the above.

84. On what issues readjustment of a repatriated employee of a multintional company is made?

(a) Changes in domestic company atmosphere.
(b) Social changes take place in parent country
(c) Proper adjustment of family members.
(d) Parent company might have already filled up the vacancy of expatriated person due to length of time spent abroad.

85. How is the repatriate programme designed?

(a) A list, relocating repatriated individuals, is prepared, which the company can undertake within its resources.
(b) Financial Tax assistance
(c) Induction of re-entry personnel and career path guidance.
(d) Academic facilities for children and assistance in new social contracts.

86. What is mentoring of repatriated persons?

(a) Usually, it is a practice that a mentor is kept in contact with the expatriated person throughout the period of assignment.
(b) Expatriated persons are given adequate information about the happenings in the parent country.
(c) Expatriated individuals are encouraged for the ongoing management development programmes and also provided assistance
(d) All the above.

87. What is performance management?

(a) It is the manner of performing the activities at international arena.
(b) Multinational companies require an effective system for managing its international operations.
(c) This is a process to evaluate the corporate business enterprises in a continuous manner so as to improve upon predetermined goals.
(d) It focuses on goals attained by an individual unit's contribution to global profitability and also with an important view on individual performance evaluation whether the outcome really commensurate with the attainment of organisational goal.

88. What is expected of an organisation through proper control and performance?

(a) Consistency (b) Coordination
(c) Compliance (d) All the above.

89. What are the important factors that affect the performance of expatriated person?

(a) Adaptability to the host country's culture for both employee and family.
(b) Environment of host country.
(c) Support from top management at Headquarters.
(d) Task and compensation.

90. How organisational goals are interpreted vis-a-vis performance appraisal criteria?

(a) Hard goals
(b) Soft goals
(c) Contextual goals
(d) Contemporary goals.

91. What is the relation between culture and organisational performance?

(a) The norms and values shared by members of an organisation create general agreement and unity that create commitment.
(b) If the organisational culture is cohesive and strong that can bring cooperation among individuals.
(c) Strong and cohesive culture can be

the focal point of a success of company.

(d) All the above.

92. What does industrial relation indicate?

(a) Sound industrial relation is based on human relations.

(b) Industrial relation and human relations are distinct and indispensable factors in an industry.

(c) It is also concerned with determination of wages and conditions of employment.

(d) All the above.

93. "A comparative study of industrial relations phenomena are very faithful expression of the society in which they operate, of its characteristic factors and the power relationship between different interest groups. Industrial relation cannot be understood without our understanding of the way in which rules are established and implemented and decisions are made in the society concerned." Who observed this?

(a) Dr. M.V. Rylee and A. Simson George

(b) Schregle

(c) Dale Yoder

(c) Dunlop John

94. What differences have been observed by Rhode in Trade Unions of various countries?

(a) Methods of Union regulation by government.

(b) Ideological differences within trade union movement.

(c) Impact of religious organisations on development of trade unions.

(d) Organisational strategies for industrial relations in large corporations.

95. What are the key issues of industrial relation policies adopted by multinational companies?

(a) High degree of integration, leading to centralisation of industrial relation function within the companies.

(b) It has been noticed that US companies exercise greater centralised control over industrialisation than the British companies.

(c) In the field of industrial relation, ethnic feelings has become a cause of conflict in many multinational companies.

(d) The attitude of management towards union seems not the real industrial relation; what is expected of multinations, where it is solely based on rational economic model. The avoidance of union by the management is also in the value system of US companies.

96. What is the structure of union in western countries?

(a) Craft unions.

(b) Conglomerate unions

(c) General unions

(d) White coloured and industrial unions.

97. Do multinationals pose any threat to trade unions?

(a) Trade union activities are not seen in multinational enterprises.

(b) Multinationals pose threat to bargaining power of labour due to considerable power and influence.

(c) Usually, multinationals are not either antiunion or strict bureaucratic in nature.

(d) There are ways and means by which multinationals have an impact on trade unions and employees' interests, they discourage collective bargaining.

98. What are the main characteristics of multinational enterprises?

(a) Great financial capability of multinationals weaken the bargaining power of unions.

(b) Alternative resource capability reduces the possibility of strike by unions in multinationals.

(c) It has the ability to transfer production capabilities to other countries.

(d) Even though authority is with the Remote Centre, multinationals take the responsibility of HRM and industrial relation at their locations. Management normally have personnel with superior knowledge of industrial relation, who carry out decentralised activities responsibly with the knowledge of Headquarters.

99. What are the factors responsible for standardisation of work practices in multinationals?

(a) Work environment at host country and process of operation method.

(b) Size of the firm, its maturity, and subsidiary mandate.

(c) Corporation culture

(d) HRM, work practices, organisational behaviour of individuals, structure and groups.

100. What are the common issues of human resource management at international level?

(a) Issues regarding language, culture and environment at the host country.

(b) Performance management and industrial relation.

(c) Issues regarding the future challenges of HRM at international level.

(d) All the above.

101. What is adherence to code of conduct of multinational companies?

(a) The code of conduct introduced by the multinationals need to be followed by the sub-contracting firms.

(b) Acceptable working conditions and barring the employment of child labour, provisioning of minimum wages.

(c) If violation of code of conduct leads to cancellation of contract.

(d) All the above.

102. What is the new universal standard of code of conduct?

(a) ISO 9000 quality standard

(b) Social accountability 8000

(c) The principles of the code are drawn from UN human rights conventions.

(d) All the above.

103. What is negotiation?

(a) Negotiation involves two levels
(i) the rational decision making and
(ii) the psychological and social level.

(b) This reveals dormant issues relevant to the negotiation process.

(c) Negotiation is a discussion between two or more persons or parties, who try to find out a solution to their problem.

(d) All the above.

104. What are the essential information data required to undertake negotiations on establishment of multinational company?

(a) Taxation, legal and commercial data.

(b) Financial and economical data along with infrastructure data.

(c) Political information and data on labour force.

(d) None of the above.

105. What are the salient points to be noted with regard to 'Profile of the company' on which negotiation is likely to take place?

(a) Ownership and legality of the parent owner.

(b) Equity structure and market distribution network.

(c) Strategic interests, scope, organisational structure and overall national structure.

(d) All the above.

106. How does a negotiation is made successful?

(a) Address the problem dispassionately, find underlying interests of both parties and both parties need to get benefit from negotiation (i.e., win-win solutions).

(b) Use result-oriented method.

(c) Understand the key factors of negotiations carefully during the process.

(d) All the above.

107. What is meant by importance of trust in negotiation?

(a) Negotiate in good faith (i.e., in the best interest) of both the parties.

(b) Not to resort to unethical behaviour, exchange all information needed for solving the problem.

(c) Preserve confidentiality of the information of negotiation, be flexible where it is necessary to arrive at a proper decision.

(d) All the above.

108. What is a project?

(a) A project requires one or more resources.

(b) It is interrelated and interdependent activity.

(c) Project is a task, which has both definable beginning and end.

(d) All the above.

109. What are the main characteristics of a project?

(a) An entity by itself and an identifiable end-product.

(b) Non-repetitive work with target date of completion.

(c) High degree of risk, uncertainty and large and complex in nature.

(d) Separate organisational structure.

110. What are the stages of project management?

(a) Defining the need and also exploration of alternative solutions.

(b) Feasibility studies (very important in foreign countries)

(c) Approval and allocation of funds, framing out work to agencies and properly planning the time schedule.

(d) Extension and evaluation.

111. What are the responsibilities of project manager, IHRM?

(a) Initiation of project and shoulder responsibilities of planning.

(b) Coordination and integration of design, modifying the project, as required.

(c) Surveillance over contract negotiations, establishing control system over project, sub-allocation and control of funds

(d) All the above.

112. What is the modern technique of project management practised globally?

(a) Critical path method (CPM).

(b) Programme Evaluation and Review Technique (PERT),

(c) MBO method.

(d) Network analysis method.

113. What is the special advantage of network project management?

(a) Planning is not only to facilitate but to force through pre-planning of work and also to prevent errors.

(b) Explicitly defines the sequences and involve relationship of all activities forming of the project.

(c) The pictorial representation of the plan facilitates communication and makes the plan easily intelligible.

(d) It enables the plan to be capable of accepting change.

114. What challenges are faced by managers in managing international projects?

(a) Duplication of functional activities and

also political factors.

(b) Physical and psychological factors of people, who are working in the establishment in a foreign country.

(c) Aspects of language, culture, communication and local laws.

(d) Risk factors related to business and personnel.

115. How are projects managed at international arena?

(a) Following European model having highly structural system.

(b) Following North American system is less centralised like European model.

(c) Japanese system is highly research oriented.

(d) The technology of the owner-country is especially adopted by developing nations.

116. What is the advantage of network in project management?

(a) Planning (b) Scheduling

(c) Control (d) Optimisation.

117. What are the areas, where employees are trained before taking up foreign assignment?

(a) Relating to work motivation, negotiating skills and special customs followed by countries abroad.

(b) Etiquettes and manners, while interacting with personnel of foreign countries.

(c) Style of conversation.

(d) All the above.

118. What is the prerequisite for a proper training programme?

(a) Analysis of training needs.

(b) Proper planning of training goals.

(c) Selection of candidates.

(d) Motivation.

119. How is the training programme implemented for expatriates?

(a) Course material for training

(b) Methods of instruction

(c) Media selected for training

(d) Sequence of the programme.

120. What are the special skills required for international managers?

(a) Capability to motivate others, trust in one's own abilities and creative abilities.

(b) Adequate knowledge, cognitive ability, desire for advancement and initiative.

(c) Flexibility, interpersonal relation and conceptual skill.

(d) All the above.

121. What are the different methods of cross cultural training?

(a) Simulation methods.

(b) Programmed instructions.

(c) Sensitivity training.

(d) Behavioural modification methods.

122. What is the purpose of training?

(a) Training can alter employees' behaviour, attitude and knowledge in such a way that it leads to profitability of the company.

(b) Training improves the existing abilities and behaviour of an individual.

(c) Development is a constant process that makes an individual capable to take future positions in his career.

(d) All the above.

123. What is meant by cross-culture training?

(a) An individual is acquainted with the environment, cultural orientation and assimilation.

(b) Language and sensitivity training.

(c) An individual is accustomed to his assignment and have adequate experience.

(d) All the above.

124. What is known by cultural assimilators?

(a) It is an important technique of cross cultural training.

(b) It is a technique designed to expose the members to another culture for understanding the basic concepts like values, attitudes, role, perception, etc., of the host culture.

(c) Learning theories are the job parameters.

(d) All the above.

125. What is known by 'job parameters' in executive development programme?

(a) Training programme must provide adequate knowledge to participants, so as to help them use it, when they return to jobs.

(b) All learning theories espeicially those related to independent learning, emphasising change in the individual, his interaction and the environment with which he is associated.

(c) Learning theories is the job parameters.

(d) None of the above.

126. What are the schools of learning theories?

(a) Behavioural school

(b) Cognitive school

(c) Humanist school

(d) Scientific school.

127. Who initiated behavioral school?

(a) Watason, Thorndike

(b) Hull and Skinner

(c) Hotstede

(d) Hail

128. Who initiated the works of cognitive school?

(a) Tolman and Ausbel

(b) Maslow

(c) Murdock, George, P.

(d) Garscombke

129. Who started humanist school?

(a) Maslow

(b) Carl Rogers

(c) Becker H. and D. Fritzche

(d) Anthony, P.D.

130. What is behavioural school?

(a) This school of thoughts emphasises an overt behaviour of an individual excluding all forms of feelings and introspection.

(b) Principles of learning are a series of stimulus-response connection.

(c) Reward and punishment are also important in learning.

(d) All the above.

131. What is meant by cognitive school or theory?

(a) Cognitive theory is concerned with intellectual growth of a person.

(b) Learning is the association of particular responses to particular stimuli.

(c) It stresses the importance of insight in learning.

(d) According to cognitive school, the most important factor, influencing learning is what the learner already knows.

132. What is humanistic approach?

(a) According to Carl Rogers, the only learning which significantly influences behaviour is self-discovered learning.

(b) Good amount of learning is acquired mostly through doing.

(c) Self-initiated learning is the most lasting and pervasive.

(d) Maslow, who developed the concept of self-actualisation through humanistic approach.

133. Why training and development of system professionals are important at international level?

(a) It is the most important aspect of managing computer system operations.

(b) System professionals are those, who

are employed in all phases of data processing system in multinationals.

(c) System professionals has become increasingly difficult and complicated because of the rapid technological changes introduced by hardware manufacturers and increased sophistication in computer and system application.

(d) All the above.

134. What is the ongoing academic training for system professionals?

(a) Academic programme attract students and also motivate to obtain the degree in system and data processing.

(b) These programmes appeal to a number of persons as the same could give basic familiarity with system concepts and data processing fundamentals.

(c) There is a vast scope of impartial study and analysis of different hardware, software and industrial practices.

(d) All the above.

135. What are the disadvantages of academic approaches to training of system professionals?

(a) Many academic programmes are too slow to develop the system to the required standard.

(b) It lacks specific goal-oriented objective to provide trained and experienced system professionals.

(c) It does not follow the demand of industries.

(d) It inherently lacks flexibility in developing specialisation within the data processing field.

136. What is OJT (on the job training) of system professionals?

(a) This training can be conducted for the specific need of the company.

(b) This helps an employee to evaluate during training for performance capability of selection process.

(c) In the training programme management has the control over the entire training, therefore, emphasis can be given to any specialised areas.

(d) This programme is flexible, as per the need.

CAREER PLANNING

137. What is meant by career?

(a) It is sequence of positions held by a person during his lifetime.

(b) One's advancement throughout one's life, specially in a profession.

(c) An individual's positive view of life, as how to lead it in his entire life period.

(d) All the above.

138. What is career planning?

(a) It is a personal function of the HRM.

(b) Concern for quality of life.

(c) Organisations to make the best use of their human resource according to the rapid growth of technology and change.

(d) All the above.

139. On what basis an individual chooses the career?

(a) Interest

(b) Need for a job and social background.

(c) Self-image

(d All the above.

140. What is a career planning process in an organisation?

(a) This depends upon how one sets goals and ability of the organisation to provide support.

(b) How far one expects his elevation in the position and also how quickly he attains that goal in the organisation.

(c) Transition is the resistance on an individual's phase during his movement towards the goal.

(d) Diligence and concerted efforts for the progress of career will pay off.

141. What factors contribute to individual's career prospects?

(a) Management skills

(b) Technical skills

(c) Security of the job

(d) Freedom of action and creativity.

142. What is career planing process?

(a) Understanding the individual needs and desires.

(b) Analysing organisational requirements.

(c) Identify the potentials of an employee and then initiate career programme.

(d) Review of the process at regular intervals.

143. What is organisational career development?

(a) Self-assessment process.

(b) Employee guidance programme

(c) Providing adequate knowledge of opportunities, assessment programmes and individual tests.

(d) All the above.

144. What is career management process?

(a) Organisational actions and individual efforts towards setting career goals.

(b) How an individual can reach the top position.

(c) Integrate organisational goals and individual needs.

(d) None of the above.

145. What is the advantage of career planning?

(a) One can understand how to bridge the gap between aspiration and achievement.

(b) Management can easily decide who have real talents and who need more training to match with the needs of organisation.

(c) Retention and replacement of employees can be decided in advance according to employees' skills.

(d) All the above.

146. What is an effective career planning?

(a) Adequate support need to be given to career planning efforts.

(b) Organisation must set its goal perspectives very clearly to enable the development of personnel for long-term and short-term plans.

(c) Placement of employees must be according to the principle of right man for the right job and provision of adequate reward system.

(d) A good career path should not have any stagnation point. Fast track promotion be made available to talented personnel.

147. What is the objective of career planning?

(a) Attract and retain the talented personnel.

(b) Use human resource at optimum level and achieve the desired results.

(c) Reduces employee turnover.

(d) All the above

148. Is career planning a function of personnel?

(a) According to organisational perspective, career planning is management function associated with human resource planning and employee development function.

(b) Human resource planners provide prediction on job vacancies to career planners.

(c) Career planners provide the data of vacancies to employees for employment opportunities.

(d) All the above.

149. What are the prerequisites of career development?

(a) Performance, exposure, and personal contacts.

(b) Loyalty to career acquisition of sponsors and becoming a key subordinate to a superior.

(c) Improving performance ability.

(d) All the above.

150. What is a career planning programme?

(a) Individual assessment abilities, career needs and goals.

(b) Assessment of the employees' potentials by the management.

(c) Communication of career options and opportunities with the organisation.

(d) Career counselling to set realistic goals and plans for achievement.

PERSONALITY

151. What is personality?

(a) It is the totality of an individual.

(b) It makes a person different from others.

(c) Which acts for fulfilment of the purpose.

(d) Characteristics traits and patterns.

152. What are the attributes of the personality of an individual?

(a) Personal bearings.

(b) Experience of an individual.

(c) Personal appearance.

(d) The nature of an individual.

153. What are the factors that help to improve upon the nature of behaviour?

(a) Self-esteem

(b) Self-consciousness and adaptability to environment.

(c) Goal orientation

(d) All the above.

154. What are the factors stressed by personality theories?

(a) Social factors

(b) Individual differences

(c) Behaviour modifications

(d) Psychological factors.

155. Who emphasised that human personality is a structure composed of various elements like 'Id', 'Ego' and 'Super ego?'

(a) Mc Clelland (b) Davidson

(c) Sigmund Freud (d) Allport

156. What is personality trait?

(a) Distinctive features of character

(b) Qualities inherited by an individual

(c) Qualities acquired by a person

(d) None of the above.

157. What are the important traits required for a successful leader?

(a) Physical and social attributes.

(b) Performance attributes, intelligence and personality

(c) The traits need to be exhibited in a variety of situations.

(d) All the above.

158. What are the key attributes to behaviour characteristics of an individual?

(a) Intelligence, ability and creativity.

(b) Attitude, adaptability and capacity to change.

(c) Flexibility and goal achievement.

(d) All the above.

159. What are the expressive traits or habitual responses of an individual?

(a) Physical traits, movement traits, perceptual traits.

(b) Style traits, age and sex.

(c) Impulsiveness, stubbornness

(d) None of the above.

160. What do you mean by personality pattern?

(a) Tendencies which are influenced by self-concept.

(b) It is a unified structure in which self is the important factor.
(c) Personality pattern consists of traits.
(d) All the above.

161. What are the characteristics of trait?
(a) Uniqueness
(b) Degree of likableness
(c) Consistency
(d) Hereditary factor.

162. What are the different types of trait?
(a) Aggressive traits
(b) Expressive traits
(c) Social traits
(d) Performance traits.

163. What are the different stages of personality formation?
(a) Primary attachment.
(b) Family role and identification.
(c) Entering of child into social world.
(d) Adolescent stage.

164. What are the ideal personality attributes of a successful executive?
(a) Persistence, honesty, hard work and goal orientation.
(b) Persistence of motivation and earnest efforts to achieve the goal.
(c) Confidence in self and the abilities to tackle the situations.
(d) Strength of one's character.

165. What are the methods used to observe the personality?
(a) Direct methods
(b) Indirect methods
(c) Subjective and objective methods
(d) Projective methods.

166. What is subjective method?
(a) Through a description of self by the individual.
(b) Questionnaire or check list method
(c) Individual discloses what he knows about himself.
(d) He makes himself an object of observation and reports his findings to the psychologist.

167. What is objective method?
(a) Objective method includes psychological responses like blood pressure rates and also verbal behaviour.
(b) Expressive physical or social response.
(c) Objective responses can easily be identified.
(d) None of the above.

168. What is projective method?
(a) Individual is encouraged to project himself the unconscious content of his personality.
(b) Subject is advised to express his feelings by writing.
(c) Direct observation on the subject by psychologist.
(d) All the above.

169. What is Thematic Apperception Test (TAT)?
(a) This is a projective test to draw out an individual's innate qualities which he otherwise cannot reveal.
(b) Psychologist assesses and evaluates the personality of an individual on the basis of stimuli and his responses.
(c) The reactions of an individual's personality are revealed in the projective method.
(d) All the above.

170. What are the methods used for judging personality?
(a) Self-assessment, projective technique and self-description.
(b) Word Association Test (WAT), Situation Reaction Test (SRT) and interview.
(c) Transactional analysis.
(d) All the above.

171. What is transactional analysis?

(a) A theory of communication process that helps and predicts the future pattern of behaviour.
(b) Behaviour analysis
(c) It has three ego-states in an individual.
(d) People possess three ego-states like Parent, Adult and Child.

172. What is perception?
(a) Facts as they are seen by a viewer, may differ from the other viewer.
(b) People normally act as they perceive.
(c) Individual perception is more influenced by his social environment than by his physical environment.
(d) All the above.

173. What is introvert nature?
(a) An individual who is very talkative.
(b) A person with inward orientation.
(c) Very shy person
(d) All the above.

174. What is value system?
(a) Value is a set of assumptions regarding facts.
(b) It is similar to attitudes.
(c) Value system is viewed as perceptual framework.
(d) All the above.

175. What are the performance traits?
(a) Intellectual abilities
(b) Special aptitudes
(c) Physical performance
(d) Non-intellectual traits.

176. What is intellectual ability of an individual?
(a) Ability to learn and understand
(b) Ability for reasoning and taking judgement.
(c) Problem solving ability
(d) All the above

177. Who designed the method of measuring mental abilities, IQ (Intelligence Quotient)?
(a) Alfred Briet
(b) Gregor Mendel
(c) G.W. Allport
(d) Peter Drucker

178. What is defensive behaviour?
(a) Individual adopts the defensive behaviour, when he feels a threat to his self-image (may be imaginary or actual).
(b) When someone attacks an individual.
(c) When an individual cannot use any defensive mechanism, he reaches to a stage of depression, which leads to catastrophe.
(d) All the above.

179. What are the processes of self-analysis?
(a) Measurement of attitude
(b) Measurement of personality
(c) Behaviour modification
(d) All the above.

180. What are the sources of understanding?
(a) Culture
(b) Life experience
(c) Religion
(d) Historical background.

ATTITUDE

181. What is attitude?
(a) Attitude is the outcome of social interaction being formed in individuals and also in groups.
(b) It has considerable influence on everyone's life
(c) It is an expression relating to people, objects and events.
(d) Attitude influences behaviour and is a comprehensive reflection of various mental activities.

182. How is the attitude formed?
(a) When an individual is associated with a group of like-minded people.

(b) Influence of values, beliefs and norms.
(c) According situations.
(d) All the above.

183. What are the salient features of attitude?
(a) Attitudes assess and understand what is seen in the environment.
(b) Attitudes act as a means to reach the desired goal or to avoid an undesired one.
(c) Attitudes influence the behaviour of the individual through perception of a situation.
(d) All the above.

184. Is there any comparison between attitude and opinion?
(a) Opinion is an expression of attitude through a common language, what we think of something.
(b) There is no much comparison between them.
(c) Public opinion is the outcome of general discussion on a particular subject concerning the interest of people at large.
(d) All the above.

185. What are the types of human behaviour?
(a) Overt symbolic (speaking, writing, etc.)
(b) Overt non-symbolic (direct muscular action, running, jumping, etc.)
(c) Covert symbolic (thought)
(d) Covert non-symbolic (emotions).

186. Who made the attitude scale?
(a) Likert and Thurston
(b) G.W. Allport
(c) Goesh, P.K. and Ghorpade, M.B.
(d) Berne, G.

187. How is the attitude measured?
(a) Interpreting the behaviour of employees by supervising staff.
(b) Attitude scale
(c) Opinion survey
(d) All the above.

188. What is attitude change?
(a) Attitude changes by advising an individual.
(b) Through training programmes
(c) The change has to be through education.
(d) Change to be of the whole person.

189. What is personality difference and attitude?
(a) Some individuals go to the extreme of anything and everything.
(b) Some may adopt conservatism.
(c) Attitude changes through experience of life and also hereditary background.
(d) All the above.

190. What are the functions of attitudes?
(a) Value oriented.
(b) Self-esteem.
(c) Provide an extensive vision.
(d) Correction and cotradiction.

INTROSPECTION

Empowerment of people can only make innovations through free thinking and expression."

ANSWERS

1(c) Procurement, allocation and utilisation of man-power from international sphere.

2 (a), (b) and (c)
- (a) The global development of business.
- (b) Power of different stake holders.
- (c) The more specific link between corporate and human resource strategies.

3 (b), (c) and (d)
- (b) International HRM deals with many functions, which are not within the scope of domestic HRM.
- (c) Responsible for functions like selection, training and management of international assignees.
- (d) IHRM has to comply with foreign cultures and laws and enhance multinational image and dealing with human rights, etc.

4 (d) All the above
- (a) International assignments, selection of proper employees.
- (b) Adjustment of employee and his family in host country.
- (c) Language and communication problems.

5 (a), (b), (c) and (d)
- (a) Staffing to the optimum level and its policy.
- (b) Management training and development
- (c) Performance rating or appraisal.
- (d) Regulation of compensation policy.

6 (a), (b), (c) and (d)
- (a) Variations in social, political and economic barriers.
- (b) Perceived value of HR activities differ according to places.
- (c) HR Management is merely viewed as an administrative function.
- (d) Cultural differences and resistance to change.

7 (b), (c), and (d)
- (b) Economic development.
- (c) Technological development
- (d) Relationship between strategy and organisational structure.

8 (d) All the above
- (a) It deals with the practices of managing people at international level.
- (b) IHRM requires quality of performance and skills.
- (c) In a global work force, a need to be studied to face the challenges in international competition of business to succeed in diverse culture.

9 (a), (b) and (c)
- (a) Quality circles, job enrichment, union of employees.
- (b) Codetermination, work council
- (c) Self-management

10 (b), (c) and (d)
- (b) Involvement in the employees' personal or informal lives to understand their needs and aspirations.
- (c) Deals with host country, parent country and third country according to the existing polices of the organisation to keep up their morale.
- (d) Provide adequate guidance to personnel on taxation and compensation aspects.

11 (b), (c) and (d)
- (b) Domestic operations.
- (c) International operations.
- (d) Multinational operations.

12 (a), (b) and (c)
- (a) In this, there is not much exposure to international arena.

(b) There can be short trips to foreign agents, and also small assignments of projects in foreign countries.
(c) Manager has to be exceptionally qualified in a particular field.

13 (a), (b) and (c)
(a) In IHRM operations, managers are assigned to foreign countries, who have requisite expertise in general, technical and financial management.
(b) In international operations, different markets require approaches as per the product, and business methods according to local conditions.
(c) Personnel deputed must have language skill, cross cultural adaptability and flexibility to various circumstances. For this purpose, managerial staff and sales personnel are usually selected from the host countries on various occasions.

14 (d) All the above
(a) It is very important to explore the cost effectiveness of the organisation for multinational operations.
(b) Management executives are selected for multinational operations on their merits.
(c) The basic aim for the corporation at multinational level is the goal integration.

15 (a), (b) and (c)
(a) IHRM comprises different workforce categories of various nations.
(b) Management has to focus on broader perspective.
(c) Considerable involvement is there in employees' personal problems and their solutions.

16 (c) Human Resource management at international level to identify skills needed for success and avoid failure.

17 (a), (b) and (c)
(a) Commitment
(b) Competence
(c) Cost effectiveness and congruence

18 (a), (b), (c) and (d)
(a) Commitment to management for human resource development.
(b) Skilled personnel of expertise in the organisation
(c) Better motivated personnel and their morale
(d) Well-developed organisational structure and system procedures.

19 (b), (c) and (d)
(b) Technological advancement and innovative process for the strategy planning is devised by the management before overseas operations.
(c) Staffing policy need to be drawn well in advance for international business.
(d) Alternative arrangements for suitable managers to be provided at international locations to help run the business smoothly.

20 (a), (b) and (c)
(a) High job commitment
(b) Quality control
(c) Flexible working relations

21 (a), (b), (c) and (d)
(a) Quality of workforce
(b) Capital available with the organisation.
(c) Technology innovations
(d) Accessibility to markets.

22 (a), (b) and (c)
(a) Acquiring perfect business performance.
(b) Development of human resource and effective use.
(c) Relation with the customers in a competitive scenario of international business sphere.

23 (c) Customer based vision must be the strategy of an organisation.

24 (b) Ostroff and Smith

25 (a) A standard to which a country can under market conditions produce goods and

services which can compete in the international market.

26 (d) All the above
(a) Government relations.
(b) Finance, competition and international conditions.
(c) Organisational challenges.

27 (a), (b), (c), and (d)
(a) Proper identification of business needs.
(b) Specify the needed skills.
(c) Structure the development process.
(d) Establish the process and improve the same as and when needed.

28 (a), (b), (c), and (d)
(a) Technical, professional and self-management
(b) Organisational management
(c) Skills for integration and competitive skills
(d) Political, social and legal skills to tackle situations at international level to manage the organisation

29 (d) All the above.
(a) Centralised human resource function of companies
(b) Decentralised human resource function of companies
(c) Transition human resource function of companies.

30 (a) Greert Hofstede

31 (a), (b), (c) and (d)
(a) Work related values are not universal.
(b) Always underlying values persist, when multinational company tries to impose the same norms on all its foreign interests.
(c) Local values are determined according to headquarters regulations are interpreted
(d) Though a multinational company tries, out of way, to insist on uniformity that may endanger the morale and efficiency of the workforce.

32 (a) and (b)
(a) Power distance, uncertainty avoidance
(b) Individualism and masculinity.

33 (b) and (c)
(b) Hofstede's respondents worked within a single multinational industry
(c) Unskilled manual labourers were not considered for the study.

34 (d) All the above
(a) Four dimensions of his study went deep into cultural values and made very important comparisons between national cultures.
(b) The connotations of each dimension are considered highly relevant to issues of importance to international managers.
(c) No other study had compared such a volume of national culture in detail.

35 (a), (b) and (c)
(a) Hall distinguished between high and low context cultures.
(b) High context cultures are Arabic, Chinese and Japanese and have indirect style of communication and ability to understand the same.
(c) Low context culture is seen in USA, Sweden and UK. In this the environment is not important and non-verbal behaviour is usually ignored. Communication is distinct and clear.

36 (a) and (b)
(a) Agreement about the importance of specific values amongst the members of organisation.
(b) If a consensus, on the important values of culture is cohesive and stable, exists amongst a large number of people.

37 (b) and (c)
(b) Management is committed to adopt the values in conformity economic and the environment of business organisations.

(c) The cultural values are known and shared by one and all business firms to adhere to business practices.

38 (a), (b), (c) and (d)

(a) Unifying corporate philosophy and goal.

(b) Access to top management and open communication with a sense of accomplishment.

(c) Employees become part and parcel of the company.

(d) High ethical standards and satisfaction with performance and reward system.

39 (a), (b) and (c)

(a) Through contingency theory approach

(b) The goal attainment approach

(c) Through competitive value approach

40 (a) and (b)

(a) It is a process of breaking up corporations in small companies and motivating them to work independently and competitively.

(b) This creates entrepreneurial responsibility, as autonomy is given to the bottom line.

41(a) and (b)

(a) Employees' awareness that their whole-hearted efforts are required for the success of company.

(b) Treat the workers with respect and dignity and make them feel that they are part and parcel of the organisation.

42 (a) Ethical conduct is within each employee and the organisation too.

43 (b) IHRM has to develop adaptability to local conditions to the maximum advantage of the organisation.

44 (b) and (d)

(b) Different languages, nationality feelings and prejudices.

(d) If the actions of management offend the feelings of the people of that country, it will culminate into failure of the business.

45 (a), (b), (c) and (d)

(a) Individual behaviour

(b) Language

(c) Social customs

(d) Business practices and etiquettes.

46 (a), (b), (c) and (d)

(a) Truth or reality influence favorably in advance and also interpersonal dynamics.

(b) Role of value of product in managing the play of indisposition.

(c) Investor's view point.

(d) Predisposition as determinant of price has multiple effect on changing pre-indisposition.

47 (a), (b) and (c)

(a) Acceptance and tolerance

(b) Adaptability and resilience

(c) Ability to induce reciprocal adoption.

48 (b), (c) and (d)

(b) Good

(c) Evil / bad

(d) Mixed opinions.

49 (b) US managers.

50 (d) Deal and Kennedy.

51 (a), (b) and (c)

(a) Verbal communication.

(b) Para-verbal communication.

(c) Non-verbal communication.

Explanation : Verbal communication is through words and also the meaning of words. Paraverbal communication- It indicates how loudly one speaks those words. Meaning of silence and importance of conversational overlap. Non- verbal communication is through body language and no use of words.

52 (a), (b) and (c)

(a) Selection and recruitment

(b) Performance, appraisal and reward

(c) Development of personnel

53 (a), (b) and (c)

(a) Parent country nationals

(b) Host country nationals

(c) Third country national

54 (d) All the above

(a) Non-availability of proper managerial talent in the host country.

(b) Multi-racial population of the host country, entails that selecting a manager of a particular race would result in social and political problems.

(c) Need to maintain organisational coordination and control.

55 (d) All the above

(a) Individuals are familiar with the customs and culture.

(b) They know the language

(c) They are economical and are aware of the routine job, and local market, hence, hiring them would bring good public relations.

56 (a) and (b)

(a) They possess requisite expertise.

(b) They were judged to be the best ones for the job.

57 (c) Remove oneself from one's native country

58 (a) and (b)

(a) Providing a chance to able managers for international exposure.

(b) It can facilitate better organisational control and coordination.

59 (b) Parent country personnel may take more time to adopt themselves to new environment.

60 (a), (b) and (c)

(a) The language problem is eliminated.

(b) Economy of hiring workers and also avoiding work permits.

(c) Continuity in management improves and also morale of host country personnel improves, as they are career oriented.

61 (b) Employing host country personnel limits opportunities for parent country nationals to gain foreign experience.

62 (d) All the above

(a) Required experience and skill for the job.

(b) Adaptability to cultural norms of host country.

(c) Special knowledge of languages of foreign countries

63 (a), (b), (c) and (d)

(a) Skills required to perform the job.

(b) Ability to communicate.

(c) Technical and managerial skills.

(d) Interpersonal skill.

64 (a) and (c)

(a) Maturity, emotional control and positive attitude.

(c) Diplomacy and adaptability.

65 (a), (b) nd (c)

(a) Technical and managerial skills.

(b) Ability, capacity and suitability for the particular job assigned to the individual.

(c) Evaluation of past performance record of the individual.

66 (a), (b), (c) and (d)

(a) Individuals must have willingness to serve in a foreign country, they need to be sufficiently motivated for the job and their families must be of supportive nature.

(b) Technical capability to perform the assigned job.

(c) They must be adaptable to situations and also flexible in their attitude.

(d) Persons must possess good interpersonal skill and communication ability.

67 (d) All the above

(a) Managers must be leaders in all respects. They must be able to develop others in the shortest period to shoulder independent responsibility.

(b) They must have broad outlook, need to have international attitude, and also be able to negotiate workforce anywhere, as and when needed.

(c) Managers need to have generalistic skills to visualise the global business perspective from all angles like-technical, financial, organisational, business related and human resource of the organisation.

68 (a), (b), (c) and (d)

(a) It involves continuous innovation within the company by utilising the knowledge and abilities of individuals.

(b) IHRM strategy to be customer-oriented.

(c) Creative talents to be procured, while making selections of people and also those who are already in service to be encouraged for creative ideas.

(d) Empowerment to people can only make innovations through free thinking and expression.

69 (a), (b) and (c)

(a) The need of empowerment, self-discretion and self-motivation.

(b) Re-engineering organisational control system.

(c) Self-monitoring and self-evaluation

70 (a) Usually corporate restructures itself once in every ten years.

71 (c) Compensation plans for Indian human resource should be made by a National Commission and must continuously update on market requirement and fluctuation of human resource and a balance to be worked out by inter-industry wage structure.

72 (a) and (c)

(a) Encourage performance to achieve the organisational goals.

(c) Create the company to optimise its complete wage-system.

73 (a), (b) and (c)

(a) Job content

(b) Career prospects

(c) Personal development (scope).

74 (a) and (b)

(a) Direct

(b) Indirect

75 (a), (b) and (c)

(a) Pension

(b) Insurance

(c) Benefits

76 (d) All the above.

(a) Basic pay

(b) Performance incentive, profit sharing

(c) Special reward for extended service

77 (a), (b) and (d)

(a) Due to income and expenditure power of the company.

(b) Institutional set-up and the wage bargaining are at variance in many countries.

(d) Possible differences between organisations and industries due to labour policy differences in productivity and labour capital ratio, etc.

78 (d) All the above

(a) Employee's cost involved.

(b) Gross benefit of the employee.

(c) Net benefit and interpretation.

79 (a), (b) and (c)

(a) Basic pay (or salary)

(b) Benefits

(c) Allowances, incentives and taxes.

80 (a), (b), (c) and (d)

(a) Basic salary

(b) Benefits and allowances

(c) Incentives

(d) Perks

81 (a) Many of the multinational companies find it difficult to establish a consistent compensation plan between countries that create credibility at domestic and overseas levels.

82 (b) On completion of international assignment of an employee is transferred to his parent country.

83 (d) All the above

(a) Preparation

(b) Relocation

(c) Transition and readjustment

84 (a), (b), (c) and (d)

(a) Changes in domestic company atmosphere.

(b) Social changes take place in parent country

(c) Proper adjustment family members.

(d) Parent company might have already filled up the vacancy of expatriated person due to length of time spent abroad.

85 (a), (b), (c) and (d)

(a) A list, relocating repatriated individuals, is prepared, which the company can undertake within its resources.

(b) Financial Tax assistance

(c) Induction of re-entry personnel and career path guidance.

(d) Academic facilities for children and assistance in new social contacts.

86 (d) All the above

(a) Usually, it is a practice that a mentor is kept in contact with the expatriated person throughout the period of assignment.

(b) Expatriated persons are given adequate information about the happenings in the parent country.

(c) Expatriated individuals are encouraged for the ongoing management development programmes and also provided assistance.

87 (a) and (c)

(a) It is the manner of performing the

activities at international arena.

(c) This is a process to evaluate the corporate business enterprises in a continuous manner so as to improve upon predetermined goals.

88 (d) All the above.

(a) Consistency

(b) Coordination

(c) Compliance.

89 (a), (b) (c) and (d)

(a) Adaptability to the host country's culture for both employee and family.

(b) Environment of host country.

(c) Support from top management at Headquarters.

(d) Task and compensation.

90 (a), (b) and (c)

(a) Hard goals

(b) Soft goals

(c) Contextual goals

Explanation : Hard, soft and contaexual goals are the basis of performance criteria of individuals.

91 (b) If the organisational culture is cohesive and strong that can bring cooperation among individuals.

92 (b) and (c)

(b) Industrial relation and human relations are distinct and indispensable factors in an industry.

(c) It is also concerned with determination of wages and conditions of employment.

93 (b) Schregle

94 (a), (b), (c) and (d)

(a) Methods of Union regulation by government.

(b) Ideological differences within trade union movement.

(c) Impact of religious organisations on development of trade unions.

(d) Organisational strategies for industrial relations in large corporations.

95 (a) and (b)

(a) High degree of integration, leading to centralisation of industrial relation function within the companies.

(b) It has been noticed that US companies exercise greater centralised control over industrialisation than the British companies.

96 (a), (b), (c), and (d)

(a) Craft unions.

(b) Conglomerate unions

(c) General unions

(d) White coloured and industrial unions.

97 (b), (c) and (d)

(b) Multinationals pose threat to bargaining power of labour due to considerable power and influence.

(c) Usually, multinationals are not either antiunion or strict bureaucratic in nature.

(d) There are ways and means by which multinationals have an impact on trade unions and employees' interests, they discourage collective bargaining.

98 (a), (b) and (c)

(a) Great financial capability of multinationals weaken the bargaining power of unions.

(b) Alternative resource capability reduces the possibility of strike by unions in multinationals.

(c) It has the ability to transfer production capabilities to other countries.

99 (a), (b), (c) and (d)

(a) Work environment at host country and process of operation method.

(b) Size of the firm, its maturity, and subsidiary mandate.

(c) Corporation culture

(d) HRM, work practices, organisational behaviour of individuals, structure and groups.

100 (d) All the above.

(a) Issues regarding language, culture and environment at the host country.

(b) Performance management and industrial relation.

(c) Issues regarding the future challenges of HRM at international level.

101 (d) All the above.

(a) The code of conduct introduced by the multinationals need to be followed by the sub-contracting firms.

(b) Acceptable working conditions and barring the employment of child labour, provisioning of minimum wages.

(c) If violation of code of conduct leads to cancellation of contract.

102 (b) and (c)

(b) Social accountability 8000.

(c) The principles of the code are drawn from UN human rights conventions.

103 (c) Negotiation is a discussion between two or more persons or parties, who try to find out a solution to their problem.

104 (a), (b) and (c)

(a) Taxation, legal and commercial data.

(b) Financial and economical data along with infrastructure data.

(c) Political information and data on labour force.

105 (d) All the above.

(a) Ownership and legality of the parent owner.

(b) Equity structure and market distribution network.

(c) Strategic interests, scope, organisational structure and overall national structure.

106 (a) Address the problem dispassionately, find underlying interests of both parties and both parties need to get benefit from negotiation (i.e., win-win solutions).

107 (a) Negotiate in good faith (i.e., in the best interest of both the parties).

108 (c) Project is a task, which has both definable beginning and end.

109 (a), (b) and (c)

(a) An entity by itself and an identifiable end-product.

(b) Non-repetitive work with target date of completion.

(c) High degree of risk, uncertainty and large and complex in nature.

110 (a), (b), (c) and (d)

(a) Defining the need and also exploration of alternative solutions.

(b) Feasibility studies (very important in foreign countries)

(c) Approval and allocation of funds, framing out work to agencies and properly planning the time schedule.

(d) Extension and evaluation.

111 (d) All the above.

(a) Initiation of project and shoulder responsibilities of planning.

(b) Coordination and integration of design, modifying the project, as required.

(c) Surveillance over contract negotiations, establishing control system over project, sub-allocation and control of funds.

112 (a) and (b)

(a) Critical path method (CPM).

(b) Programme Evaluation and Review Technique (PERT).

113 (a), (b), (c) and (d)

(a) Planning is not only to facilitate but to force through pre-planning of work and also to prevent errors and omissions to the minimum.

(b) Explicitly defines the sequences and involve relationship of all activities forming of the project.

(c) The pictorial representation of the plan facilitates communication and makes the plan easily intelligible.

(d) It enables the plan to be capable of accepting change.

114 (a), (b), (c) and (d)

(a) Duplication of functional activities and also political factors.

(b) Physical and psychological factors of people, who are working in the establishment in a foreign country.

(c) Aspects of language, culture, communication and local laws.

(d) Risk factors related to business and personnel.

115 (a), (b), (c) and (d)

(a) Following European model having highly structural system.

(b) Following North American system is less centralised like European model.

(c) Japanese system is highly research oriented.

(d) The technology of the owner-country is especially adopted by developing nations.

116 (a), (b) and (c)

(a) Planning

(b) Scheduling

(c) Control.

117 (a) and (b)

(a) Relating to work motivation, negotiating skills and special customs followed by countries abroad.

(b) Etiquettes and manners, while interacting with personnel of foreign countries.

118 (a) and (b)

(a) Analysis of training needs.

(b) Proper planning of training goals.

119 (a), (b), (c) and (d)

(a) Course material for training

(b) Methods of instruction

(c) Media selected for training

(d) Sequence of the programme.

120 All the above.

(a) Capability to motivate others, trust in one's own abilities and creative abilities.

(b) Adequate knowledge, cognitive ability, desire for advancement and initiative.

(c) Flexibility, interpersonal relation and conceptual skill.

121(a), (b), (c) and (d)

(a) Simulation methods.

(b) Programmed instructions.

(c) Sensitivity training

(d) Behavioural modification methods

122 (a) and (b)

(a) Training can alter employees' behaviour, attitude and knowledge in such a way that it leads to profitability of the company.

(b) Training improves the existing abilities and behaviour of an individual.

123 (d) All the above.

(a) An individual is acquainted with the environment, cultural orientation and assimilation.

(b) Language and sensitivity training.

(c) An individual is accustomed to his assignment and have adequate experience.

124 (a) and (b)

(a) It is an important technique of cross cultural training.

(b) It is a technique designed to expose the members to another culture for understanding the basic concepts like values, attitudes, role, perception, etc., of the host culture.

125 (a) and (b)

(a) Training programme must provide adequate knowledge to participants, so as to help them use it, when they return to jobs.

(b) All learning theories especially those related to independent learning, emphasising change in the individual, his interaction and the environment with which he is associated.

126 (a), (b) and (c)

(a) Behavioural school

(b) cognitive school

(c) Humanist school.

127 (a) and (b)

(a) Watason, Thorndike

(b) Hull and Skinner

128 (a) Tolman and Ausbel

129 (a) and (b)

(a) Maslow

(b) Carl Rogers

130 (a) This school of thoughts emphasises an overt behaviour of an individual excluding all forms of feelings and introspection.

131 (a) Cognitive theory is concerned with intellectual growth of a person.

132 (a) According to Carl Rogers, the only learning which significantly influences behaviour is self-discovered learning.

133 (b) System professionals are those, who are employed in all phases of data processing system in multinationals.

134 (d) All the above

(a) Academic programme attract students and also motivate to obtain the degree in system and data processing.

(b) These programmes appeal to a number of persons as the same could give basic familiarity with system concepts and data processing fundamentals.

(c) There is a vast scope of impartial study and analysis of different hardware, software and industrial practices.

135 (a) and (b)

(a) Many academic programmes are too slow to develop the system to the required standard.

(b) It lacks specific goal-oriented objective to provide trained and experienced system professionals.

136 (b) and (c)

(b) This helps an employee to evaluate during training for performance capability of selection process.

(c) In the training programme management has the control over the entire training, therefore, emphasis can be given to any specialised areas.

137 (b) One's advancement throughout one's life, specially in a profession.

138 (a) and (c)

(a) It is a personal function of the HRM.

(c) Organisations to make the best use of their human resource according to the rapid growth of technology and change.

139 (c) Self-image

140 (a), (b), (c), and (d)

(a) This depends upon how one sets goals and ability of the organisation to provide support.

(b) How far one expects his elevation in the position and also how quickly he attains that goal in the organisation.

(c) Transition is the resistance on an individual's phase during his movement towards the goal.

(d) Diligence and concerted efforts for the progress of career will pay off.

141 (a), (b), (c), and (d)

(a) Management skills
(b) Technical skills
(c) Security of the job
(d) Freedom of action and creativity.

142 (a), (b), and (c)

(a) Understanding the individual needs and desires.
(b) Analysing organisational requirements.
(c) Identify the potentials of an employee and then initiate career programme.

143 (d) All the above

(a) Self-assessment process.
(b) Employee guidance programme
(c) Providing adequate knowledge of opportunities, assessment programmes and individual tests.

144 (a) Organisational actions and individual efforts towards setting career goals.

145 (b) and (c)

(b) Management can easily decide who have real talents and who need more training to match with the needs of organisation.

(c) Retention and replacement of employees can be decided in advance according to employees' skills.

146 (b), (c) and (d)

(b) Organisation must set its goal perspectives very clearly to enable the development of personnel for long-term and short-term plans.

(c) Placement of employees must be according to the principle of right man for the right job and provision of adequate reward system.

(d) A good career path should not have any stagnation point. Fast track promotion be made available to talented personnel.

147 (d) All the above.

(a) Attract and retain the talented personnel.

(b) Use human resource at optimum level and achieve the desired results.

(c) Reduces employee turnover.

148 (a) According to organisational perspective, career planning is management function associated with human resource planning and employee development function.

149 (d) All the above

(a) Performance, exposure, and personal contacts.

(b) Loyalty to career, sponsors acquisition of and becoming a key subordinate to a superior.

(c) Improving performance ability.

150 (a),(b), (c) and (d)

(a) Individual assessment abilities, career needs and goals.

(b) Assessment of the employees' potentials by the management.

(c) Communication of career options and opportunities with the organisation.

(d) Career counselling to set realistic goals and plans for achievement.

151 (a) It is the totality of an individual.

152 (d) The nature of an individual.

153 (b) and (c)

(b) Self-consciousness and adaptability to environment.

(c) Goal orientation

154 (d) Psychological factors.

155 (c) Sigmund Freud.

156 (a) Distinctive features of character.

157 (c) The traits need to be exhibited in a variety of situations.

158 (a) and (b)

(a) Intelligence, ability and creativity.

(b) Attitude, adaptability and capacity to change.

159 (a) and (b)

(a) Physical traits, movement traits, perceptual traits.

(b) Style traits, age and sex.

160 (b) It is a unified structure in which self is the important factor.

161 (a) and (b)

(a) Uniqueness

(b) Degree of likableness

162 (b) and (d)

(b) Expressive traits

(d) Performance traits.

163 (a), (b), (c) and (d).

a) Primary attachment.

(b) Family role and identification.

(c) Entering of child into social world.

(d) Adolescent stage.

164 (b), (c) and (d)

(b) Persistence of motivation and earnest efforts to achieve the goal.

(c) Confidence in self and the abilities to tackle the situations.

(d) Strength of one's character.

165 (c) and (d)

(c) Subjective and objective methods

(d) Projective methods.

166 (c) and (d)

(c) Individual discloses what he knows about himself.

(d) He makes himself an object of observation and reports his findings to the psychologist.

167 (a) and (b)

(a) Objective method includes psychological responses like blood pressure rates and also verbal behaviour.

(b) Expressive physical or social response.

168 (a) Individual is encouraged to project himself the unconscious content of his personality.

169 (a) and (b)

(a) This is a projective test to draw out an individual's innate qualities which he otherwise cannot reveal.

(b) Psychologist assesses and evaluates the personality of an individual on the basis of stimuli and his responses.

170 (a) and (b)

(a) Self-assessment, projective technique and self-description.

(b) Word Association Test (WAT), Situation Reaction Test (SRT) and interview.

171 (a) A theory of communication process that helps and predicts the future pattern of behaviour.

172 (d) All the above

(a) Facts as they are seen by a viewer, may differ from the other viewer.

(b) People normally act as they perceive.

(c) Individual perception is more influenced by his social environment than by his physical environment.

173 (b) A person with inward orientation.

174 (a) Value is a set of assumptions regarding facts.

175 (a), (b), (c) and (d)

(a) Intellectual abilities

(b) Special aptitudes

(c) Physical performance

(d) Non-intellectual traits.

176 (d) All the above

(a) Ability to learn and understand

(b) Ability for reasoning and taking judgement.

(c) Problem solving ability

177 (a) Alfred Briet

178 (a) Individual adopts the defensive behaviour, when he feels a threat to his self-image (may be imaginary or actual).

179 (d) All the above

(a) Measurement of attitude

(b) Measurement of personality

(c) Behaviour modification.

180 (a), (b) and (c)

(a) Culture

(b) Life experience

(c) Religion

181(a) and (d)

(a) Attitude is the outcome of social interaction being formed in individuals and also in groups.

(d) Attitude influences behaviour and is a comprehensive reflection of various mental activities.

182 (a) and (b)

(a) When an individual is associated with a group of like-minded people.

(b) Influence of values, beliefs and norms.

183 (d) All the above

(a) Attitudes assess and understand what is seen in the environment.

(b) Attitudes act as a means to reach the desired goal or to avoid an undesired one.

(c) Attitudes influence the behaviour of the individual through perception of a situation.

184 (a) Opinion is an expression of attitude through a common language, what we think of something.

185 (a), (b), (c) and (d)

(a) Overt symbolic speaking, writing, etc.

(b) Overt non-symbolic direct muscular

action, running, jumping, etc.

(c) Covert symbolic (thought)

(d) Covert non-symbolic (emotions).

186 (a) Likert and Thurston

187 (b) and (c)

(b) Attitude scale

(c) Opinion survey

188 (c) and (d)

(c) The change has to be through education.

(d) Change to be of the whole person.

189 (d) All the above

(a) Some individuals go to the extreme of anything and everything.

(b) Some may adopt conservatism.

(c) Attitude changes through experience of life and also hereditary background.

190 (a), (b), (c) and (d)

(a) Value oriented

(b) Self-esteem

(c) Provide an extensive vision

(d) Correction and contradiction.

◆◆◆◆◆

BIBLIOGRAPHY

1. **Ahuja, K.K.** "Human Resource Management." Kalyani Publishers, 1998.
2. **Armstrong, Michael.** A Handbook of "Human Resource Management", London Kogan Page Ltd., 1984.
3. **Aswathappa, K.** "Human Resources and Personnel Management." Tata Mc Graw-Hill, New Delhi, 1997.
4. **Bennis, Warren G.** "Organisational Development" Addison Welsey Publishing Company, 1969.
5. **Blum, M.L. and Nylor.** "Industrial Psychology," Yew York Haper and Row, 1968.
6. **Brewster C. and Tyson, S**. "International Comparisons in Human Resource Management," London, Pitsman.
7. **Byars, L. Leoyd and Rue W. Leslie.** "Human Resource and Personnel Management," USA, Richard D Ivawani, INC, 1989.
8. **Cowling, Alen and Mailer Chole.** "Managing Human Resources" (Ed), London Edward Arnold, 1990.
9. **D. Voich and D.A. Wren.** Principles of Management-Resources and Systems,
10. **Dale, P.N.** "The Myth of Japanese Uniqueness," Croom Hdm London, 1986.
11. **Dowling, P.J. and Schular, R.S.** "International Dimensions of Human Resource Management," Boston, PSW Kent, 1990.
12. **Dowling, P.J., Welck, D.E. and Schuler, R.S.** "International Human Resource Management-Managing people in an international context Cincinnati, OH South-Western College Publishing ITP (1999).
13. **Eliot, John.** "Human Development and Cognitive processes," New York. Holt, Rinebart & Winston, INC, 1971.
14. **Freud, Sigmund.** "Introductory Lectures on Psychoanalysis." London Penguin Books, 1974.
15. **Greenwood, W.T.** "Management and Organisational Behaviour theories." Cinemnate, South Western, 1965.
16. **Guthrie, E.R.** "The Psychology of Human Conflict." Boston, Beacon Press, 1938.
17. **Hofstede, G.** "Culture Consequences International differences in work related values," Beverely Hills Calif Sage (1980).
18. **Menon, P.K.S.** Human Resource Management and Organisational Behaviour, Himalaya Publishing House, Mumbai, 2005.
19. **Mudock, George, P.** "Culture and Society" University Press, Pittsburgh, 1965.
20. **Richard Tanner Pascale and Anthony G. Athos.** "The art of Japanese Management." Warner Book Inc. 666, Fifth Avenue, New York.
21. **Richard, R.C.** "Cross Cultural Business Behaviour, Marketing, Negotiating Across Cross Culture" Copenhagen Business School Press-Indian Edition, New Delhi, 2000 (Viva Books).
22. **Rustom S. Davar.** "The Management Process." Progressive Corporation Pvt. Ltd., Bombay, Madras, 1982.
23. **Sanford, F.H.** "Psychology- A study of man", Teachers' College, New York.
24. **Sayadin, M.S.** "Human Resource Management," Tata Mc Graw-Hill Publishing Co., New Delhi, 1988.
25. **Singh, Warrier** "Organisational Behaviour," Himalaya Publishing House, 1982.
26. **Summers, G.F.** "Attitude Measurement," Chicago Rand, 1970.
27. **S.K. Bhatia.** International Human Resource Management. Global Perspective – Deep and Deep Publications Pvt. Ltd. F-159 Rajori Garden, New Delhi – 2005.
28. **S.C.Gupta.** Text Book of International HRM. MACMILLAN India Ltd. 2006.
29. **Kaith Davis** "Human Behaviour at Work, Tata Mc. Graw Hill Publishing Company Ltd. New-Delhi. 1984.